D0455089

THE END OF AUTHORITY

THE END OF AUTHORITY

How a Loss of Legitimacy and Broken Trust Are Endangering Our Future

Douglas E. Schoen

ROWMAN & LITTLEFIELD
Lanham • Boulder • New York • Toronto • Plymouth, UK

Published by Rowman & Littlefield
4501 Forbes Boulevard, Suite 200, Lanham, Maryland 20706
www.rowman.com

10 Thornbury Road, Plymouth PL6 7PP, United Kingdom

Distributed by National Book Network

Copyright © 2013 by Douglas E. Schoen

All rights reserved. No part of this book may be reproduced in any form or by any electronic or mechanical means, including information storage and retrieval systems, without written permission from the publisher, except by a reviewer who may quote passages in a review.

British Library Cataloguing in Publication Information Available

Library of Congress Cataloging-in-Publication Data

Schoen, Douglas E., 1953–
The end of authority : how a loss of legitimacy and broken trust are endangering our future /
Douglas E. Schoen.
pages cm
Includes index.
ISBN 978-1-4422-2031-7 (cloth : alk. paper) — ISBN 978-1-4422-2032-4 (electronic)
1. Legitimacy of governments. 2. Government, Resistance to. 3. Power (Social sciences) 4. State, The. 5. Income distribution—Political aspects. 6. Political corruption. I. Title.
JC497.S36 2013
320.01'1—dc23
2013024949

♾™ The paper used in this publication meets the minimum requirements of American National Standard for Information Sciences Permanence of Paper for Printed Library Materials, ANSI/NISO Z39.48-1992.

Printed in the United States of America

CONTENTS

INTRODUCTION

The Crisis of Authority

If the folks in power want leeway to pursue their solutions, they're going to need somehow to convince the public that the fortunes of the people and the powerful are once again intertwined.

—Ezra Klein

People have lost confidence in all of these institutions they trusted will make a difference, like the unions and the ANC. The new institutions of democracy—Parliament, the courts—people have also lost confidence that those can protect them and help them. That is why they go for violence and take law into [their] own hands.

—William Gumede, political analyst, South Africa

Many Japanese feel they've been lied to by their government. In a time of disaster, people wanted the government to help them, not lie to them. And many wonder whether it could happen again.

—Mitsuhiro Fukao, professor, Keio University in Tokyo

Our ambition is to get our rights. Our problem is not the high prices. It is the audaciousness of the corruption. It is about democracy, freedom, and social justice.

—Ali Ababene, Jordanian protester

Consider the state of the world at the end of 2012: In Washington, the Democratic and Republican parties finally agreed on a deal to avoid the much-dreaded "fiscal cliff" of tax hikes and massive spending cuts—but only for the short term, and only after haggling into the wee hours of New Year's Day while global markets anxiously awaited an outcome.

Those global markets had enough to worry about without Washington adding to the concern: though it had made clear its long-term commitment to the stability of the euro, the European Union nevertheless remained on the brink of economic and fiscal calamity. The Continent's uncertain fate, amid a stagnant economy and high unemployment, has given rise to extremist movements in nearly every major country. Some of these movements have made substantial gains toward real political power.

Elsewhere, repression or instability seems the norm: in Russia, having retaken the presidency in 2012, Vladimir Putin is moving aggressively to clamp down on the nation's vibrant protest movement. Africa remains fraught with brutal civil wars, health crises, and humanitarian catastrophes. Extremist Islamist militants took control of northern Mali, brutalizing the population, while large portions of the African continent have struggled to contend with massive famines.

Even outside of the Third World, global health and well-being seem newly threatened: virulent new strains of drug-resistant tuberculosis gained strength in Europe, and in the United States the devastation wrought by the killer storms of recent years has made it clear that the issue of climate change cannot be ignored much longer.

While the fiscal cliff was being temporarily averted in Washington, thousands in New Delhi gathered in protest of the Indian government's ineffectual response to the brutal rape of a young woman on a private bus—merely the latest awful incident in a country in which sexual violence has become a national scandal (the woman eventually died). The Indian government responded to these protests by closing off portions of the capital, invoking emergency policing powers, and clashing with protesters.

"I'm now beginning to feel that my government is not capable of understanding the situation, let alone solving it," said one activist.[1]

That's a view that citizens around the world share today, and for good reason: we face a crisis of authority that threatens the political and economic foundations of the global order.

Around the world, citizens no longer trust their governments to solve the enormous problems facing them. They no longer have confi-

st-Mubarak, however, the quest for justice in Egypt has a long
 go. That became particularly evident in November 2012, when
 issued a decree that essentially placed him above the courts and
her legal entity as the guardian of the Egyptian revolution. Morsi
s supporters claimed the steps were taken to break political dead-
nd address Egyptians' many demands more effectively. But crit-
 the outlines of a new dictatorship: "An absolute presidential
," as Amr Hamzawy, political activist and former liberal member
 parliament, wrote online. "Egypt is facing a horrifying coup
legitimacy and the rule of law and a complete assassination of
nocratic transition."[8]

an rebels, with the aid of foreign military intervention, were
replace Mu'ammar Gadhafi and his government and eventually
 and kill him. They fought against Gadhafi's atrocious human-
ecord and for a freer and fairer society. Syrians are still fighting
nt Bashar al-Assad's army, battling against high unemployment
ernment corruption. Even with significant UN efforts, Assad's
es of agitators and innocents won't likely end soon.

popular unrest extends beyond Egypt or Tunisia or Libya or
democratic India, citizens have organized a massive grassroots
nt against political corruption, crony capitalism, and the un-
stribution of wealth. In South Africa, nearly twenty years after
can National Congress took power in a peaceful transition
the end of apartheid, government institutions have failed to
massive unemployment, spiraling levels of income inequality,
nsider system of crony capitalism that threatens the country's
 well-being as well as its investment climate.

very disappointed in this government," said a truck driver in
who cannot afford more than a "fetid shack" for a home, even
 is one of the lucky ones with a job. "I lost faith in them. They
ng too much and leaving us with nothing."[9] The collapse of
nt leadership was symbolized tragically in August 2012, when
Marikana opened fire on striking platinum miners, killing thir-
e worst incident of government violence in the country since
eid era.

ope, country after country faces public unrest in the face of
rises that may yet lead to the end of the "European project."
us side, 2012 offered cause for optimism, especially when

dence in the institutions of their societies to manage and lead effectively. A profound cynicism and anger prevails at a time in history when
nations desperately need public unity and morale. The crisis of authority stems from the failure of institutions, especially of government but
also of business, to provide effective leadership.

They have failed to produce equitable, stable economies untainted
by crony capitalism and financial speculation. Too many countries lack
reliable, fair administrations of justice and stable systems of governance. Election fraud is pervasive, especially in Russia—and even many
Americans doubt the validity of their elections. Educational systems
remain hugely deficient, whether due to failing public school models—
as in the United States—or, in the developing world, a refusal to educate young girls or to extend educational opportunities to the poor more
generally. Again and again over the last several years, we have seen
governments fail in providing basic services from health care, water
delivery, and electric power to competent disaster relief. The results:
economic turmoil, human hardship and misery, growing political extremism, and a mounting sense that there is nowhere to look for answers—no higher authority to appeal to, because the authorities themselves have failed.

At the heart of these failures is broken trust—with constituents, with
the law, and with the essential compact between government and citizen, wherein the citizen cedes some autonomy in exchange for princi-
pled leadership in the national interest. Having repeatedly broken this
trust in nations across the globe, governments, as well as other institutions—particularly business and media—have lost legitimacy in the
eyes of the public. And without legitimacy, there can be no authority.

The public loss of trust in political and economic institutions has led
to unprecedented political instability and economic volatility, from
Moscow to Brussels, from Washington to Cairo. The failure of democracies and autocracies to manage the fiscal and political crises facing us
has led to profound disquiet, spawning protest movements of the left,
right, and center around the globe.

The mood might be best summarized by South African political
scientist William Gumede. Referring to his country's widening inequality between rich and poor, massive unemployment, and sometimes-
violent labor unrest, he said, "People have lost confidence in all of these
institutions they trusted will make a difference, like the unions and the

ANC. The new institutions of democracy—Parliament, the courts—people have also lost confidence that those can protect them and help them. That is why they go for violence and take law into [their] own hands."[2]

Fortunately, the violence Gumede refers to has generally been the exception rather than the rule, at least so far. But note his words about the lack of trust in institutions: this diagnosis applies to countries around the world, and its consequences are as dire as any terminal disease that gestates for a long period and then explodes into symptomatic activity. Unless addressed comprehensively, the breakdown of authority could lead to massive social unrest, continued economic stagnation, and even the collapse of our global system.

Are things really this serious? Look around.

"REGULAR PEOPLE GOING CRAZY ABOUT WHAT'S GOING ON"

You can see it in the cries of protesters fighting for democratic reform in Russia, where elections widely regarded as fraudulent have prompted a mass movement, and in Iran—where the Green Movement has forged ahead, even after its brutal repression by the government in 2009.

"[Putin's] popularity is on the wane, and in this instance the true wishes of the Russian people have been ignored," said Ruslan Susdiko, a young Russian, after the March 2012 elections returned Vladimir Putin to power. "Most people view today's victory with a degree of cynicism. For the moment we have resigned ourselves to a Russia where Putin is in charge. Everyone knows these elections merely gave us the illusion of free choice."[3]

"I'm just an ordinary person, and I'm fighting for my rights," an Iranian protester, "Sarah," told Anderson Cooper on CNN in 2011. When Cooper asked her if she was afraid to speak out, she replied, "Yes, I am afraid to talk, but I really want to be doing this. One of our friends was killed; he was, like, twenty-six . . . and that could be me. He was shot randomly. It's a Persian expression I've translated into English because I don't know the equivalent: 'we are not allowing his blood go to waste.'"[4]

You can see the breakdown of authority all acr
in the eyes of the rioters who rose up against
Tunisia, Egypt, Libya, Yemen, and Syria—and
where thousands of protesters crowded city stree
demanding the end of King Abdullah II's rule.
other Arab countries over the last few years, a b
was sparked by a seemingly minor grievance: an
Yet the gas issue served as a catalyst for the
anger against a whole range of injustices, and th
when police killed one of the protesters. Demo
gans against King Abdullah II that previously
whispered," reported the *New York Times*.[5]

"This is the beginning of the Jordanian Spri
political science professor Hassan Barari. "Bec
political thing; this is the lives of the people."
nian blogger and activist, said of the budding
and spontaneous; it was not called by activi
regular people going crazy about what's going

That's an apt description for the protes
around the world, particularly for the region-w
has come to be known as the Arab Spring. Its
powerful dramatization, came in Tunisia in J
vendor Mohamed Bouazizi set himself ablaz
ment and humiliation suffered by the lower
sian officials. In nation after nation in the
were born to protest the gross human-righ
unfairness perpetrated by autocratic govern
treatment triggered mass movements for d
governance.

In Egypt today, even under the first d
dent, Mohamed Morsi, thousands continue
pression and assembly, key democratic ten
under Hosni Mubarak. As Tom Friedm
Times, "When I talked to Egyptians, it w
their protest, first and foremost . . . wa
Egyptians were convinced that they live
where the game had been rigged by the
capitalists."[7]

Pc
way t
Mors
any o
and h
locks
ics sa
tyrann
of the
agains
the de
Lib
able to
captur
rights r
Preside
and gov
massac
But
Syria: i
movem
equal d
the Afr
marking
address
and an i
economi
"I am
Tembisa
though h
are steal
governm
police in
ty-four, t
the apart
In Eu
financial
On the p

European Central Bank head Mario Draghi made a full-out pledge of support for the euro, staving off—perhaps for good—fears that the currency might fail. Draghi's move, which I discuss in greater detail in chapter 11, showed just the kind of leadership that has been lacking around the world and that will be needed to restore stability and trust. In itself, however, it does not spell the end of the Continent's troubles. Fiscal distress in multiple countries has triggered rollbacks in public spending, arousing intense popular opposition, especially since many see these "austerity" programs as unevenly applied—burdening ordinary people while elites suffer little. In Italy, for instance, students have demonstrated and clashed with police over cuts to the education budget—cuts begun under former prime minister Silvio Berlusconi and continued by his successor, Mario Monti. Italians see Berlusconi's alleged mafia collusion and other illegal practices as illustrations of an unjust political system.

"We take to the streets not only to say that we reject these austerity politics but also to bring to the public's attention the problems of our education system, to remind people that schools are an important part of society and we can't do without them," said a student protester.[10] And Italians aren't protesting just austerity in the education budget. Activists and demonstrators have also targeted Equitalia, the tax-collection office, as multiple Italian citizens, unable to pay their tax bills, have committed suicide. Protesters have hurled red paint and eggs at officers guarding Equitalia, and police in riot gear have had to quell rock- and bottle-throwing protesters.[11]

In May 2012, France joined Spain and Italy in the list of European government turnovers—the right-leaning government of Nicolas Sarkozy was voted out and the Socialist François Hollande took power. The French government, like Italy and Spain, had failed to react effectively to the economic crisis, and the electorate punished its leaders at the polls. Meanwhile, tough austerity policies in response to the EU fiscal crisis, and the pending bankruptcy of nations like Greece and Spain, have sparked furious, and sometimes violent, public protests.

Greece has endured years of street demonstrations against the German-dictated austerity measures. In fall 2012, Greek citizens were grappling with their third round of austerity in as many years. Huge protests broke out again in Athens, involving a cross section of Greek society—"civil servants, teachers, medical personnel, bank employees, and lawyers," according to the *New York Times*. The protests began peacefully but then degenerated into violence, as black-masked protesters hurled gasoline bombs at police, at the Finance Ministry, and into the National Gardens near Parliament. When police responded with batons and tear gas, the protesters screamed at them, calling them "Merkel's pigs"—a reference to German chancellor Angela Merkel, whom many Greeks blame for the austerity policies. Trade unions called for a nationwide strike to protest billions of dollars in proposed new salary and pension cuts. [12]

"Our message is one," said Greek opposition leader Alexis Tsipras. "The democratic tradition in Europe will not allow the Greek people to be turned into crisis guinea pigs and for Greece to become a social cemetery. We'll win in the end, because justice is on our side and we're growing in number." [13]

In Spain, the protesters, or *indignados*, have been in the streets for the last several years, protesting the corrupt Spanish political system and the nation's cripplingly high unemployment rate. "We are not just asking for jobs. We are asking for a change in the political system," said Carlos Gomez, a Spanish protester, in May 2011. "We have no option but to vote for the two biggest parties in Spain, who are more or less the same. They are unable to solve any problems; it is just a nest of corruption. We are tired. In short, we want a working democracy. We want a change." [14] In September 2012, tens of thousands of protesters flooded the Spanish Parliament building to protest austerity measures proposed by the government of Mariano Rajoy.

Even in neighboring Portugal, which had long avoided major public discord, citizens rose up in anger against punishing austerity policies. In October 2012, when President Pedro Passos Coelho announced a budget with new tax increases and further cuts to public-sector jobs, tens of thousands of Portuguese citizens took to the streets. [15] A month earlier, half a million people marched in cities across Portugal to protest an increase in employee social-security contributions. [16] Trade unions planned a general strike.

It's no coincidence that these movements, as diverse as they are, are happening at the same time. As author and longtime international observer Guy Sorman writes, "It might seem far-fetched to compare the Arab Spring, which toppled authoritarian regimes, to protests in democratic countries. But the similarities are striking. In the Arab world, too, the enemy was 'the system'—in this case, one that combined political oppression with crony capitalism. And behind the rebellions were youthful crowds demanding change, jobs, and social justice."[17]

At the core of these mass public movements is a pervasive loss of trust and confidence in national and global institutions. While a rejection of institutional authority can often inspire idealistic and hopeful efforts for change, it can also provoke anger, extremism, rootlessness, and cynicism. Above all, in country after country, the crisis of authority has brought instability, unpredictability, and a looming sense that the worst may lie ahead. It's heartening that for the most part we've seen little overall violence—but there is no guarantee that this restraint will hold. In the absence of meaningful change, we could soon see less peaceful movements.

The situation in the United States is not much better. As the long-time model of democratic governance, the United States has stood as a beacon for nations around the world. Millions have looked to the day when their nations might adopt some form of the democratic institutions and practices that made America the envy of the globe.

Unfortunately, the crisis of authority is deep seated in the United States as well, impairing Washington's ability not only to solve its own problems but also to set an example for others. In October 2011, a year before the next presidential election, a *New York Times*/CBS poll found that "Americans' distrust of government at its highest level ever."[18] The poll was taken at a time when the Occupy Wall Street movement was headline news in the United States and around the world: thousands of protestors camped out in Zuccotti Park in downtown Manhattan, protesting bank bailouts, income inequality, and the collusive relationship between Wall Street financiers and Washington politicians.

Nearly half of the poll respondents agreed that the sentiments of the Occupy movement reflected the views of "most" Americans. Two-thirds said that wealth in the United States should be distributed more evenly—a stunningly high proportion in a nation devoted to rugged individualism and the notion that one should be able to rise as high as one's efforts can take him or her. Two-thirds of respondents also opposed tax cuts for corporations and favored higher taxes on millionaires.

The predominant mood in the poll was one of skepticism: 89 percent of Americans said they distrusted government to do the right thing, 74 percent said the country was on the wrong track, and 84 percent disapproved of both parties in Congress.[19] Looking at this poll and others like it, Paul Volcker, former Federal Reserve chairman, wrote, "In other words, four out of five Americans don't instinctively trust our own government to do the 'right thing' even half of the time. That's not a platform upon which a great democracy can be sustained."[20]

When the Occupy protests took off, U.S. unemployment numbers remained at crippling levels, while income inequality had reached levels viewed by many as unsustainable. As it stands, the top 1 percent takes in 24 percent of U.S. national income and holds 40 percent of the national wealth.[21] Only Chile, Mexico, and Turkey have higher income inequality than the United States among OECD countries.[22] Occupy's famous slogan—"We are the 99 percent"—has become a battle cry of antielite movements across the world.

American discontent becomes even starker when you remember that Occupy was not the first but the second mass political movement in the country in the last four years. The first was the conservative Tea Party movement, which arose in early 2009 in response to the government bailouts of financial institutions and massive government spending. The federal government's decision to spend over $700 billion bailing out major banks sent a signal that the financial industry was the country's top priority while average citizens were losing their jobs (and their homes). The Tea Party represented a backlash against government protection of the financial industry as well as the practice of crony capitalism—in which businesses, supposedly operating in a "free market," collude with Washington for special favors and anticompetitive advantages. Instances of crony capitalism have become increasingly common in the United States, whether it's special treatment that allowed government-sponsored "companies" Fannie Mae and Freddie Mac to dominate mortgage underwriting or the Obama administration's grant of a $535 million loan guarantee to the solar-panel firm Solyndra.

"I want Congress to be afraid," said Keldon Clapp, forty-five, an unemployed marketing representative, at a 2009 Tea Party event in Washington, D.C. "Like everyone else here, I want them to know that we're watching what they're doing. And they do work for us."[23]

Both movements, either in spirit or in name, have spread around the world: the Tea Party has influenced right-wing, conservative parties in Europe, and Occupy has launched an international movement against financial and social inequality. While they may be opposites in their goals, Occupy and the Tea Party arrived at a common diagnosis shared by protest movements around the world: elites in every institution, from government to finance to education to media, have failed.

AUTHORITY BETRAYED

The government knew the flood was coming, but it didn't notify its citizens—it didn't even bother to disturb their sleep. By morning, citizens were fighting for their lives as the floodwaters overwhelmed their homes, washed away their property and belongings, and killed hundreds. Only after the fact did the government acknowledge that it had early warning of the approaching disaster and had, inexplicably, failed to protect the people for whom government is supposed to work.

In the southern Russian town of Krymsk, this is what happened in July 2012.

"If they knew at eleven, why didn't they warn us? What are we, hunks of meat? Are we not people?" asked Sergei Viktorovich, forty-five, who, as the *New York Times* reported, "described waking in the darkness to the sensation of moisture in his bed, then reaching for his phone on a bedside table to find that it was already lost in the water." Viktorovich would not offer his surname for fear of retribution. "We are the young people, so we swam, but what about our grandmothers? How many grandmothers drowned?"[24] Town residents described not only their grief but also their rage—and their utter lack of trust in anything their government officials tell them.

That same distrust is now rampant in Japan nearly two years after the disaster at the Fukushima nuclear plant, where the worst nuclear meltdown since Chernobyl's in 1986 occurred after the massive Tōhoku earthquake and tsunami. Having already lost twenty thousand to the earthquake and tsunami, the Japanese still live in fear for their lives. A Tokyo fisherman said, "I tell them the government checks the fish for radiation, but they don't trust elected officials or anyone. A year after the disaster, Japan is still afraid of its own food."[25] Japan's government has been unable to restore the broken trust that resulted from this tragedy. The crucial issue between citizens and the government is not whether food is safe to eat but whether citizens will believe anything their government says.

Almost as frightening as the damage done to lives, property, and economies is the sense of governmental paralysis. In July 2012, Sir Mervyn King, the governor of the Bank of England, testified before the Treasury Select Committee. He shared his pessimistic outlook on the U.S. and Asian economies as well as the eurozone crisis. Political leaders, he said, seemed to have no viable plan to address the short-term or long-term implications. As for the financial crisis, he didn't think we were even *halfway* through it.[26]

The reaction? Nothing. Just your average day in Armageddon. The members of the Treasury Committee asked a few perfunctory questions, but King's forecast didn't seem to strike any fear in their hearts or even rankle the markets. Apparently his testimony, by now, is just par for the course. The fact that we're in a dangerous situation and no one knows what to do about it seems something like a new status quo.

Despite an endless stream of negotiations within and between national governments and a string of policies—from industry bailouts to austerity plans—we have not come close to remedying this crisis. In fact, I think things have actually gotten worse—because the longer these problems, ranging from pending insolvency to chronic, generational unemployment, are permitted to fester, the more damaging their ultimate impact will be. We seem to have no cogent plans for the future, no accountability from our leaders, and, most important, no good will or trust left in our institutions. We may someday look back at this time and say that all the signs of imminent collapse were there but that we ignored them.

With some exceptions like the European Central Bank's Draghi, too many leaders don't seem to understand the true nature of the crises they are fighting, including the broken trust that they must repair. Beyond the financial crisis, we see failures of governance in our inefficient, bureaucratic, and undemocratic international institutions, which seem unable to mobilize and successfully coordinate relief and mediation efforts where we need them most: Syria, where an ongoing civil war threatens to destabilize an already troubled Middle East; Congo, where the "African world war," a conflict begun in 1998 that continues to rage on today, has become the deadliest conflict since World War II;[27] Haiti, where the effects of the cataclysmic 2010 earthquake, including an ongoing cholera outbreak, continue to ravage the population; and nations in both West and East Africa, which have seen deadly famines in

2011 and 2012. To this list could be added many other trouble spots in a world never lacking for hardship or danger.

THE FAILURE OF GOVERNANCE
AND THE LOSS OF TRUST

The political movements for change that we have seen in nations around the world arise, at core, out of a sense of betrayal. Poll after poll makes clear the extent and severity of public discontent and the loss of trust in authority and leadership.

In this year's Edelman Trust Barometer survey, for example, trust in government plummeted among informed publics in Spain, France, and Italy by twenty-three points, eighteen points, and fourteen points, re-spectively. The Trust Barometer, which surveys twenty-five countries, examines citizen trust in four main institutions: government, business, media, and nongovernmental organizations (NGOs) worldwide. The year 2011 was a terrible one for public trust, with three of the four institutions losing support globally.[28] Trust in government ranked at 43 percent globally in 2011—a nine-point drop from 2010 and the largest drop in the survey's history. In 2011, trust in government in the United States hit historic lows: a CNN poll found that just 15 percent of Americans said they "trust the government in Washington to do what's right just about always or most of the time," the lowest figure ever recorded in response to that question.[29]

"We have lost our gods. We lost [faith] in the media. . . . We lost it in our culture. . . . We lost it in politics, because we know too much about politicians' lives. We've lost it—that basic sense of trust and confi-dence—in everything," says Laura Hansen, an assistant professor of sociology at Western New England University.[30]

Indeed, around the world, people have nowhere to turn for the truth. Political leaders' claims tend to have credibility only on their side of the aisle—everywhere else, they are regarded as deceptive, meaning-less, or both. Business and the private sector generally are regarded as self-interested and unreliable in regulating themselves or protecting consumers; churches are overrun by scandals; the largest media organ-izations are continually exposed for duplicitous and politically slanted reporting or for simple incompetence; the most empirical and objective information available—economic data, say, or political polling results—is widely dismissed as "cooked" or "skewed," manipulated to fit the agendas of whomever controls the information.

In fact, in the run-up to the 2012 U.S. presidential election, it was widely declared on both the right and the left that, if the other side won, the election would be illegitimate or "stolen" through some corruption of the voting process. Some on the left objected to the fact that a company that owned the voting machines in several key Ohio counties had links to Mitt Romney, speculating openly about stolen votes.[31] The left also argued that Republican efforts to enact voter ID laws amounted to efforts to disenfranchise Democratic voters. On the right, meanwhile, allegations about voter fraud—whether it's dead people voting, illegal immigrants, or others not properly registered—abounded.[32] Thus even the gold standard of democracy—an American presidential election—is seen as a sham, or at least as highly suspect, by growing numbers of Americans.

How has it happened? In the simplest terms, it comes down to a failure of governance and leadership.

Elites in government have utterly failed to address the enormous challenges facing their electorates—political, economic, social, and environmental. These issues range from the crushing problem of debt and illiquidity to the global economic slowdown, from income inequality to the mounting threats of environmental damage and energy shortages. Citizens around the world have learned that they cannot depend on politicians to protect their interests and respond to their needs.

Consider the European Union's financial crisis. With the exception of Draghi's bold stand to stabilize the euro, little else has been resolved. The twenty-seven member states have consistently failed to reach agreement on a way to move forward to address debt relief and containment, unemployment, and a sustainable budget for the union. To some extent, the EU's struggles may be inevitable at this point: an organization founded as six member states, all with highly developed economies, has more than quadrupled in size to include enormously divergent states and economic histories. The result is vastly different agendas among the member states, perhaps best symbolized by British prime minister David Cameron's lament in November 2012, after the breakdown of another budget summit: "Brussels continues to exist as if in a parallel universe."[33] For Cameron, and for German chancellor Angela

Merkel, deep cuts are necessary to the EU's multiannual budget, but France and other EU states, especially in the south, are much more averse to that idea. Meanwhile, the specter of Greece hangs over every EU proceeding: the Mediterranean nation has stood on the brink of leaving the eurozone for two years, and no agreement has been reached on how the EU should move forward.

Meanwhile, Americans have watched their revered two-party system become a pathetic sideshow of partisan warfare, culminating in 2011's debt-ceiling crisis and the historic downgrade of the U.S. credit rating. President Obama's reelection in 2012 brought cautious optimism that perhaps he might be able to work with Republicans to avert the much-dreaded "fiscal cliff"—wherein tax rates were to go up and deep spending cuts were to kick in, both in January 2013, unless some deal were made in the meantime. Beyond the fiscal cliff, American political leaders in Washington face the same long-term, structural crisis: something must be done to reach agreement on deficit reduction and unsustainable entitlement costs. Yet there seems nothing like the political will necessary to find solutions to these problems.

Business leaders, too, have been unaccountable for years, proving themselves to be exclusively self-interested, driving us deeper into the financial crisis and paying themselves bonuses in the meantime. Politicians have cushioned their fall, protecting their interests over those of the average citizen and refusing to pursue any form of punishment or accountability.

If there is a silver lining, it is this: by and large the global discord reflects the popular hunger for democratic governance and individual freedom. Different as their national situations are, millions share, broadly speaking, a common aspiration: basic rights and a more equitable society. These struggles take different forms in different regions and cultures.

The Muslim world has seen explosions against authoritarian rule and rebellion in pursuit of these basic human rights. Perhaps the most agonizing recent example was the October 2012 Taliban shooting of Malala Yousufzai, a fourteen-year-old Pakistani activist for girls' education and a fierce critic of the extremist Islamist group, which governs the country's northwest Swat Valley, where she lived. Yousufzai's shooting was a grim illustration of how far the foes of modernity and Western political ideals will go to press their case—as the Taliban demonstrated by celebrating their deed. [34]

Protests in Western democracies have not been so much about the absence of civil and political rights, but rather against economic mismanagement and deteriorating material conditions. The deep-seated, systemic problems of prosperous Western nations have made clear that democratic governments don't automatically enjoy higher levels of public trust. The Western democracies have plummeted from stable, prosperous societies with strong public trust in government to wildly unequal, insecure societies where trust feels like a naïve and nostalgic idea.

In this book, I'll explore at length some of the drivers of this loss of trust—including economic instability, income inequality, democratization, globalization, and developments in technology and communications. And I'll document how corrosive practices, ranging from political corruption to crony capitalism, have eroded public faith in institutions in countries as diverse as Russia, China, the United States, and Spain.

But the one event that overrides all others—the single most important episode in the erosion of authority—is the financial crisis. This is because it has simultaneously destroyed the reputations of both political and economic institutions.

The worldwide recession has exposed governments as unable to fulfill their responsibility to protect millions of ordinary, hardworking citizens from the inequities of free-market capitalism. Millions who spent lifetimes accruing savings and improving their homes have seen both vanish. Meanwhile, those who profited most from the financial crisis continue to flourish, seemingly unaffected and mostly unpunished.

It is this overarching sense of inequity, unfairness, and injustice that created the crisis of authority and the loss of trust. Only serious efforts to rebuild public trust in government and other institutions can provide hope for a more secure global future.

GLOBAL SOLUTIONS, AMERICAN LEADERSHIP

Restoring trust and putting the international community back on a solid footing, both politically and economically, will take hard, focused work and the recognition that this moment is crucial. Leaders must lead.

Only through a firm commitment to advancing the cause of democracy and creating a class of responsive elites can we change the current state of affairs.

At the broadest level, what we need is a renewed commitment to multinational institutions and solutions—not "one-world government," as some think of it, but a newly effective and efficient international system that can work together responsively to solve common problems. This means both bolstering existing organizations—whether the UN or the World Health Council, the International Monetary Fund or the World Bank—and creating new ones as needed. These might include international institutions that will deal with problems like climate change, the narcotics trade, terrorism, AIDS, and others. We may need new institutions specifically devoted to enhancing public trust, fostering governmental transparency, and enabling greater civic participation. NGOs have a crucial role to play: in the Edelman Trust surveys, they were the only large institutions that saw gains in trust. In my concluding chapter, I'll explore some reforms in detail.

Despite the failings and obvious limitations of Western democracies, the nascent freedom movements around the world all advocate democratic change and the kinds of civic values Americans hold dear. In an important 2012 *New York Times* column, Tom Friedman pointed out that the United States could build bridges to these movements, and enhance its own credibility as a force for positive change, by making clear its support for governments that uphold six core values:

1. educate their people up to the most modern standards
2. empower their women
3. embrace religious pluralism
4. have multiple parties, regular elections, and a free press
5. maintain their treaty commitments
6. control their violent extremists with security forces governed by the rule of law[35]

Of course, another way for the United States to play a leading role is to get its own house back in order. The U.S. model is in a dangerous state of disrepair, both at home and abroad. Citizens in the United States don't trust their government or most other institutions of society; at least one Supreme Court justice doesn't even think that our Constitu-

tion is worth emulating. The longer the crisis in U.S. governance continues, the more global confidence in the U.S. model will deteriorate.
Less democratic, and often antidemocratic, models stand ready to fill
the breach—like the autocratic Russian model or the consumerist but
brutally undemocratic Chinese model.

In fact, some damage has already been done to the prestige of the
American example. In February 2012 the *New York Times* ran the
article "'We the People' Loses Appeal with People Around the World,"
which argued that the U.S. Constitution, for so long the guide for every
democratic movement, no longer occupies such a primary place in the
world's imagination. The article pointed to a new study that showed a
steep drop in the last few decades in the percentage of countries using
the Constitution to write their own governing charters. The article spec-
ulated that the U.S. Constitution, "parsimonious" in the explicit rights it
grants, may have fallen out of step with a time of much more expansive
democratic aspirations.[36]

Perhaps most damagingly, Supreme Court justice Ruth Bader Ginsburg, whose job is to interpret and protect the Constitution, has stated
that our governing document isn't such a good model for countries
today. "I would not look to the United States Constitution if I were
drafting a constitution in the year 2012," she said in a TV interview in
Egypt. She recommended instead "the South African Constitution, the
Canadian Charter of Rights and Freedoms, or the European Convention on Human Rights."[37]

I don't think I need to explain why a Supreme Court justice's doubts
about the Constitution's merits should be so troubling. But in some
ways Ginsburg's comments perfectly encapsulate the end of authority:
voiced by someone at the highest echelons of the U.S. democratic system, they reflect a loss of confidence, a loss of faith, and a sense of
confusion about the U.S. mission in the world. When elites themselves
talk like this, how are the American people supposed to feel any confidence?

It is my contention, however, that there is nothing wrong *intrinsical-
ly* with U.S. democracy that cannot be fixed. Perhaps it is getting late in
the day—our problems are mounting up—but the problem is not, as
some have argued, a "failure of democracy" or even a "failure of capitalism." The failure of *leadership* is the ultimate cause of the crisis of

authority. And leadership will be needed if the United States is to reclaim its role as beacon of hope and freedom.

While political dysfunction in the United States has prompted extensive analysis, comparatively little commentary has focused on a fundamental point: that the trust breakdown in the United States has significance beyond our shores. Whether it wants to or not, the United States is fated to lead at this time in history. We must do better to improve conditions at home and set an example abroad.

Many in the United States today are skeptical of that point of view, but their denial of U.S. responsibility is mostly wishful thinking. Consider the remarks by a Jordanian journalist at a recent Clinton Global Initiative meeting in New York:

> It's not just that we simply read about your news from afar. We use the United States as a reference point, a focal point. And a central reference for our own actions. When you fail, it makes failure here easier. When American politicians are corrupt, it signals to politicians around the world that it's okay for them to be corrupt. When the American legislature is paralyzed in never-ending gridlock, it says that intraparty cooperation is an unattainable goal and gives politicians a way to avoid working together to find solutions.[38]

"We're still indispensable," the *New York Times*'s Tom Friedman reminds us, "but the problems are much more intractable. Our allies are not what they used to be, and neither are our enemies, who are less superpowers and more superempowered angry men and women. A lot of countries will need to go back to the blackboard, back to the basics of human capacity building, before they can partner with us on anything."[39] But they want and need to partner with us.

The longer the United States puts off confronting the real issues, the more tempted citizens in other countries will be to believe that the American system—and with it Western democracy—no longer works. If we are to restore democratic legitimacy around the world, America must lead.

WHAT THIS BOOK IS ABOUT

Most people in the West understand that democracy, the rule of law, and free-market capitalism have produced the greatest wealth, the greatest opportunity, and the broadest individual freedoms in the history of the world. The question is this: How do we adapt our institutions—international, national, and local—to address the challenges of the twenty-first century? How do we solve the problems of slow economic growth, unemployment, income inequality, environmental degradation, energy shortages, and unequal educational opportunity?

It is not, as some radical voices insist, a matter of ridding ourselves of outdated institutions and values. Far from it: we must revitalize them in order to restore authority and legitimacy and thus rebuild public trust.

The purpose of this book will be to systematically analyze the crises facing democracies and autocratic governments alike; present a first-hand, detailed assessment of why this has happened; and offer a blueprint for how we can restore public trust in government and economic institutions.

In 2012, I published a book called *Hopelessly Divided*, which analyzed the breakdown in governance in the United States, just as the problems facing the country—debt, unemployment, high energy prices, falling incomes, and income inequality—were metastasizing. After describing the deep-seated, systemic problems facing the American political system, from Super PAC money and hyperpartisanship to excessive lobbyist influence and redistricting abuses, I wrote, "I want to conclude by suggesting that, unless we have a broad-based commitment to change and to a national conversation and dialogue about the systemic problems we face, we are going to fail. . . . If we don't recognize the threat we face from the corruption of our system, and work to change that system, we *will* fail—all of us. That much is certain."

I believe the same argument applies globally today, and the same urgency: time is growing short, and we need to articulate our best ideas and act on them. It is my hope that this book serves as a contribution to that effort.

NOTES

The epigraphs in this chapter are drawn from the following sources: Ezra Klein, "A Breakdown of Trust," *Washington Post*, October 11, 2011, http://www.washingtonpost.com/blogs/ ezra-klein/post/a-breakdown-of-trust/2011/10/07/gIQAVCjrSL_blog.html; Lydia Polgreen, "Upheaval Grips South Africa as Hopes for Its Workers Fade," *New York Times*, October 14, 2012, http://www.nytimes.com/2012/10/14/world/africa/unfulfilled-promises-are-replacing-prospects-of-a-better-life-in-south-africa.html; John Glionna, "A Year after Tsunami, a Cloud of Distrust Hangs over Japan," *Los Angeles Times*, March 11, 2012, http://articles.latimes. com/2012/mar/11/world/la-fg-japan-quake-trust-20120311; and David Kirkpatrick, "Protests in Jordan Continue, with Calls for Ending King's Rule," *New York Times*, November 16, 2011, http://www.nytimes.com/2012/11/16/world/middleeast/protesters-in-jordan-call-for-ending-king-abdullah-iis-rule.html.

1. Jim Yardley, "Leaders' Response Magnifies Outrage in India Rape Case," *New York Times*, December 29, 2012, http://www.nytimes.com/2012/12/30/world/asia/weak-response-of-india-government-in-rape-case-stokes-rage.html.

2. Polgreen, "Upheaval Grips South Africa."

3. "Russian Elections: Your Views," BBC News, March 5, 2012, http://www.bbc.co.uk/news/world-europe-17260711.

4. "CNN: Iranian Protestor 'Sarah' Speaks Out," YouTube, February 15, 2011, archived at http://www.youtube.com/watch?v=oWRveQ8ikG8.

5. Jodi Rudoren and Ranya Kadri, "Protests over Gas Prices in Jordan Turn Deadly," *New York Times*, November 14, 2012, http://www.nytimes.com/2012/11/15/world/middleeast/jordan-protests-turn-deadly-on-second-day.html.

6. Ibid.

7. Thomas L. Friedman, "Did You Hear the One about the Bankers?" *New York Times*, October 29, 2011, http://www.nytimes.com/2011/10/30/opinion/sunday/friedman-did-you-hear-the-one-about-the-bankers.html.

8. David Kirkpatrick and Mayy El Sheikh, "Citing Deadlock, Egypt's Leader Seizes New Power and Plans Mubarak Retrial," *New York Times*, November 22, 2011, http://www.nytimes.com/2012/11/23/world/middleeast/egypts-president-morsi-gives-himself-new-powers.html.

9. Polgreen, "Upheaval Grips South Africa."

10. "Italy Student Protests Turn Violent in Several Cities," Euronews, May 10, 2012, http://www.euronews.com/2012/10/05/italy-student-protests-turn-violent-in-several-cities/.

11. "Hundreds of Protestors Clash with Police in Naples," RT, May 11, 2012, http://rt.com/news/italy-protests-police-clashes-041/.

12. Liz Alderman and Niki Kitsantonis, "Markets Falter in Europe amid Protests on Austerity," September 26, 2012, http://www.nytimes.com/2012/09/27/world/europe/greece-faces-national-strike-to-protest-austerity.html.

13. "Anti-Merkel Protestors Clash with Police in Athens," Euronews, September 10, 2012, http://www.euronews.com/2012/10/09/anti-merkel-protesters-clash-with-police-in-athens/.

14. "Spain Protests: 'We Want Change,'" BBC News, May 21, 2011, http://www.bbc.co.uk/news/world-europe-13482778.

15. Raphael Minder, "Austerity Protests Are Rude Awakening in Portugal," *New York Times*, October 14, 2012, http://www.nytimes.com/2012/10/15/world/europe/portugal-readies-budget-with-job-cuts-and-tax-increases.html.

16. "Europe's Austerity Protests: Mad as Hell," *The Guardian*, September 26, 2012, http://www.guardian.co.uk/commentisfree/2012/sep/26/europe-austerity-protests-mad-hell.

17. Guy Sorman, "The New Rebellions," *City Journal* Online. http://www.city-journal.org/2012/22_1_tech-empowered-protesters.html.

18. Jeff Zeleny and Megan Thee-Brenan, "New Poll Finds a Deep Distrust of Government," *New York Times*, October 25, 2011, http://www.nytimes.com/2011/10/26/us/politics/poll-finds-anxiety-on-the-economy-fuels-volatility-in-the-2012-race.html.

19. Ibid.

20. Paul Volcker, "What the New President Should Consider," *New York Review of Books*, December 6, 2012, http://www.nybooks.com/articles/archives/2012/dec/06/what-new-president-should-consider/.

21. Klein, "A Breakdown of Trust."

22. Harry Bradford, "10 Countries with the Worst Income Inequality: OECD," Huffington Post, updated July 23, 2011, http://www.huffingtonpost.com/2011/05/23/10-countries-with-worst-income-inequality_n_865869.html#s278244&title=1_Chile. The OECD is the Organisation for Economic Co-operation and Development.

23. Jeff Zeleny, "Thousands Rally in Capital to Protest Big Government," *New York Times*, September 12, 2009, http://www.nytimes.com/2009/09/13/us/politics/13protestweb.html.

24. Ellen Barry, "After Russian Floods, Grief, Rage, and Deep Mistrust," *New York Times*, July 10, 2012, http://www.nytimes.com/2012/07/11/world/europe/after-russian-floods-grief-rage-and-deep-mistrust.html.

25. Glionna, "A Year after Tsunami."

26. Becky Barrow and Hugo Duncan, "We're Not Even Halfway through Economic Crisis, Warns King . . . and Interest Rates Could Be Slashed to Zero," *MailOnline*, June 26, 2012, http://www.dailymail.co.uk/news/article-2164863/Were-halfway-economic-crisis-warns-king--rates-slashed-zero.html.

27. Joe Bavier, "Congo War–Driven Crisis Kills 45,000 a Month: Study," Reuters, January 22, 2008, http://www.reuters.com/article/2008/01/22/us-congo-democratic-death-idUSL2280201220080122.

28. "Trust Barometer Executive Summary," Edelman Trust Barometer 2012 Annual Global Study, January 19, 2012, http://www.scribd.com/doc/79026497/2012-Edelman-Trust-Barometer-Executive-Summary.

29. "CNN Poll: Trust in Government at All Time Low," CNN, September 28, 2011, http://politicalticker.blogs.cnn.com/2011/09/28/cnn-poll-trust-in-government-at-all-time-low/.

30. Ron Fournier and Sophie Quinton, "In Nothing We Trust," *National Journal*, April 26, 2012, http://www.nationaljournal.com/features/restoration-calls/in-nothing-we-trust-20120419.

31. Keith Thomson, "Could Romney-Linked Electronic Voting Machines Jeopardize Ohio's Vote Accuracy?" Huffington Post, October 26, 2012, http://www.huffingtonpost.com/kcith-thomson/could romney linked elect_b_2025490.html.

32. Ray V. Hartwell III, "Bring Out Yer Dead!" American Spectator, August 14, 2012, http://spectator.org/archives/2012/08/14/bring-out-yer-dead.

33. James Kanter and Andrew Higgins, "New Setback for European Union as Budget Talks Falter Over Administrative Costs," *New York Times*, November 23, 2012, http://www.nytimes.com/2012/11/24/world/europe/european-union-budget-talks-collapse.html.

34. NBC News and News Services, "Thousands Rally in Karachi for Malala, 14-Year-Old Pakistani Girl Shot by Taliban," MSNBC News, October 14, 2012, http://worldnews.nbcnews.com/_news/2012/10/14/14431038-thousands-rally-in-karachi-for-malala-14-year-old-pakistani-girl-shot-by-taliban.

35. Thomas Friedman, "It's Not Just about Us," *New York Times*, October 9, 2012, http://www.nytimes.com/2012/10/10/opinion/friedman-what-romney-didnt-say.html.

36. Adam Liptak, "'We the People' Loses Appeal with People Around the World," *New York Times*, February 6, 2012, http://www.nytimes.com/2012/02/07/us/we-the-people-loses-appeal-with-people-around-the-world.html.

37. Ibid.

38. Private conversation with Jordanian journalist.

39. Thomas Friedman, "My Secretary of State," *New York Times*, November 27, 2012, http://www.nytimes.com/2012/11/28/opinion/friedman-my-secretary-of-state.html.

I

WHY THE CRISIS OF AUTHORITY MATTERS

The state has lost a lot of its capacity to govern effectively.
                    —Rob Malley, International Crisis Group

The current predicament of the world economy is all the more poignant because it is unnecessary. This is a political and ideological crisis, not a technocratic one.
                    —Alan Beattie, *Who's in Charge Here?*

If we are really able to address these mega-challenges of the future then we would be able to restore the trust in leadership—and I believe the world needs leadership.
                    —Werner Wenning, Supervisory Board chairman, Bayer

This book is fundamentally different from other books about trust. It's not just about documenting a loss of confidence as reflected in declining poll ratings, though we've seen that, too (in the next chapter I'll examine several important international surveys that chronicle this loss of trust, especially the Edelman Trust Barometer). It's also about the wholesale loss of authority of government and financial institutions and its implications for the international order—tangible and dangerous implications. And it's about how this crisis, coming at this time in history, has the potential to be much more destructive than most people realize.

Given what the world has accomplished since the end of the Cold War—after nearly half a century of worrying about nuclear apocalypse—it's tempting to assume that the international community will somehow get it together in time and stave off disaster. But the future is unwritten: there are no guarantees that these problems will be resolved or that the world won't devolve into chaos. After all, we live in a time of unparalleled number and variety of extremist or antisystemic movements, many the direct outgrowth of institutional failures. We face real challenges, real risks, and real scenarios. The most significant global crisis since the 1930s could lead in any number of damaging directions if governments don't work to regain the trust of their citizens.

Already we can see the effects, in real-world events, of systems that fail to function. But there's a still larger issue: *the loss of trust is rendering us, in a collective sense, impotent and inactive in the face of enormous global challenges.*

A SOMBER SURVEY

In September 2012, the world got a raw glimpse of what happens when, as William Butler Yeats famously put it, "things fall apart": in over twenty countries around the world, but especially in the Middle East, anti-American and anti-Western rioting and demonstrations erupted. While the rioting and violence had specific political contexts, they also illustrated a much broader issue: apart from local politics or religious grievances, this is what happens when institutional authority breaks down and public anger and rage have no other outlet.

The consequences of the September riots were gravest in Libya, where a terrorist attack on the U.S. embassy on the eleventh anniversary of the September 11 attacks took the lives of four Americans, including the respected American ambassador Chris Stevens. The Libyan attack turned out to have been premeditated by terrorist groups, but the demonstrations in dozens of other countries had nothing to do with terrorism; they were driven by public outrage over the Internet release of an anti-Muslim film.

The movie, only the trailer of which played on YouTube, was a crude propaganda film slandering the Prophet Muhammad. As with the Danish cartoons in 2006 and other similar incidents, the anti-Muslim movie created a rallying point for mass unrest in the Arab world and in other countries with large Muslim populations. Clearly the massive international unrest in response to this film indicates that freedom of expression has a long way to go in the Muslim world.

Looking beyond the immediate causes, however, the riots also showed the consequences of the breakdown in institutional authority: the rioters' and hooligans' religious grievances were a convenient pretext for more intractable real-world problems like massive unemployment and political disenfranchisement. "We have, throughout the Arab world, a young, unemployed, alienated, and radicalized group of people, mainly men, who have found a vehicle to express themselves," declared Rob Malley of the International Crisis Group. Across the Middle East, he said, especially in countries like Egypt and Tunisia, "the state has lost a lot of its capacity to govern effectively. Paradoxically, that has made it more likely that events like the video will make people take to the streets and act in the way they did."[1]

Yet it isn't just in the Middle East that states have lost their capacity to govern. Recent years have offered one example after another of large-scale governance failures with the direst results. To take just a few:

- In Japan, the Fukushima nuclear disaster of March 2011 released about one-fifth as much radioactive cesium as the 1986 Chernobyl disaster in the Soviet Union. Traces of radiation were found in Tokyo's water and agricultural products, 90,000 residents lost their homes, and the cleanup of the evacuated areas could take decades. An independent investigative commission later called the incident a man-made disaster and declared that "its effects could have been mitigated by a more effective human response."[2]
- In 2012, the Russian government failed to provide either a competent early-warning system or effective relief for flood victims in Krymsk. Over 150 people died amid government refusal to release information on death toll, causes of the flood, and its own poor response.
- In July 2012, massive power outages in India affected up to 620 million people, the largest power failure in world history.
- Monsoons, mostly affecting the Sindh province, overwhelmed Pakistan in summer 2012, affecting 4.5 million people and forcing hundreds of thousands to seek shelter in relief camps—yet the

Pakistani government refused foreign assistance, claiming it had matters well in hand.

- In 2011 and 2012, countries in East and West Africa—Somalia, Djibouti, Ethiopia, and Kenya in the East and nations in the Sahel region of West Africa, including Burkina Faso, Chad, and Niger—suffered debilitating famines, with death tolls in the hundreds of thousands, including countless children.
- The global community faces an enduring health and clean-water crisis: according to the World Health Organization, about 2.6 billion people—half the developing world—lack even a simple "improved" latrine, and 1.1 billion people have no access to any type of improved drinking source of water. As a result, 1.6 million people—90 percent of them children—die every year as a result of diarrheal diseases (including cholera).[3]
- The European Union, once touted as the most inspiring political creation to come out of the Second World War, continues to face enormous uncertainty about its future. In November 2012, a summit meeting of European leaders collapsed after failure to reach agreement on the EU's Multiannual Financial Framework, its seven-year budget plan.
- And in the United States, where the national debt will shortly exceed the GDP for the first time in history, even an impending catastrophe of unsustainable entitlement costs is not sufficient motivation to bring Democrats and Republicans to a workable compromise.

The crisis of authority has implications for every country in the world, because in a global political environment there is no such thing as an isolated event.

In another time, the breakdown of authority across societies would be a serious but containable problem—one that individual nations could address (or ignore) from the relative safety of their own borders, with little risk of spillover effects or international ramifications. Today, however, the global crisis of trust within an interconnected global political system affects everyone, and it threatens potentially catastrophic consequences—from a breakdown of our international economic system to a weakening of international political institutions for conflict resolution and mediation. The global proportions of the crisis make it imperative that societies and governments reform and remake themselves for the challenges of our young century.

Consider just one: cyber security.

In an October 2012 speech, U.S. defense secretary Leon Panetta warned that Americans faced the possibility of a "cyber Pearl Harbor" in the near future unless significant new safety measures were implemented. He warned that increasingly sophisticated computer hackers—especially from Russia, China, and Iran—could initiate an attack that would bring down portions of the nation's infrastructure, causing catastrophic damage.

"An aggressor nation or extremist group could use these kinds of cyber tools to gain control of critical switches," Panetta said. "They could derail passenger trains or, even more dangerous, derail passenger trains loaded with lethal chemicals. They could contaminate the water supply in major cities or shut down the power grid across large parts of the country."[4] Issues like cyber security make it clear how vital multinational cooperation, joint efforts, and information sharing will be in the twenty-first century, when small groups—like nineteen Arab men in September 2001—can affect the course of history.

THE THREAT BROKEN TRUST PRESENTS

Anyone reasonably conversant in world events would probably agree that we're living in a time of great international challenge, when the stability of everything from the global economy to basic governance is under threat. The most urgent problems, to my mind, include:

- income inequality and global poverty;
- the ongoing challenge of restarting economic growth and sustainability;
- crony capitalism and the corruptions of global aid;
- public-health problems, including pandemics and famines;
- climate change, deteriorating polar ice caps, and environmental degradation;
- nuclear and cyber security and other challenges in a multipolar world;
- international drug trafficking and money laundering; and

- disaster relief and the challenge of securing global food and energy supplies.

Unless some semblance of trust in government and other important institutions can be restored, these problems will only get worse. Some of them have reached a point of such severity that we really have no more time to lose. Consider the problem of global poverty: over three billion people, nearly half of the Earth's population, live on less than $2.50 a day.[5] Compounding this issue is the particularly grim fate of girls in many developing countries. Whether being forced into child marriages or prevented from getting even a rudimentary education, young girls face enormous barriers. According to the Population Reference Bureau, "child marriages are especially common in South Asia, sub-Saharan Africa, and in some parts of Latin America, where one in seven girls marr[ies] before the age of fifteen and as many as 38 percent marry before they turn eighteen." Furthermore, despite the oppression they suffer, "adolescent girls today do not benefit proportionally from development programs designed for women; simply because they are often invisible in their communities, adolescent girls might be among the hardest-to-reach populations in the developing world."[6]

One of the issues preventing a better and more effective response to global poverty is the chronic and often scandalous problem of corruption in foreign aid. It's a problem with a long history that unfortunately shows little sign of changing. The problems of the world's poor require such vast efforts, and coordination between so many interest groups, that corruption may well be inevitable—at least to some degree.

But something must be done to reduce it: global-aid and delivery groups—and nongovernmental organizations more broadly—are widely perceived as the world's good guys, and yet they also often fall far short of this mark and even become villains themselves. How can we ever expect to regain our trust in politicians and financiers when we often can't even trust NGOs?

Many Americans remember the corruption of the UN's Oil for Food Program during the 1990s and early 2000s, for instance. It was a program initiated by President Clinton to be administered through the UN on behalf of the Iraqi people, then under stiff sanctions for Saddam Hussein's actions after the First Gulf War. It would allow Iraq to sell oil on the world market in exchange for critical food and medical supplies.

But the program was soon rife with corruption and abuse and with allegations that profits were skimmed off the top by Iraqi officials and UN officers. Oil for Food is a classic example of all that can go wrong in foreign aid.

A decade and a half later, depressingly little has changed. The $20 billion Global Fund to Fight Aids, Tuberculosis and Malaria, which has usually enjoyed positive press, faced allegations in 2012 that nearly *two-thirds* of some of its grants went unaccounted for. As the *Economist* reported, "For Fund insiders, that was nothing new: evidence of the misuse of $34m paid out in Mali, Mauritania, Djibouti, and Zambia became public knowledge in October."[7]

Multilateral organizations have likewise failed grievously when it comes to addressing food shortages and famines. The problem is not the international community's inaction but the fact that many of its actions have, in fact, exacerbated problems. Abdoulaye Wade, the ex-president of Senegal, referred to the UN Food and Agriculture Organization (FAO) as a "bottomless pit of money" that should be abolished for its inability to increase global food production.[8] Indeed, decades of agricultural neglect by major institutions—the FAO, World Bank, and World Food Program (WFP)—have left rural countries with less food for their people.

As a Stanford University scholar of food security explains, "Everybody understands that 80 percent of the world's poor are in rural areas. But the World Bank for thirty years has basically said that market signals don't support agriculture, so we can't support agriculture."[9]

U.S. food-aid policy has inadvertently made hunger worse in many disaster areas. By shipping cheap, subsidized U.S. staples that flood the markets of these countries, the United States has undercut local farmers, ultimately hurting the countries' ability to feed themselves. A consensus has emerged that, in order to encourage local production, donor nations should instead purchase relief food as close as possible to disaster locations. In June 2012, antihunger activists worked with legislators to reform the main vehicle for American food aid, the U.S. Farm Bill, in that direction.[10] But a bipartisan Senate bill containing those revisions died in the House in September 2012. At this writing, America is without a farm bill for the first time in nearly fifty years.[11]

The World Food Program's scandal in Somalia in 2010 is a stark reminder of what can go wrong in the management of food crises. The internal UN report that accused the WFP of failing to get food to starving Somalis suggested collusion between WFP staffers, Islamist militants, and food transporters. The result was that up to half of the food the WFP shipped to Somalia was diverted, with some of it going to jihadists. Though the WFP denied the charges of corruption, facts are facts: desperately needed food did not reach Somalia. Two years later, a report by aid groups Oxfam and Save the Children blamed the deaths of thousands of Somalis and needless wasting of millions of dollars in aid on the international community's slow response. The report argued that governments, donors, aid groups, and the UN need to change their approach to such disasters.[12] That seems like an understatement.

The problem with corruption in global aid is threefold: first, it's obviously immoral to steal benefits meant for needy people; second, it causes additional trust issues among populations, who see little reason to believe in continued promises of assistance; and third, it diminishes the willingness of developed countries to offer such aid.

In the developed world, of course, such dire poverty and food shortages seem remote, but wealthier nations have their own version in the form of spiraling income inequality. It's an issue popularly associated with the United States, home to the world's leading economy and the most visible proponent of free-market economics. But while the inequality gap has grown to disturbing dimensions here, the United States is far from alone. Most of the major EU countries have seen gaps between rich and poor jump as well over the last generation, and, in developing free-market "tigers" like India, the gap is more like a chasm. According to a May 2011 report from the Organisation for Economic Co-operation and Development—which comprises thirty-four democratic, market-oriented countries—"the gap between rich and poor in OECD countries has reached its highest level for over thirty years."[13]

Needless to say, whether one is out of work and seeing no income or laboring with a stagnant income or falling behind as others race ahead, the income and wealth disparities of the last generation have had devastating effects on public confidence. Poll after poll across multiple countries shows that people have less trust in their governments in part as a result of income inequality. That shouldn't be hard to understand: if you were working hard for years at a time and getting nowhere while a small group of others prospered beyond their wildest dreams, you would probably think something was wrong too.

People do: everywhere you look, they do.

And as much as they blame the rich, greedy bankers, the super elites—take your pick regarding what to call the villains—they also reserve a substantial portion of blame for their governments, because they believe that these governments have collaborated with and aided those at the top at the expense of everyone else.

Even if it's somewhat overdrawn, this fundamental supposition— "the government doesn't care about people like me, only those with power and wealth"—might be one of the only things people all around the world agree on. They agree on it in unprecedented numbers. And until that fact changes, we will continue to face a deeply uncertain future.

WHY IT'S DIFFERENT TODAY

If you want to get a sense of how this time is different, why national and international systems seem to have broken down and ceased functioning, compare today's predicament with the U.S. government's response to the Great Depression—not in a policy sense but in a sense of overall effectiveness, action, and vision. In the 1930s, the systemic problems were arguably worse than today's, especially since institutions like the Federal Deposit Insurance Corporation and the Security and Exchange Commission were not yet in existence—let alone Social Security or anything resembling a public safety net. Getting old in America, as getting old anywhere back then, generally meant falling on the good graces of one's children or, failing that, dying in poverty. When the U.S. economic collapse had gone into its third year—mirroring a global downturn—Americans went to the polls and elected Franklin Roosevelt. Time has raised many questions about the effectiveness of Roosevelt's New Deal solutions in addressing the hardships of the Depression, but the important point, for my purposes, is this: the majority of the nation trusted the government, even if they didn't agree with everything FDR did, to take steps that might alleviate the problem.

They saw government as the legitimate mechanism by which economic and political crises should be managed, and they had some degree of faith that it could do so.

Without that trust, Roosevelt would never have been able to implement the New Deal, which made a genuine impact on people's lives (again, we can disagree on its overall effectiveness, as many critics do).

Similarly, on December 7, 1941, when the United States was attacked at Pearl Harbor, the nation rallied around Roosevelt as war leader and made the sacrifices necessary to win the war. Again, time and history have raised plenty of questions about Roosevelt's judgment, but he had the support and trust of the American people, who recognized a national emergency when they saw one. Whatever the flaws in FDR's leadership, just imagine how much less effective it would have been had he not been able to count on a baseline of public trust and confidence. He earned that trust by showing that he understood the struggles of ordinary Americans.

We often hear laments today that "What we need is another Roosevelt" or another Churchill or some other great leader's name—fill in the blank. But we're not going to get one. Some say this is because the quality of leadership is much lower today; perhaps that is true. But why shouldn't we have more effective leaders today, in a better-educated world? The reason, it seems to me, is that no one, at a national or global level, enjoys the trust and legitimacy necessary to *become* a leader like Roosevelt.

Trust is the element missing today, not just in the United States but also internationally—and it presents a danger of the first order, because unless it is remedied the enormous challenges facing governments and societies simply cannot be solved.

The challenges extend well beyond the issue of inequality or the ongoing economic and fiscal struggles brought on by the financial crisis.

Health

Consider problems of international and global health. We have an ongoing AIDS crisis in Africa that will continue to require massive financial and human efforts to contain. The use of cheap, less effective drugs has led to resistant strains of malaria and the continuation of this epidemic disease, which kills between one and two million each year.[14]

It's clear that international institutions have a ways to go in terms of effectively handling global health epidemics like these. In the West, some serious attempts have been made to fight AIDS, such as President

Bush's PEPFAR, but no comparable and successful effort has come from the EU or UN. Funding, as usual, is an important element in combating these diseases, but lack of coordination and cooperation on the institutional level represents a clear failure of governance.

Meanwhile, a 2008 report from the World Health Organization warned that new diseases were emerging at a "historically unprecedented" rate—more than one per year. Just since the 1970s "the WHO has identified thirty-nine new diseases, including Ebola, SARS, bird flu, Nipahvirus, and Marburg hemorrhagic fever," according to a Natural-News report. [15] "It would be extremely naive and complacent to assume that there will not be another disease like AIDS, another Ebola, or another SARS, sooner or later," the WHO report says. Infectious-disease epidemics and pandemics remain a major concern globally, especially in an era of global travel, with over two billion airline passengers annually. WHO warns that diseases once thought confined to history—cholera, epidemic meningococcal disease, and yellow fever—are once again posing a threat, "while new diseases such as bird flu have the potential to infect as much as 25 percent of global population." [16]

What does this have to do with trust? Just listen to the appeal made by WHO director general Margaret Chan: "Given today's universal vulnerability to these threats, better security calls for global solidarity. International public-health security is both a collective aspiration and a mutual responsibility." [17]

Chan's vision won't be achievable, though, without a reconstruction of baseline levels of trust. For one thing, some countries, like Indonesia, don't want to participate in global efforts of this kind. Indonesia refused to share strains of the bird flu with the health organization, for example, and it's not the only nation to resist such cooperation. Further, unless governments can get their acts together on their own shores—and until their own people feel more secure economically—ambitious international efforts to improve global health are bound to fail, both politically and financially.

Given the role that travel plays in spreading epidemics and pandemics, it's also well to consider the impact of health problems on another issue that influences trust: immigration. Already we've seen the rise of intense nationalist and nativist parties around the globe, especially in Europe. These parties have a range of viewpoints, but one principle they share is opposition to immigration from countries not considered part of the dominant national culture. In most European countries this means opposition to immigration from Muslim-dominated nations in the Middle East or Africa—the latter, in particular, being a locus point for many of these diseases.

So long as the trust crisis goes unaddressed, don't expect the twenty-first-century challenges of epidemic and pandemic alleviation to take major steps forward—unless your idea of progress is closing all national borders and even deporting "foreigners" from the European continent. That's what the most extreme nationalist parties want to do, and, as their national governments continue to flounder, these groups are attracting more support.

Climate Change and Environmental Degradation

Climate change is another problem in its roots and scope that has yet to be properly addressed by international institutions. On both the global and the state level, there has been a wayward and meandering path to curb emissions and to implement effective environmental policy. Like global health, the issues of climate change and environmental degradation will require multinational cooperation.

Heading into this year's international energy summit in London, Maria van der Hoeven, the executive director of the International Energy Agency, wrote that "the world's energy system is being pushed to breaking point . . . the current state of affairs is unacceptable precisely because we have a responsibility and a golden opportunity to act."[18] But to date, little progress has been made. The expectation that this crisis can be put off until next year, or that other matters are more pressing, underlies too much of global inaction on climate change.

The urgency of the situation was underscored in September 2012, when the National Snow and Ice Data Center in Boulder, Colorado, announced that Arctic sea ice had reached its "lowest seasonal minimum extent in the satellite record since 1979," thus reinforcing "the long-term downward trend in Arctic ice extent."[19] As Elizabeth Kolbert reported in the *New Yorker*, the sea-ice level the center reported was down 20 percent just from 2007. "We are now seeing changes occur in a matter of years that, in the normal geological scheme of things, should take thousands, even millions, of times longer than that," she wrote, pointing to a forecast by an Arctic ice-cap expert that, based on current conditions, the Arctic Ocean could be "entirely ice-free in summer by 2016."[20]

One shouldn't have to be an ardent environmentalist to find this alarming.

In June 2012, the United Nations Conference on Sustainable Development held its twentieth annual conference, dubbed Rio+20 to commemorate the first event in Rio de Janeiro in 1992—the first Earth Summit, which produced a global treaty on climate change. Unfortunately, the conference concluded with little in the way of tangible progress. From the start, delegates' plans for international action were constrained by the global economy and financial crises or other matters back home. Those noticeably absent from Rio+20 included President Obama, German chancellor Angela Merkel, and British prime minister David Cameron.

The absent sense of urgency to the climate-change crisis and the preoccupation with the financial crisis has eclipsed an issue of tremendous importance. The meeting did produce an agreement called "The Future We Want," which contains many commendable goals—but also few, if any, enforceable mechanisms on global warming or other issues. As a result, some critics denounced the conference as all show, including the antipoverty organization CARE, which called it "nothing more than a political charade." Greenpeace called it an "epic failure," while the World Wildlife Fund deemed it a "colossal failure of leadership and vision." Even Pew's environmental group, trying to be charitable, could only muster this: "It would be a mistake to call Rio a failure," the group said, "but for a once-in-a-decade meeting with so much at stake, it was a far cry from a success."[21]

Despite the hard scientific data demonstrating the persistent threat that climate change represents to our health, economic well-being, and survival, we lack a concerted international approach to address it. In the decision between choosing pain now or more pain later, the international community has seemingly opted for more pain later. An editorial in the *Guardian* published at the close of the summit lambasted the leaders of the Rio+20 for a wasted opportunity to lead: "Global leadership has failed lamentably to develop answers or institutions capable of charting a just route through the global jungle."[22] The UN's December 2012 meeting in Doha likewise offered little hope for optimism.

Part and parcel of climate change is the even broader problem of environmental degradation—the generalized depletion or despoliation of the Earth's resources, whether water, air, or soil, along with species eradication and destruction of habitats and ecosystems. In 2004, the UN's High Level Threat Panel listed environmental degradation as one of its ten threats to future international well-being and security.

Concerted, coherent international action is also needed to guard against another potential global food crisis. In part due to extreme weather, droughts in the United States and Russia sent food prices soaring in 2012 and prompted UN agencies to urge a series of measures to hold commodity prices down—including resisting the urge to restrict exports and holding down panic buying. But concerted action has the best chance of succeeding when governments are stable, don't find cooperation threatening, and enjoy public trust—the lack of which underlies national and international problems on a much broader scale than many commonly understand.

Perhaps the best way to think about it is that trust is, ultimately, an issue of *security*—financial, economic, health, military, legal, and civic.

Nuclear Security: The Challenge of Iran and North Korea

The most broad-ranging global-security challenge is the issue of nuclear proliferation and the potential of state or nonstate actors to fashion crude (and not-so-crude) nuclear weapons. It's an issue that gets plenty of discussion, but no coherent global solution exists. The coming showdown over the Iranian nuclear program, for instance, in which the Iranians have enjoyed support from the Russians and Chinese, will once again test American (and Western) resolve—as will the ongoing issue of the North Korean nuclear program.

The Iranian situation has been an international-security crisis at least since 2009, when Iran first accepted, and then reneged on, an agreement to send 75 percent of its low-enriched uranium to Russia and France, where it would be converted into a special fuel for a reactor making medical materials in Tehran. Shortly afterward, Iran announced it wouldn't do that after all, at least not until it had gotten additional nuclear fuel for a reactor in Tehran. And then UN nuclear inspectors discovered a new enrichment site being built in the Shiite holy city of

Qom. When the UN demanded it freeze the project, Iran refused, even pledging to build ten more such sites.[23]

Since then, the West and Iran have faced off on the issue of Iran's nuclear ambitions. The United States has imposed unilateral sanctions, which have done real damage to the Iranian economy but have so far done little to persuade the regime to reconsider its position. In addition, the UN and the International Atomic Energy Agency have been unable to deliver a conclusive report on Iran's nuclear-energy program and its purposes, thus leaving the issue, for better or worse, in the hands of the American president.

Contemplating a nuclear Iran is a frightening prospect, since it would give Iran unrivalled regional power and the potential to project its power beyond the Middle East—and even sell nuclear weapons to terrorists. During the American 2012 presidential campaign, neither President Obama nor his Republican challenger, Mitt Romney, disavowed the possibility of using precision strikes to destroy Iran's major nuclear sites. At least from a rhetorical standpoint, an American bombing strike on Iran remains a possibility. Israel, for its part, has been even more confrontational in its language, particularly under the leadership of Prime Minister Benjamin Netanyahu.

Of course, the problems with such a strike, both technical and otherwise, cannot be underestimated. First, the strike might not be successful. While U.S. and Israeli intelligence know more or less where Iran's major nuclear sites are, destroying them all would be quite a challenge. Secret sites could exist as well. If the United States were to attack, the political and strategic fallout would be considerable. An attack on Iran would earn sympathy for Tehran's regime, both inside and outside Iran, likely provoking even more anti-American opposition in Islamic countries. The price of oil would spike drastically if Iran ceased its exports or if conflict caused its production facilities to shut down. A war between Israel and Iran would be nearly inevitable, and it could very well draw in the entire region. The question will hinge on whether Israel and the United States believe that anything but a strike will prevent Iran from going nuclear.

In short, the failure of international structures to put into place and implement an effective inspection regime for Iran could lead the region to the brink of war.

In North Korea, too, the limits of international diplomacy and multinational institutions are all too apparent. North Korea has long sought nuclear armaments as a source of security against the United States and a potential leveraging tool against South Korea. A special negotiation series, called the six-party talks, has brought together most of the countries with high stakes in the issue to discuss a common way forward.

At best, however, the six-party talks have a mixed record of success. Their fortunes reflect the difficulty of finding consensus among six nations with competing interests and goals; in some cases (as with the Asian neighbors), there is a long trail of historical mistrust and bad blood. After years of six-party talks, the issue has not been resolved to anyone's satisfaction—except perhaps North Korea's, given that the isolated dictatorship continues to keep its adversaries, and even its Chinese sponsor, off balance. The parties don't trust one another, and they're painfully aware of their diverging interests.

At the same time, the six-party talks, however inadequate their record, show diplomacy's potential, even when it goes unrealized. In spite of vigorous posturing from all parties, practically no blood has been shed and tensions have been contained. One can look at the six-party talks and see the outline for a much broader international effort at solving these problems. The more buy-in from more nations, the more diluted the various national rivalries would become, and the better our chances of possibly reaching a lasting resolution.

One of the major problems facing such efforts, however, is an American-made one, and also has to do with trust: in the post-Iraq decade, after an American president had made claims about weapons of mass destruction and links to the 9/11 attacks that turned out to be untrue, how likely is it that another president will be able to call upon public support for necessary action? The skepticism stems from the widespread sense among the public that the government is no longer *worthy* of trust in its national-security policy. Thus the world's only superpower faces the future under a cloud about its role in the world—and the world, which needs American leadership now more than ever, faces a leadership vacuum.

Broader Security Challenges in a Multipolar World

Lack of trust will impact every other important international-security effort among the Western democracies—the ongoing and building threat of a Russian-Chinese axis, for instance, in which both countries are collaborating to exercise their strength on a whole range of territorial and economic issues. How will the West offset this power if citizenries believe almost no exercise of military power can be justified? How will Western citizenries, with their corrosive attitude toward their own elites, ever again come to accept arguments for U.S. and Western primacy in important international conflicts?

These disputes range from the multiparty Asian disputes over several island archipelagos—some of which are said to have lucrative energy deposits—to the pervasive and seemingly eternal stare-down between Pakistan and India, nuclear-armed superpowers on a collision course shaped by nationalism, religion, and history.

Another area that will undoubtedly become more prominent in the years ahead is cyber security. U.S. defense secretary Leon Panetta, whom I quoted at the outset of this chapter, has warned of a "cyber Pearl Harbor." Among other adversaries, he was thinking of Vladimir Putin's Russia, which has already made substantial and devastating use of cyber war, as in its 2008 conflict with Georgia, when Internet-service attacks crippled Georgian communication networks and helped short-circuit a rebellion. More broadly, the Chinese (also cited by Panetta) have been implicated in broad-ranging cyber warfare and industrial espionage. The U.S. government is racing to keep up with Chinese cyber-war innovations. For example, as John Avlon reported in 2009, "spies from Russia and China have cracked into the U.S. electrical grid and left behind software programs that could be used to disrupt or destroy critical infrastructure. 'If we go to war with them,' an intelligence official told the *Wall Street Journal* this April, 'they will try to turn them on.'"[24]

Avlon also reported that recovered Al-Qaeda computers contained information on Supervisory Control and Data Acquisition (SCADA) systems in the United States. SCADA systems, never meant to be accessible to the public, control a huge range of critical infrastructure, from electrical grids and nuclear plants to fiber-optic cables and water storage and distribution facilities. Finally, there is the problem of "hack-

tivists," lone individuals with the technological know-how and the motivation—whatever it may be—to do serious damage to systems. Their
potential for mayhem became apparent in 2007, when an IBM Security
Services researcher test hacked into a nuclear power plant and found it
to be "one of the easiest penetration tests I've ever done."[25]

The new age of cyber warfare highlights a central truth about our
multipolar world: smaller nations and even small, nonstate groups can
cause havoc, and any one region could affect any other. It's not just
cyberspace or terrorists, either: look at the growing problem of international piracy on the high seas once protected by U.S. naval authority, for
instance. Security concerns can no longer be contained regionally.

Once again, we see the need for a broad-based international security
umbrella that can only be formulated and instituted through cross-
national alliances—which, in turn, require the kinds of public support
that any important government initiative requires. How can the United
States expect, however, that the EU will be there for that struggle when
the Brussels-based institution is regarded with such contempt by so
many on the Continent? Besides, how will the EU be able to sustain
such a project financially when several of its member states stand on the
brink of financial ruin?

The loss of trust also presents obstacles in the security area that
dominated global imaginations in the post–9/11 decade—counterterrorism. The United States, for example, has been able to prevent another catastrophic attack domestically since 9/11 in large part because,
in this one crucial area, the American people have maintained a solid
basis of trust in their government. The Obama administration has striv-
en to maintain its antiterror bona fides, vastly expanding such President
Bush–instituted measures as assassination of terrorists by drone attack.
Institutions like the NYPD, which may well be better than the FBI
when it comes to counterterrorism, have the broadest buy-in from New
Yorkers that it is possible to imagine for a public institution. Their
successes, now crystallized into "best practices," are emulated worldwide. Even the much-derided "security theater" at airports is accepted
by most Americans as a price to be paid for freedom of travel in a
post–9/11 age.

When President Obama gave an executive order to take out Osama
bin Laden, and the operation was carried out successfully, few critics

objected that the Al-Qaeda mastermind hadn't been captured instead and put on trial.

But beyond these crucial points of consensus, the lack of trust in government is making its presence felt in the security area and will continue to do so. Already, we have seen the near-total abandonment of American support for our military efforts in Afghanistan and Iraq. The Obama administration has ended one war officially (Iraq) while laying the groundwork to abandon the other (Afghanistan). In fact, U.S. combat deaths in both theaters have long since become nearly invisible to U.S. media and to the American people. Beyond their own families, the fallen men and women of the U.S. military may as well be fighting an invisible war, a conflict fought on some alternate plane of reality. This surely has to be a first in American history: regular, ongoing troop deaths in difficult military conflicts, with an almost total absence of public concern or awareness.

In my view, the United States will pay a price for its decision to step away from its international commitments in Iraq and Afghanistan in at least two respects: first, because we risk the failure of our objectives in both places, a failure that will be enormously bitter given the high price paid in blood and treasure; and second, because our abandonment of these efforts signals to the rest of the world that the United States may be serious about stepping away from its customary role as global leader. President Obama's "leading from behind" formulation, while well meaning, only strengthens this impression.

To some extent, an American pullback was inevitable. Pre–9/11, the world had seen a decade of *uni*-polarity, with the United States as the world's sole superpower. U.S. hegemony forged Western-friendly trade agreements and economic policies, some of which also coexisted with double standards on human rights in the developing world. All of this created considerable resentment around the world, which the immediate aftermath of 9/11 obscured. We had the world's sympathy for a time, but that time passed quickly.

The problem is, American paralysis is likely to have a very unfortunate impact on international conflict resolution. Distrust in governing institutions and generalized public cynicism about elites, however justified, will not help solve the massive challenges facing the international community.

Multinational Crime Rings

Security issues don't end with terror, nukes, and military disputes. Recent years have made clear that the international community faces mounting threats from multinational crime rings—everything from narco trafficking to money laundering, weapons sales, and even human trafficking. As summarized by the United Nations Office on Drugs and Crime:

> Organized crime has diversified, gone global, and reached macroeconomic proportions: illicit goods may be sourced from one continent, trafficked across another, and marketed in a third. Transnational organized crime can permeate government agencies and institutions, fuelling corruption, infiltrating business and politics, and hindering economic and social development. And it is undermining governance and democracy by empowering those who operate outside the law.[26]

It's not terribly surprising that money laundering would become an increasingly intractable problem in the twenty-first century, when computer and communications technology allow money to move all around the world rapidly and easily. As the United Nations Office on Drugs and Crime puts it, "There are two reasons why criminals—whether drug traffickers, corporate embezzlers, or corrupt public officials—have to launder money: the money trail is evidence of their crime and the money itself is vulnerable to seizure and has to be protected." The UNODC estimates that global money laundering now totals somewhere between $800 billion and $2 trillion—or 2 to 5 percent of global GDP.[27]

The problem we face today with crime rings is exacerbated by a problem deeply familiar to most Americans: the lack of a coherent or effective drug policy. I don't think it's unfair to say that Washington really doesn't have a policy. Crime overruns Central America, much of which is essentially ungovernable. Narco gangs control northern Mexico and parts of Honduras. No clear consensus exists on what the problem is—demand or production?—or what to do about it. We have no drug-prevention or interdiction strategy, and the problem of drug infestation, already acute on the Texas-Mexico border, has gone unaddressed. Parts of California, especially Los Angeles, are overrun by traffickers. Again, we see a huge problem with no clear solution—and, worse, no evidence of serious attempts to find one.

THE SPECTER OF INSTABILITY

Partly in response to the failures of their governments to provide effective leadership, protest movements have risen up in almost every major country: the *indignados* in Spain; the Russian protest movement; the protest movement in India; the antisystemic, budding political parties like the Pirates in Germany or the Five Star Movement in Italy. I'll also allude briefly to the two major protest movements in the United States: the Tea Party and Occupy Wall Street. All reflect, to some degree, a fundamental rejection of the prevailing system and its failures.

Up to now, almost none of these movements has engaged in political violence or insurrection. In fact, the main violent reactions have come from the government forces—as when Hosni Mubarak's forces moved against protesters in Cairo's Tahrir Square, Putin's police attacked Moscow protesters, and South African police opened fire on striking miners.

This is very heartening, of course, for what it says about the popular movements in so many nations around the world. I'm concerned, however, that the longer the problems I've described here go unaddressed, the greater the risk of broad-ranging political and social instability. The longer an unsustainable state of affairs is allowed to persist—whether it's a debt ratio incompatible with economic functioning, an unemployment rate destructive of social stability, or a political system that rewards insiders and ignores the needs of its law-abiding citizens—the more likely that something will explode.

Instability doesn't necessarily have to mean violence: some of the nations in Europe, like Greece and Spain, have come to the brink of a complete government meltdown due to insolvency. The rise of extremist parties across Europe has been—with one horrible exception, in Norway—mostly free of violence. But the growing allegiance many have to such socially divisive and often bigoted groups presents major challenges to the social fabric. African countries like Angola and South Africa look, on the surface, to be doing much better economically than their unfortunate neighbors, but political discontent is swelling in both countries, fueled by a growing sense that their governments don't deal honestly and fairly with their people. And even in the United States, secessionist petitions from half a dozen states flooded the White House website in the week after the 2012 election. While these petitions don't reflect serious, broad-based political movements—at least not yet— such efforts are profoundly troubling.

Put another way, we are seeing the credibility and legitimacy of our world system and way of life threatened. Some will think this mere fearmongering and believe that I am overstating the case in these instances. I'll leave that to the reader's judgment. Nonetheless, each of the issues that I've raised here, or any combination of them, has the potential to destabilize the world system that we have come to know and rely on. And this is the ultimate significance of the end of authority and why solutions are so essential to our future: nothing less than global stability and a functioning international order are at stake.

I very much hope that I am wrong about this. But I have been writing and commenting on politics for many years, and I have never seen the world, or the United States, so primed for dissolution.

Genuine solutions won't be forthcoming until institutions find a way to restore, at least in part, the public trust they once enjoyed. Unlike *authority*, a term that can seem abstract, *trust* is not only more visceral but also more measurable. In the last decade, Edelman has been tracking trust internationally through polls and surveys. Its recent results make clear how broadly trust in fundamental institutions has eroded around the world. Let's take a closer look at the data on loss of trust.

NOTES

The epigraphs in this chapter are drawn from the following sources: Rick Gladstone, "Anti-American Protests Flare beyond Mideast," *New York Times*, September 14, 2012, http://www.nytimes.com/2012/09/15/world/middleeast/anti-american-protests-over-film-enter-4th-day.html; Alan Beattie, "Book Extract: *Who's in Charge Here?*" *Financial Times*, March 8, 2012, http://www.ft.com/intl/cms/s/0/92022d64-6933-11e1-956a-00144feabdc0.html; and Simon Hooper, "Davos: Annan Warns of Global Governance 'Crisis,'" CNN Money, January 28, 2009, http://money.cnn.com/2009/01/28/news/economy/davos/index.htm.

1. Gladstone, "Anti-American Protests."

2. Hiroko Tabuchi, "Japan Declares Fukushima Crisis a Man-Made Disaster," *New York Times*, July 5, 2012, http://www.nytimes.com/2012/07/06/world/asia/fukushima-nuclear-crisis-a-man-made-disaster-report-says.html.

3. World Health Organization, "Health through Safe Drinking Water and Basic Sanitation," accessed July 3, 2013, http://www.who.int/water_sanitation_health/mdg1/en/index.html.

4. Elisabeth Bumiller and Thom Shanker, "Panetta Warns of Dire Threat of Cyberattack on U.S.," *New York Times*, October 11, 2012, http://www.nytimes.com/2012/10/12/world/panetta-warns-of-dire-threat-of-cyberattack.html.

5. Anup Shah, "Poverty Facts and Stats," Global Issues, last updated January 7, 2013, http://www.globalissues.org/article/26/poverty-facts-and-stats.

6. Kata Fustos, "Despite Wide-Ranging Benefits, Girls' Education and Empowerment Overlooked in Developing Countries," Population Reference Bureau, April 2010, http://www.prb.org/Articles/2010/girlseducation.aspx.

7. "Cleaning Up," *Economist*, February 17, 2011, http://www.economist.com/node/18176062.

8. Thaliff Deen, "Development: UN Bodies Under Fire for Food Crisis," Inter Press Service, May 5, 2008, http://www.ipsnews.net/2008/05/development-un-bodies-under-fire-for-food-crisis/.

9. Colum Lynch, "World Food Agencies Faulted in Food Crisis," *Washington Post*, May 19, 2008, http://www.washingtonpost.com/wp-dyn/content/article/2008/05/18/AR2008051802233.html.

10. Ron Nixon, "Senate Passes Farm Bill with Bipartisan Support," *New York Times*, June 21, 2012, http://www.nytimes.com/2012/06/22/us/politics/senate-passes-farm-bill-but-tougher-road-seen-in-house.html.

11. Jonathan Weisman, "Congress Heads for Home with Rancor Still Evident," *New York Times*, September 21, 2012, http://www.nytimes.com/2012/09/22/us/politics/lawmakers-going-home-with-rancor-still-evident.html.

12. Katharine Houreld, "Somalia Famine Response Too Slow, Thousands of People Died Needlessly: Report," Huffington Post, January 18, 2012, http://www.huffingtonpost.com/2012/01/18/somalia-famine-response_n_1212799.html.

13. Newsroom, "Society: Governments Must Tackle Record Gap between Rich and Poor Says OECD," OECD, May 12, 2011, www.oecd.org/newsroom/societygovernmentsmusttacklerecordgapbetweenrichandpoorsaysoecd.htm.

14. Nicholas White, "Antimalarial Drug Resistance," *J Clin Invest* 113 (April 2004), http://www.ncbi.nlm.nih.gov/pmc/articles/PMC385418/.

15. David Gutierrez, "WHO Warns of High Risk of Global Epidemic from Emerging Diseases," Natural News, January 5, 2008, http://www.naturalnews.com/022457_emerging_disease_World_Health_Organization.html.

16. Ibid.

17. Ibid.

18. Fiona Harvey and Damian Carrington, "Governments Failing to Avert Catastrophic Climate Change, IEA Warns," *Guardian*, April 25, 2012, http://www.guardian.co.uk/environment/2012/apr/25/governments-catastrophic-climate-change-iea.

19. "Arctic Sea Ice Extent Settles at Record Season Minimum," National Snow and Ice Data Center, September 19, 2012, http://nsidc.org/arcticseaicenews/2012/09/arctic-sea-ice-extent-settles-at-record-seasonal-minimum/.

20. Elizabeth Kolbert, "Hotter than Paul Ryan," *New Yorker*, September 28, 2012, http://www.newyorker.com/online/blogs/comment/2012/09/candidates-ignore-an-arctic-disaster.html.

21. Simon Romero and John Broder, "Progress on the Sidelines as Rio Conference Ends," *New York Times*, June 23, 2012, http://www.nytimes.com/2012/06/24/world/americas/rio20-conference-ends-with-some-progress-on-the-sidelines.html.

22. "Rio+20: Mañana, Mañana," *Guardian*, June 19, 2012, http://www.guardian.co.uk/commentisfree/2012/jun/19/rio-summit-manana-manana-editorial.

23. "Timeline: Iran's Nuclear Program since October 2009," Reuters, January 12, 2011, http://www.reuters.com/article/2011/01/12/us-iran-nuclear-events-idUSTRE70B7DQ20110112.

24. John Avalon, "The Cyber-Threat Grows," *City Journal* 19, no. 4 (Autumn 2009), http://www.city-journal.org/2009/19_4_snd-cyber-threat.html.

25. Ibid.

26. "Organized Crime," United Nations Office on Drugs and Crime, http://www.unodc.org/unodc/en/organized-crime/index.html.

27. "Money-Laundering and Globalization," United Nations Office on Drugs and Crime, accessed July 3, 2013, https://www.unodc.org/unodc/en/money-laundering/globalization.html.

2

DOCUMENTING AND UNDERSTANDING
THE LOSS OF TRUST

The 2012 Edelman Trust Barometer sees an unprecedented nine-point global decline in trust in government. . . . Business leaders should not be cheered by government's ineptitude, especially as trust in the two institutions seems to move in sync.
—Richard Edelman, Edelman Trust Survey

While the statistics on trust that I'll review in this chapter have been documented and, to some extent, reported in the media, it is my sense that their significance is not well understood or recognized. For all that has been written over the last five years on various crises, political and economic, I've seen little sign of recognition of the importance of trust. Trust is one of the most beneficial byproducts of effective leadership; it underpins any successful functioning of a government, an economy, and a functioning civil society. Correspondingly, its absence indicates leadership that has failed or gone awry. We've had explanations aplenty of how the financial crisis got started or who was to blame for the sub-prime-mortgage meltdown; we've had much less reflection on what it means when such large proportions of the public in multiple countries make it clear that they don't trust their government or other key institutions of their society.

What we'll see in this brief chapter is that trust has, for the most part, suffered a precipitous, across-the-board drop over recent years. It shouldn't require deep political philosophizing to grasp the basic significance of this development: any government, democratic or autocratic, will struggle to work effectively without a baseline of trust and approval from the public. Up to now I've discussed the failure of governance and leadership as the key factor in eroding authority and thus destroying public trust. But the relationship between these factors doesn't flow in just one direction: the corresponding loss of trust works as an ongoing disabler of leadership and governance, too. When governments no longer have buy-in from the electorate, they find it immeasurably more difficult to win support for, and to implement, policies that might address serious national problems.

TRUST AND ITS CONNECTION TO GOVERNANCE

A little over a decade ago, a group of us saw the trust crisis coming and decided to put trust on the agenda. We created the Edelman Trust Barometer as a way to gauge trust in institutions, industries, and societies. We were ahead of the curve, in many respects, in our recognition of trust as a central issue to our political and economic well-being—but none of us foresaw the trust breakdown escalating to this level. It has exceeded all expectations. And it is truly dangerous.

We haven't observed public anger like this in decades. Atop the list of public complaints are unaccountable politicians and institutions that treat their power as a right, not a privilege. The time of reliable government, strong international institutions, and effective global elites has long passed.

In their recent book, *Why Nations Fail*, MIT economist Daron Acemoglu and Harvard political scientist James A. Robinson argue that institutions are the key factor distinguishing successful nations from unsuccessful ones. What they call "inclusive" political and economic institutions are those that "enforce property rights, create a level playing field, and encourage investments in new technologies and skills." By contrast, noninclusive or "extractive" institutions "are structured to extract resources from the many by the few."[1]

Acemoglu and Robinson make a strong case for the role of institutions in national success, but what they're really talking about, it seems to me, is *trust*—since the institutions they praise will invariably foster trust in their constituents, while institutions that act otherwise will invariably erode trust and create dissension and withdrawal. The truth of these insights has been understood for some time.

In 2007, for instance, the United Nations authored a report titled *Building Trust in Government in the Twenty-First Century*. The report acknowledged falling levels of trust in government across the world and argued that trust and good governance are mutually reinforcing. The more people trust their government, the more effectively it can govern; the more the state delivers effective policies, the more the people will trust it. However, in the current environment, in which so many governments have lost the trust of their citizens, successful policymaking becomes much more difficult.

Look at the United States: public trust has waned in both the Democratic and the Republican parties, as confirmed consistently by polls. This lack of public trust, in turn, extends to the politicians themselves, who, knowing that the public sees through them, resolve to do the only thing left: win their political battles, regardless of the cost to the public good.

The UN report identified three causal mechanisms that connect trust to good governance: a vibrant civil society, an equitable and efficient economy, and political legitimacy.[2] This resembles the vision Secretary of State Hillary Clinton articulated in a 2012 interview:

> I have this view, which I articulated in a speech in 1998 at Davos, that a successful society is like a three-legged stool: You have an effective, functioning, accountable, responsible government; you have a dynamic, free-market economy creating wealth and opportunity; and you have civil society, which is an equal player in promoting what makes life worth living. Because it's in civil society that we have our families, that we exercise our faith, that we engage in volunteerism, that we try to make a contribution to help another person or improve our community.[3]

We often forget the importance of civil society—and in the United States today, with so much political division, that's easy to do. Civil society creates the interest groups and citizen groups that can mediate between governments and citizens. If citizens don't want to form these types of groups because they don't trust one another or the government to acknowledge their needs, then the link between citizens and government will be difficult to sustain.

Civil society, in turn, depends heavily on a perception of political and economic fairness. People won't trust their government if it does not distribute economic benefits equitably. Thus, even a competent government will fail to gain the trust of its citizens if segments of the population lack access to what they perceive as their "fair share" of economic gains. In the United States, for instance, we have seen spiraling levels of income inequality over the last decade, though this is a problem not confined to America (I will address the problem of income inequality in chapters 5 and 6).

Finally, trust flows from *legitimacy*—and it is legitimacy that so many governments, including our own, struggle to assert with their citizens. As the UN report put it, "Legitimacy embodies the consent that citizens accord to the ruling government and/or state institutions. If citizens think that a government rightfully holds and exercises power, then that government enjoys political legitimacy."[4]

As I will show in the following chapter, trust functions differently in democracies and autocracies. In the context of declining American trust, we can say with confidence that the United States cannot indefinitely remain the world's leading democracy with the plummeting trust levels Americans currently display. All of our historic gains in the past have relied in no small part on American *confidence* in our institutions—even as Americans continued to see themselves as self-governing individuals. Those who dismiss the trust breakdown in the United States today as just another manifestation of American individualism miss the point: while Americans have always had a healthy distrust of government, for the majority of our history we have believed that our government could accomplish the things it set out to do. We believed, in other words, in its legitimacy.

Stable and effective governance becomes much more difficult when a government's constituents don't trust its decisions—in significant part because they doubt the very legitimacy of the government itself.

This is, in fact, what we see today, both in the United States and around the world.

DOCUMENTING THE DECLINE IN TRUST

Let's take a close look at the numbers on the decline in trust around the world. Few sources track this issue more diligently than the 2012 Edelman Trust Barometer, which for over a decade has conducted a highly respected international survey of citizen trust in government, business, media, and nongovernmental organizations such as relief groups and other charities. The survey covers twenty-five countries, with over thirty thousand respondents—approximately one thousand "general-population" respondents in each country and a smaller sample of "informed-public" respondents. The survey respondents are over twenty-five, college educated, and in the top 25 percent of household income in their countries. The informed-public respondents report extensive media consumption and awareness of business news and public policy. The Trust Barometer surveyed five hundred such people in the United States and China and two hundred in each of the other countries in the survey.

The Trust Barometer thus combines a broad mix of population from these twenty-five countries. And in its 2012 edition, the Trust Barometer uncovered some truly startling findings, which make clear the extent of the breakdown in legitimacy and trust.

As figure 2.1 shows, in eighteen of the twenty-five countries Edelman surveyed, *less than half of respondents trusted their government to do what is right*. Trust in government globally now ranks at 43 percent—a nine-point global decline from the previous year and the worst drop in the barometer's history. Only Ireland and India saw substantial gains in government trust; eight other countries, including the United States, saw their trust levels holding fairly steady, and for many of these "steady" means little change from a low level of trust. All others saw trust declines.

The U.S. trust measure in the 2012 survey exactly mirrored the 43 percent global average, hardly a measure of confidence for the country that considers itself the world's leading democracy. Several other countries—especially Japan, Brazil, Indonesia, and Spain—saw precipitous trust declines, likely due to specific circumstances. Japan, of course, is recovering from the brutal aftermath of the Fukushima nuclear disaster, and millions of citizens have lost their confidence in the national government. Spain's austerity measures have been hugely unpopular.

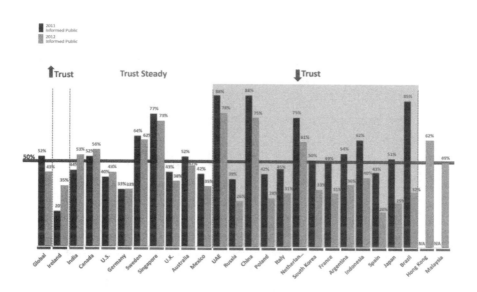

Figure 2.1. Majority of Countries Now Distrust Government. (© Edelman, 2012. All rights reserved.)

Indonesia suffered calamitous floods in 2011 in which government response left much to be desired, and the public is also skeptical about government efforts to fight corruption.[5] Edelman attributed Brazil's previous high-trust ranking to a robust economy and the impact of being selected to host the 2016 Olympics and the 2014 World Cup. In 2011, the economy declined, the Olympics selections were over, and the government had to deal with scandals and a postal strike.[6]

Figure 2.2 offers a good indication of this global loss of confidence. Respondents were asked to rate eight actions that the government can take in building trust with citizens on a nine-point scale of importance. A score of 1 meant that the action was "not at all important to building your trust," while 9 meant "extremely important to building your trust." Then respondents were asked to rate their governments on how they were performing these attributes on another nine-point scale—in which 1 means "extremely poorly" and 9 means "extremely well." The discrepancies between importance and performance speak for themselves.

But government was not the only institution to suffer from declining trust. As figure 2.3 shows, Edelman's "informed-public" respondents showed declining confidence in three of the four major institutions they were asked to evaluate—government, business, media, and NGOs.

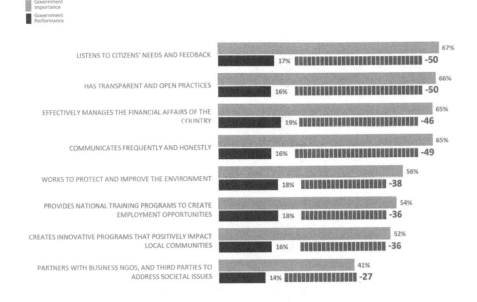

Figure 2.2. Government Not Meeting Public's Expectations. (© Edelman, 2012. All rights reserved.)

Only media, somewhat surprisingly, saw a slight rise in confidence among this subgroup. Note, though, that the Trust Barometer's "general-public" respondents showed less confidence in media—and, in fact, they showed less confidence in each of these four institutions than the "informed-public" respondents did. This shouldn't be too surprising, as it reflects an ongoing and widening divide in perception and attitude between the better-off and the majority of less-well-off citizens.

(Though they saw a slight dip in trust, NGOs remain the most trusted institutions worldwide, at 58 percent—a stark comment on the public loss of confidence, broadly and globally speaking, in the institutions of government and business.)

For critics of government who tend to prefer a greater and greater role for the private sector, government's plummeting trust levels might seem like cause for celebration. But business trust levels, while better than government's, are hardly robust. Globally, trust in business stands at just over the halfway mark—53 percent—but 49 percent of respondents globally said that government doesn't regulate business enough. And figure 2.4 shows that several mature, flourishing economies, in-

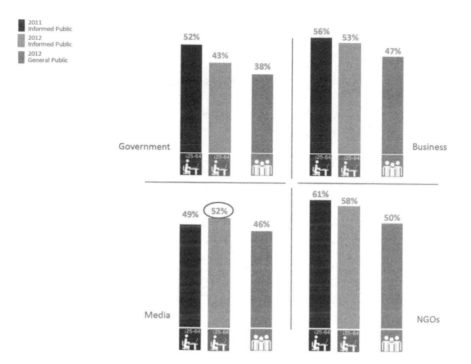

Figure 2.3. Trust in Three of Four Institutions Declines; Only Media Rises.
(© Edelman, 2012. All rights reserved.)

cluding South Korea, Germany, Brazil, and France, saw double-digit drops in business trust. In the United States, longstanding champion of business, trust levels stand at just 50 percent.

And, in any event, the government's declining ratings are not a cause for celebration in the business world, according to Richard Edelman. "Business leaders should not be cheered by government's ineptitude, especially as trust in the two institutions seems to move in sync," he said. Figure 2.5 shows how, at least in major Western economies, the two tend to follow the same broad trends. Figure 2.6 reveals how, worldwide, the credibility of CEOs and government officials plummeted among survey respondents—while that of ordinary people or lower-level employees rose dramatically. This is in keeping with the general move toward greater skepticism of established institutional authority, a consistent trend around the globe.

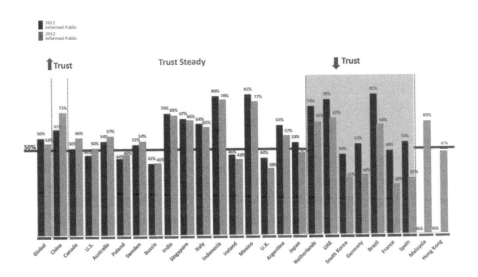

Figure 2.4.   Several Mature Markets See Double-Digit Drops in Business Trust.
(© Edelman, 2012. All rights reserved.)

United States

A few brief words on the plummeting trust in government in the United States, which has been documented by other organizations as well: A survey conducted by the Pew Research Center in August 2010 revealed that Americans' faith in their elected officials had reached its lowest levels in history. More than 80 percent of Americans reported that they trusted the federal government to do the right thing "only sometimes or never."[7] Pew charted a half-century of steadily dropping American faith in government. In the late 1950s and early 1960s Americans trusted their government to do what was right just about always or "most of the time" at rates nearing 80 percent; by 2011, that figure hovered at barely 30 percent. Frustration with the federal government is nothing new in America, but the level of anger expressed in the survey *is* new—the percentage of people who say that they are "angry" has doubled since 2000, as shown in figure 2.7.

These trends show little sign of dissipating, and the rancorous 2012 presidential election only heightened the sense around the country that effective governance in the United States was largely a thing of the past.

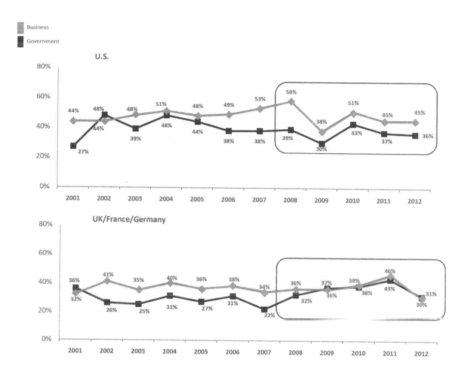

Figure 2.5.   Trust in Business and Government Move In Sync since 2008 in Western Economies. (© Edelman, 2012. All rights reserved.)

Internationally

It's more difficult to generalize about trust internationally, given that one is talking about hundreds of nations, each with its own unique history, political culture, and demographics. But it seems clear from the data that the most prosperous industrialized nations have experienced losses in public trust over the last half century—mirroring in some ways the American experience. The Edelman Trust Barometer notably listed as government distrusters the United States, the United Kingdom, France, Germany, Japan, and Russia—some of the most vital economies in the world.[8] And Edelman's 2012 survey found that nearly twice as many countries are skeptics—listed as either "distrusters" or "neutral"—than are "trusters" (see figure 2.8).

Sociologist Russell J. Dalton has categorized the rise and fall of trust throughout the industrial world and concluded that literally every in-

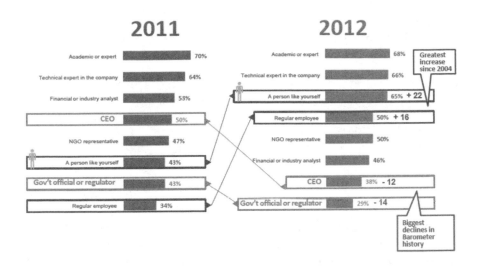

Figure 2.6. Credibility of CEOs and Government Officials Plummet; Peers and Regular Employees See Dramatic Rise. (© Edelman, 2012. All rights reserved.)

dustrialized democracy has experienced a decline in trust over the last several decades:

> The first striking empirical finding is the wide-scale erosion of trust in government across the advanced industrial democracies during the later third of the twentieth century. Even though national experts vary in the factors they cite as potential causes of the decline, the pattern is generally apparent across nations, which tends to discount "proper name" explanations that are linked to the unique history or policy performance of the nation. For instance, Austrians point to the collapse of the collectivist consensus, Canadians discuss the tensions over nationality and Quebec, Germans point to the strains of unification, and the Japanese explain these trends in terms of the prominent scandals and the economic recession of the 1990s. In every case there are national explanations for the drop in trust in government. But to assume that a simultaneous decline of trust throughout advanced industrial democracies during the late twentieth century was purely coincidental seems unlikely.[9]

In non-Western or developing nations, the situation is somewhat more complex. It's important to recognize that trust often functions differently in democracies than it does in autocracies. In less democratic soci-

**Frustration with Government Is Nothing New –
Growing Anger Is**

Feeling about federal government	Oct 1997 %	Feb 2000 %	Nov 2001 %	Mar 2004 %	Oct 2006 %	Jan 2007 %	Mar 2010 %
Basically content	29	33	53	32	21	21	19
Frustrated	56	54	34	52	54	58	56
Angry	12	10	8	13	20	16	21
Don't know	3	3	5	3	5	5	5
	100	100	100	100	100	100	100

Pew Research Center March 11-21 Q20. Figures may not add to 100% because of rounding.

Figure 2.7. *Source:* "Distrust, Discontent, Anger, and Partisan Rancor," Pew Research Center, April 18, 2010, http://pewresearch.org/pubs/1569/trust-in-government-distrust-discontent-anger-partisan-rancor.

eties, trust in government institutions often has more to do with "making the trains run on time" or with protecting citizens against external threats than it does with more idealistic notions, common in the West, of a government operating in accord with constitutional principles, or with an economy that provides a level playing field.

In the Edelman Trust Barometer, for instance, as shown in figure 2.8, three of the four BRIC nations (Brazil, Russia, India, and China) are listed as either "trusters" or "neutral" (only Russia is on the negative side with the noted distrusters of the West). There are some likely explanations for this: China's economy continues to flourish, leading substantial numbers of Chinese to believe that their government is making things better (as I'll argue in chapter 3, though, there is reason to doubt this picture of Chinese public confidence).

A GLOBAL PROBLEM

Around the world, leadership failures have eroded the basic relationship between citizens and governments. Governing institutions have been demonstrating an often self-confessed inability to solve the crises

Figure 2.8.   Distrust in Growing; Nearly Twice as Many Countries Are Now Skeptics; Fewer Countries Now in Neutral Zone. (© Edelman, 2012. All rights reserved.)

we face, and their constituents have long since made their displeasure known. The past few years have made clear that most countries face this problem in some form and that governing elites will be forced to contend with civilian opposition no matter the political system. The loss of trust has truly gone global.

In the broadest sense, the trust breakdown occurs among both nations that are more or less democratic and nations that are more or less autocratic. While the trust crisis has affected them all, it functions differently in different political systems. Efforts to address it, then, must be informed by an understanding of these differences. In the next chapter I will examine how trust works in democracies and autocracies and how the trust breakdown has manifested itself in these divergent societies.

NOTES

The epigraph in this chapter is drawn from the following source: "Trust Barometer Executive Summary," Edelman Trust Barometer, January 19, 2012, http://trust.edelman.com/trust-download/executive-summary/.

1. Daron Acemoglu and James A. Robinson, *Why Nations Fail: The Origins of Power, Prosperity, and Poverty* (New York: Crown Publishers, 2012), 430.

2. "Trust Barometer Executive Summary," Edelman Trust Barometer.

3. Richard Wolf, "One on One with Hillary Rodham Clinton," *USA Today*, May 19, 2012, http://www.usatoday.com/news/washington/story/2012-05-16/hillary-clinton-interview/55055334/1.

4. Peri K. Blind, *Building Trust in Government in the Twenty-First Century: Review of Literature and Emerging Ideas*, United Nations Department of Economic and Social Affairs, November 2006, http://unpan1.un.org/intradoc/groups/public/documents/un/unpan025062.pdf.

5. Agus Triyono and Ulma Haryanto, "Trust in Indonesian Government on Corruption at New Low," *Jakarta Globe*, January 9, 2012, http://www.thejakartaglobe.com/archive/trust-in-indonesian-government-on-corruption-at-new-low/.

6. Gisela Antakly Martinez, "Brazil—Does Decline in Trust Mean Distrust?" Edelman Public Affairs Blog Latin America, March 12, 2012, http://publicaffairslatinamerica.com/2012/03/brazil-is-decline-in-trust-distrust/.

7. "Distrust, Discontent, Anger, and Partisan Rancor," Pew Research Center, April 18, 2010, http://pewresearch.org/pubs/1569/trust-in-government-distrust-discontent-anger-partisan-rancor.

8. "2012 Edelman Trust Barometer Global Results," Edelman Trust Barometer, January 19, 2012, http://trust.edelman.com/trust-download/global-results/.

9. Russell J. Dalton, "The Social Transformation of Trust in Government," *International Review of Sociology* 15, no. 1 (March 2005): 138, http://unpan1.un.org/intradoc/groups/public/documents/un-dpadm/unpan044542.pdf.

3

HOW TRUST WORKS IN DEMOCRACIES AND AUTOCRACIES

The implosion of financial capitalism has become a crisis of political authority in the West. Behind this lies an unequal contest between a globalized economy and politicians struggling to answer the demands of national electorates.

—Philip Stephens, *Financial Times*

The recipe for regaining lost trust is conviction, openly talking, creating a dialogue.

—Russian president Dmitry Medvedev

The biggest difference between a dictatorship and democracy is not how they oppress or respect their people. The biggest difference is in the magnitude of their mistakes.

—Anonymous Iranian blogger

One of the reasons I wanted to write this book is because I was struck by how, across the world, in nations as dissimilar from one another as can be imagined, citizens from every kind of racial and ethnic group and with every kind of political affiliation have lost confidence in their governing institutions. While the standard of living and individual freedoms of those living in the Western democracies continue to be the envy of the world, we share with citizens nearly everywhere a loss of trust in those charged with the task of governance. As the Edelman survey has made clear, this loss of trust is a worldwide phenomenon.

It has become so self-evident, in fact, that in March 2012, then–Russian president Dmitry Medvedev did an astonishing thing: he publicly admitted that Russian citizens had lost trust in their government.

"There is a crisis of trust between government and society, and there always has been. The question is, how deep is it?" Medvedev asked at his Open Government forum. He called for a more open dialogue and increased transparency in government.

But while the forum was intended to reverse declining public trust in Russia, the government's initiatives so far have mostly been ceremonial.[1] In November 2011, Russian prime minister Vladimir Putin also admitted that Russians had lost faith in their government and promised to introduce more "direct democracy" in his third term.[2] He suggested that undemocratic measures taken in the past had been necessary but that these steps could slowly be reversed. So far there has been little sign of change. In fact, his 2012 jailing of an all-female punk band, Pussy Riot, for staging a public protest at Moscow's cathedral can only be seen as a step backward.[3] This and other moves have eroded any sense among Russians that they can rely on the government to deal with citizens in a forthright and democratic manner.

The stillborn struggle of the Russian government to reestablish trust with its people may be one of the more extreme examples of the authority crisis today, but many other nations face similar challenges. At their core, authority and trust involve a government's ability to function.

Weak governments are ultimately provocative. Their inability to resolve competing group claims, provide economic stewardship, ensure equal justice, or guarantee sufficient access to the political process creates tensions that can escalate into violent conflict. Mature democracies can often defuse tensions through political inclusion, but autocratic regimes are more comfortable repressing dissent and managing conflict through force. The most vulnerable states are those in transition—like those in the Middle East undergoing political change—or ones like Russia, where public discontent has reached dangerously high levels.

In the West, too, the ongoing financial and economic crisis has eroded faith in governance, sparked the rise of fringe movements, and created a permanent sense of instability that makes social and political harmony difficult. Europe's ongoing agonies with government deficits and sovereign debt have endangered the future of the European Union, and the long-running euro crisis wrought havoc on financial markets. In the United States, no solutions have been found for the country's ongoing fiscal crisis—papered over by the short-term debt-ceiling deal of summer 2011 and the early 2013 deal that avoided a broad-based "Taxmageddon" but imposed a painful sequester of government spending while hiking top-bracket income taxes. Neither party has embraced a balanced, bipartisan plan to reduce the deficit. In such a climate, protest movements like Occupy Wall Street have all but called for the abolition of market capitalism.

The true crisis, however, is less systemic than it is a matter of will. As Philip Stephens put it in the *Financial Times*, it is "not so much a crisis of capitalism but of the capacity of politicians to manage it." The problem stems, he writes, from a "mismatch between global economics and local politics. States have been shedding power to globalization. The big lesson has been about the extent to which globalized capitalism has outstripped the capacity of national governments to manage it."[4]

I agree. The global economy has become practically all-powerful in shaping our lives, and, as governments fail to devise effective remedies for the negative consequences, public anger and distrust grow. Buffeted by huge changes in global economics and technology, citizens expecting some government relief from their troubles have found precious little. This is one reason why so many in the United States—for example, in the Tea Party—tend to blame government itself for the crisis. The sense is that if government had acted more effectively—which, in some cases, would have consisted of doing nothing—then so many people wouldn't be hurting.

I wrote about this problem in my recent book, *Hopelessly Divided*, arguing that many political pundits had their diagnosis backward: where they saw the parties' hardening toward their right- and left-wing extremes as the cause of government breakdown, I saw the rise of ideological populism, left and right, as *the result of government breakdown*. Stephens also sees it that way:

> It is this gap between the supply and demand for governance that fuels popular discontent and gives impetus to the temptation for states to look in on themselves. It explains the rise both of rightwing populism and the anticapitalist movements of the left and risks fuelling a dangerous revival of the politics of identity on both sides of the Atlantic. The response of many governments has been to turn inward

and seek to defy the realities of interdependence by elevating narrow definitions of national interest. Old concepts of mutual interest and solidarity have cracked even in the eurozone, the most closely integrated group of rich nations.[5]

Given the depth of the problem, we need to understand the different ways trust functions in regimes around the world. In this chapter, I'll briefly examine how trust works in some Western democracies as well as in various autocratic regimes. In the following chapter, I'll analyze how the consequences of broken trust are playing out in democracies and autocracies.

TRUST IN DEMOCRACIES

In a democratic society, the notion of trust is inherently complex. On the one hand, no democratic government can function effectively without what Jefferson called "the consent of the governed"—the sense of authorization from citizens, even those who disagree with the administration in office, that the established authority is legitimate. On the other hand, democracy itself, and especially the American version, is founded in substantial degree on the power of dissent and the assumption of ongoing political change. America was born, after all, out of a revolution.

In operation, however, these two democratic strands existed in relative harmony until fairly recently. Especially in the twentieth century, with World War II and the Cold War years that followed, Americans had a strong instinct to trust the federal government. It was only during the 1960s and afterward, with the shocks and traumas of Vietnam, Watergate, the oil crisis, and the massive societal change brought about by the various protest movements, that public views of the U.S. government changed for the worse. Ever since, the U.S. government has struggled to build a solid sense of trust among the American people. In one sense, there was a kind of innocence lost: most Americans, as polls showed, genuinely believed that whatever the government said was true up until about the mid-1960s. The newly dissident culture that emerged after the Vietnam War and Watergate made any kind of widespread trust of government seem unhip, naïve, and even foolhardy.

Still, in good times Americans have regarded their government relatively positively. In the 1980s and 1990s, under robust economies with low unemployment, and in the period after 9/11, trust in government spiked up as Americans rallied behind their political leaders.

These trends suggest that in democratic societies, trust will probably never again reach the heights of the postwar era but can still rally impressively when the right conditions are met. These conditions would include a strong economy, a sense of common goals and purpose (as in the early post–9/11 period), and a general sense that the nation's leaders were more or less honest and making a genuine effort to solve the nation's problems.

In both democracies and autarchies, citizens value *performance*. They want sound economies, growing GDP, rising incomes, effective foreign policy, and so forth. When governance fails in these tangible areas, public trust and confidence erode.

In most democracies, however, *intangible* criteria also apply: citizens want to believe that the nation's leaders are governing in a way consistent with the nation's deepest values, that elections are fair and free, that the rule of law is being upheld, that individual rights are respected, and that opportunity is open to all. In the United States and in the Western European democracies, these values have enormous power and influence on the way people see their governments. True, when the economy is struggling or in a time of war, citizens will worry somewhat less about these things, but they won't forget about them.

In recent years, both the United States and Europe have struggled mightily to reverse their economic downturns, and the public mood, not surprisingly, has been bleak. But that hasn't been the only reason why the citizenry in both places has tended to see the sky falling: there is a deeper dynamic at work that transcends a harsh economy and high unemployment. On both sides of the Atlantic, citizens share a sense that the societies they have long known are vanishing—that all they once believed in and counted on from their government and their way of life might soon end.

Such fears are exacerbated by the widening gap—in background, educational attainment, and cultural views—between the governors and the governed. Politicians worldwide are increasingly technocrats educated at elite institutions and lacking much awareness of how their constituents live. Instead of ordinary people of exceptional talent rising to become political leaders, we get economists from Brussels.

This combination—poor governing performance along with a pervasive decline in the perceived *character* of governance—accounts for the authority crisis in the West.

TRUST IN AUTOCRACIES

Westerners don't always know how to react when they see an autocratic government losing the trust of the public. At one level, it can only be good: when a lawless or undemocratic regime can no longer convince citizens of its legitimacy, its days are almost certainly numbered. At another level, the consequences of that trust breakdown—including revolution or war—may well lead to even greater repression.

Case in point: the triumph of the Muslim Brotherhood in Egypt's first presidential elections in June 2012. Afterward, Egyptian president Mohamed Morsi sent some worrisome signals: he dismissed the nation's longtime defense minister, who had been running the country since Hosni Mubarak's ouster, along with other military leaders, thus consolidating his own political power; he suppressed newspapers and television stations critical of the Muslim Brotherhood; and he sought to remove non-Islamist judges from the judiciary.

Finally and most dramatically, in November 2012 Morsi granted himself sweeping powers—"to take all necessary measures and procedures" to secure the Egyptian revolution—including removal of judges and the nation's public prosecutor, a Mubarak crony. Morsi also ordered the retrial of Mubarak himself.[6] He insisted, however, that these new powers would only last until the country had ratified a new constitution. But the list of political leaders who seized dictatorial powers and then voluntarily relinquished them is unsurprisingly short.

Trust in the Middle East

Until 2011, democracy in the Middle East did not exist in the practical sense, despite the holding of plebiscites. Princeton's Amaney Jamal, who has examined the relationship between the citizenry and authoritarian governments of Egypt, Jordan, and Morocco, notes that these countries—all of which enjoy little political freedom—show considerably less social trust than Western democracies:

> Compared to levels of trust in Western democracies, levels of social trust in these three Arab countries are quite low. When asked whether most people can or cannot be trusted, only 38 percent of Egyptians said that most people could be trusted. Only 27.65 percent of Jordanians, and an even lower percentage of Moroccans (22.8 percent), felt that others could be trusted. In comparison, 59.6 percent of Swedes, 65.1 percent of Norwegians, and 48.6 percent of Americans report that they trust others in their societies. . . . All in all, it does not appear that Arabs in these countries hold high levels of trust for others.[7]

Yet, just as democracies do, authoritarian governments require substantial citizen trust to legitimate themselves and rule effectively. Their efforts to foster trust, in turn, often undermine attempts at democratization, because a population with a positive view of its rulers is less likely to seek to replace them. As Jamal writes, "Higher levels of trust in authoritarian settings, therefore, can pose a threat to democratization more broadly."[8] He concludes, "Trust, conventionally understood to support democratic outcomes, is in fact linked to stronger support for the authoritarian governments in power."[9]

For a long time, too, many countries that would one day host Arab Spring movements had governments that fulfilled the baseline level of trust most common in autocracies: they provided work, food, shelter, and national security. They did not provide freedom or genuine growth in the sense of expanding economic opportunity in the way it is understood in the West. The relative stability of such societies, however, allowed a young, educated middle class to develop—one that would eventually be willing to rebel, especially when their government began to fail at delivering even these goods. That's what happened in Tunisia in early 2011, setting the stage for the revolutions to come. Whether these movements would have arisen if the governments had been able to maintain a baseline performance—especially in the face of a newly insistent younger population—is a question to which there is no clear answer.

So it's important to recognize that when I talk about trust as vital for democratic governance, I mean it as it applies to democracies: it allows democratic governments to function effectively while also providing a positive example to citizens of nondemocratic regimes. In autocratic societies, popular trust in the ruling regime usually reinforces the status quo. So while we typically view trust as good and distrust as bad, it appears that in the authoritarian Arab context, social and certainly governmental trust work *against* both democracy and human rights.[10]

Thus, democracy advocates should take encouragement from the fact that authoritarian regimes in the Arab world inspired such low levels of social trust by early 2011, when the Arab Spring movements began. If Jamal is correct, this means that these governments are scarcely viewed as legitimate and democratizing them should be possible. At their most hopeful, the Arab Spring movements held out that promise. Those on the front lines of these movements emphasized their common desire for government responsiveness and, most of all, democracy.

As political activist and codirector of the Activist News Association Alexander Page tweeted from Syria, "It's a war zone out there but, despite all the difficulties, people are risking their lives for a common goal: freedom."[11] Ahmed Raafat Amin, a twenty-two-year-old Egyptian protester from Cairo, was at first afraid to take part in the demonstrations, but the corruption, injustice, and inequality in Egypt became too much for him to bear. He said, "I was also like many other Egyptians who were dreaming of change but never believed it could happen. . . . Someone had to stand up and say 'enough is enough'—and that is why I decided to take part in the revolution. . . . As I realized the demands of the revolution were my own demands, I was willing to pay whatever price our freedom would cost."[12]

There is unquestionably a new sense of dissidence within the Muslim world, a sense that decades of governmental failure and deceit are no longer tolerable. This dissidence has even made itself known, at least to a small degree, on that most explosive of issues: Israel. Consider the following editorial in the English-language newspaper *Arab News*, published in Saudi Arabia, a nation that has promulgated no shortage of anti-Israel attitudes and propaganda. Taking issue with the ubiquitous notion of Israel as the enemy of the Arab people, the writer, Abdulateef Al-Mulhim, a retired commodore of the Saudi navy, describes the Middle East carnage he sees regularly in news reports:

The common thing among all what I saw is that the destruction and the atrocities are not done by an outside enemy. The starvation, the killings, and the destruction in these Arab countries are done by the same hands that are supposed to protect and build the unity of these countries and safeguard the people of these countries. So, the question now is that who is the real enemy of the Arab world? . . .

The real enemies of the Arab world are corruption, lack of good education, lack of good health care, lack of freedom, lack of respect for the human lives, and, finally, the Arab world had many dictators who used the Arab-Israeli conflict to suppress their own people. These dictators' atrocities against their own people are far worse than all the full-scale Arab-Israeli wars.

In the past, we have talked about why some Israeli soldiers attack and mistreat Palestinians. Also, we saw Israeli planes and tanks attack various Arab countries. But do these attacks match the current atrocities being committed by some Arab states against their own people?[13]

Editorials like these may or may not represent a realization among growing numbers of Arab citizens. But the fact Al-Mulhim's piece was even printed is surely heartening, and few would argue that high levels of trust exist in most of the Arab world's authoritarian governments. The question now is this: What will be the result of the crisis engulfing the region from Syria to Egypt and beyond—some tentative steps toward democracy, or defiant authoritarianism?

Russia

As it emerged from the ashes of the Soviet Union, Russia has provided a good case of the relationship between trust and the sustainability of a democratic transition. In this case, an unstable, partially democratic regime that has become considerably less free over time replaced an authoritarian one in which there was no freedom at all. The current limitations on freedom have influenced the way Russian citizens see their government: with a composite score of 32, Russia claimed the lowest spot in the Edelman trust survey. In the survey, 26 percent of respondents said they trusted their government, compared with 36 percent in 2011.[14] Russia performs poorly across the board in NGO rankings. It ranks 143 out of 182 countries in Transparency International's

Corruption Index,[15] with a score of 2.4, and 142 out of 179 countries in Reporters Without Borders' Freedom Index.[16]

In the Russian context, William Mishler of the University of Arizona and Robert Rose of the University of Strathclyde propose a relationship between trust and performance, not trust and democratization—of which Russians have seen little. Their findings underscore the fact that governments with few sources of legitimacy must perform competently and transparently if they are to win the trust of the people. The most important area of performance, not surprisingly, is economic. As they conclude, "Although attitudes about democracy appear to be culturally conditioned, Russians appear more likely to judge the current regime in terms of its honesty and effectiveness in addressing the problems that matter to them at the moment, especially the economy."[17] Essentially, people judge an existing regime by its performance rather than by whether or not they "trust" it (a point I made earlier in reference to the Arab Spring countries).

We will see how this dynamic plays out in Russia in the next chapter.

China

Probably the most complicated case here is that of China, which has consistently scored high in surveys, including Edelman, that assess citizen trust in government. I must state up front that I don't buy it—and I'm hardly alone. But the issue is complicated, so let's first give the devil his due and acknowledge what the surveys say.

China ranked number one in the 2012 Edelman Trust Index, with 81 percent of respondents saying they trust their government, a decline from 88 percent in 2011, but still significantly higher than in Western democracies.[18] Some have questioned these results, noting that the survey was conducted online and includes only college-educated citizens from top income brackets, resulting in a less-than-representative sample.[19] However, research from the East Asian Institute in Singapore in 2009 found that trust actually *declines* in urban areas of China and among those with more education, suggesting that, if anything, trust levels could be understated. The Edelman results are also consistent with other surveys suggesting trust in the Chinese government is unusually high.[20]

To some degree, cultural inclinations in China may foster obedience to authority and traditional hierarchies. As *Forbes*'s Helen Wang, an expert on Chinese middle-class issues, writes, "Blind obedience to authority is still deeply rooted in the Chinese psyche. We don't need to look very far to see that this core of Chinese culture has remained the same. I have heard many times from people in China that the central government is good and wise, that only some officials, especially local officials, are evil."[21]

As we've seen, trust plays a very different role in democratic countries than in autocratic or semiautocratic regimes. Generally speaking, if citizens in an autocratic regime like China's believe the government is managing affairs competently, they will not seek to replace it. China's supercharged economic growth of the last decade is generally given as the main reason—and perhaps the only reason—that accounts for popular support of the Communist regime. China's booming economy has pulled millions out of poverty and has allowed it to escape the effects of government mistrust that have plagued other democratic and nondemocratic countries.[22]

According to this school of thought, if China maintains its robust economic growth, even while providing few freedoms, its citizens will continue to trust their government based on its competence, rather than other factors. China's economic growth will likely continue for the foreseeable future, although it may one day develop a class of prosperous citizens for whom "performance" is no longer sufficient to excuse the regime's serial political crimes and oppressions. Needless to say, if China cannot sustain its growth, we may well see a drop-off in political trust.

Some argue that this is already happening.

Putting the economic debate aside, it's worth questioning the purported high trust levels in China. In assessing Chinese-citizen survey responses, we have to ask to what extent people are answering questions honestly. Given the vast surveillance and censorship that China's government oversees, it would not be surprising to discover that millions are giving the responses they assume the regime wants to hear. After all, they have a lot of practice doing this in their daily lives.

In addition, there is also the fact of China's incredible vastness— with a population of some one billion in its interior, among them hundreds of millions of peasants not yet enjoying the nation's supposed economic miracles. As I'll describe in my China section in the following chapter, there is much to the argument that public trust in China is essentially a government-concocted fiction.

Elsewhere, including the West, governments don't even pretend to have the trust of the public anymore. The consequences of their poor performance have been laid bare for all to see. Let's take a brief look at some real-world examples of how broken trust is playing out in specific countries and regions.

NOTES

The epigraphs in this chapter are drawn from the following sources: Philip Stephens, "Leaders Who Generate Diminishing Returns," *Financial Times*, January 18, 2012, http://www.ft.com/intl/cms/s/0/36297676-413f-11e1-8c33-00144feab49a.html; "Only Dialogue Can Fix Lack of Trust in Govt. —Medvedev," RIA Novosti, March 22, 2012, http://en.rian.ru/society/20120322/172327797.html; and "What Went Wrong?" Iran Rigged Election, July 10, 2009, http://iranriggedelect.blogspot.com/2009/07/what-went-wrong.html.

1. "Only Dialogue Can Fix Lack of Trust."
2. David Hearst, "Putin: We Have Lost Russia's Trust," *Guardian*, November 11, 2011, http://www.guardian.co.uk/world/2011/nov/12/putin-russia-lost-trust.
3. Miriam Elder, "Putin Says Pussy Riot 'Got What They Asked For' as Jailed Women Appeal," *Guardian*, http://www.guardian.co.uk/world/2012/oct/08/putin-backs-pussy-riot-conviction.
4. Stephens, "Leaders Who Generate Diminishing Returns."
5. Ibid.
6. David KirkPatrick and Mayy El Sheikh, "Citing Deadlock, Egypt's Leader Seizes New Power and Plans Mubarak Retrial," *New York Times*, November 22, 2012, http://www.nytimes.com/2012/11/23/world/middleeast/egypts-president-morsi-gives-himself-new-powers.html.
7. Amaney Jamal, "When Is Social Trust a Desirable Outcome? Examining Levels of Trust in the Arab World," *Comparative Politics* 40 (2007): 1336.
8. Ibid.
9. Ibid., 1342.
10. Ibid., 1345.
11. Dhruti Shah, "The Big Stories Affecting You in 2011," BBC News, December 26, 2011, http://www.bbc.co.uk/news/world-middle-east-16275176.
12. Ibid.

13. Abdulateef Al-Mulhim, "Arab Spring and the Israeli Enemy," Arab News, October 6, 2012, http://www.arabnews.com/arab-spring-and-israeli-enemy.

14. "Trust Barometer Global Results," Edelman Trust Barometer, January 19, 2012, http://trust.edelman.com/trust-download/global-results/.

15. "Corruption Perception Index 2011," Transparency International, November 2012, http://www.transparency.org/cpi2011.

16. "Press Freedom Index 2011–2012," Reporters Without Borders, January 25, 2012, http://en.rsf.org/press-freedom-index-2011-2012,1043.html.

17. Ibid.

18. "FY12 Citizenship Report," Edelman, September 18, 2012, http://www.edelman.com/news/trust/2011/; "2012 Edelman Trust Barometer: China Results," Edelman APCACMEA, accessed July 3, 2013, retrieved from http://www.slideshare.net/EdelmanAPAC/2012-edelman-trust-barometer-china-results.

19. Rebecca Chao, "China, Singapore Earn High Marks in Trust-in-Government Survey," Asia Society, February 2, 2012, http://asiasociety.org/blog/asia/china-singapore-earn-high-marks-trust-government-survey.

20. Shan Wei, "How Much Do the Chinese Trust Their Government," East Asia Institute, August 28, 2009, http://www.eai.nus.edu.sg/BB472.pdf; Peter Drysdale, "In China, Trust in Government Depends on Where You Look," *Jakarta Global*, July 29, 2011, http://www.thejakartaglobe.com/opinion/in-china-trust-in-government-depends-on-where-you-look/455855; Zhengxu Wang, "Before the Emergence of Critical Citizens: Economic Development and Political Trust in China," *International Review of Political Science* 15, no. 1 (2005): 155–71.

21. Helen H. Wang, "Blind Activist's Blind Faith Reveals Chinese Attitude toward Authority," *Forbes*, June 19, 2012, http://www.forbes.com/sites/helenwang/2012/06/19/blind-activists-blind-faith-reveals-chinese-attitude-toward-authority/.

22. Wang, "Before the Emergence of Critical Citizens."

4

BROKEN TRUST IN DEMOCRACIES AND AUTOCRACIES

The overwhelmingly significant finding of this year's survey, exemplified above all in Europe, was a decline in trust of governments at any level—the biggest decline in the survey's history. European countries are now defined as distrusting of government.
                                  —Martin Porter, managing director, Edelman

This society has bred mistrust and violence. Leaders know you have to watch your back because you never know who will put a knife in it.
                    —Roderick MacFarquhar, historian of Communist China

In Western democracies, as we have seen, trust is bound up not only with performance but also with democratic principles and national ideals. Most vitally, it affects the ability of government to address collective problems. Most autocracies don't face this obstacle: in China or even in Russia, despite substantial political distrust, the government can act unilaterally. Censorship, arrests of political opponents, interference with the judiciary—autocratic governments have used all of these tactics, among others, in recent years, often to considerable international condemnation. Yet the tactics have proven effective in preserving their hold on power.

In the West, of course, such abuses remain shocking to most observers. But the Western democracies, including the United States, face other problems that have eroded public trust: failures of governance, corruption, and political polarization, to name a few. The latter problem, in particular, afflicts the United States, where political cooperation has almost completely broken down in a time of enormous uncertainty.

CONSEQUENCES OF BROKEN TRUST: UNITED STATES

Consider the long-running impasse over the federal budget, taxes, and deficits. A constructive long-term agreement would decrease long-term interest rates, spur economic growth, lessen the chances of another economic crisis, and allow for lower taxes in the future as the U.S. debt burden is reduced. However, to get there, each stakeholder must bear a portion of the costs: the defense budget will probably have to be cut; tax hikes on the wealthiest Americans might be necessary to defray some of the costs of government and cut deficits; social-welfare programs may need to be trimmed back. To be put on a stable, long-term footing, the foundational safety-net programs—Social Security, Medicare, and Medicaid—will have to be reformed, if not reinvented; we may need to raise the retirement age, for example, or increase the Medicare tax. Everyone will have to give up certain sacred cows and make hard choices.

These would be challenging tasks in any environment, but in today's Washington climate they loom like Mount Everest. The federal government is so overcome with partisan warfare that just about nothing constructive outside of the realm of foreign policy can be pursued. Partisanship overwhelms any possibility of legislative coalitions, once a staple of Washington governance, and makes impossible the efficient functioning of government departments. Most of the time, we cannot even have a constructive debate about reform. Vested interests oppose any of the solutions I mentioned above, as well as many others. Trust is absent: the two parties seek only to "win," not to achieve compromises that will benefit the country.

One example of the effects of this intransigence can be shown in figure 4.1. It shows the Congressional Budget Office's long-term budget projections. The Extended Baseline Scenarios line takes into account what current law dictates (meaning laws stipulating that some top-bracket tax cuts will expire). The Extended Alternative Fiscal Scenario takes into account current policy—a strong military and low taxes supported by Republicans and a strong social safety net supported by

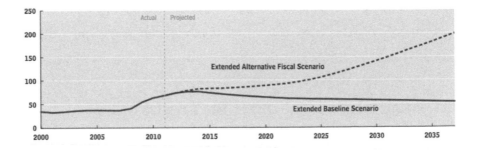

Figure 4.1. Federal Debt Held by the Public Under CBO's Long-Term Budget Scenarios. *Source:* **Congressional Budget Office.**

Democrats. Given the total absence in cooperation between the parties, the alternative scenario is more likely.

To illustrate how much has changed in Washington, consider two of the most famous fiscal commissions ever formed: the recent Bowles-Simpson Commission, convened by President Obama, and the Greenspan Commission, formed in the 1980s at President Reagan's request. Bowles-Simpson was created to address our long-term fiscal challenges, while the Greenspan Commission was formed to address the long-term solvency of Social Security. Both commissions faced potential fiscal calamities and exponential growth in costs. Both were bipartisan, and both called for unpopular decisions: Democrats opposed benefit cuts, while Republicans resisted tax hikes.[1]

The difference? One commission succeeded and the other failed.

Formed in an age when *trust* and *bipartisanship* were not dirty words, the Greenspan Commission voted 12–3 for changes that raised the retirement age and cut benefits by as much as 30 percent—drastic recommendations that somehow gained the endorsement of both President Reagan and Democratic Speaker Tip O'Neill.[2] But the Bowles-Simpson Commission could not gain the necessary supermajority of votes, with only eleven of eighteen votes in favor of its tough-medicine recommendations, and it failed to gain the full endorsement of either President Obama or the Republicans.

The failure of Bowles-Simpson, especially in contrast to earlier bipartisan efforts, illustrates the impact of the trust breakdown on actual, real-world governance. The astonishing thing is that the fiscal challenges that the U.S. government faces now are much more severe than they were in 1983—yet still our leaders refused to make a deal.

Instead, we fight. If we keep it up much longer, we're going to go bankrupt.

CONSEQUENCES OF BROKEN TRUST: EUROPE

Meanwhile, perhaps the world's greatest collective-action crisis is in Europe, where the European economy has for all intents and purposes stopped growing and some of the Continent's lesser economies, especially Greece and Spain, teeter on the edge of collapse. Like the United States, Europe faces a kind of Armageddon without anything resembling unity in how to deal with it. The only thing everyone agrees on is that this state of suspended animation cannot continue forever.

Europe, like the United States, suffers from a governing paralysis originating in the loss of legitimacy and trust, and, as such, all of its attempts at remedies have failed thus far. Economists, European leaders, and even the population at large seem to recognize that preserving the European monetary system is vital. But the steps and cost necessary to do so place disproportionate burdens on different countries.

Until the European Central Bank's Mario Draghi stepped forward in September 2012 to guarantee the euro, Germany stood to lose the most from dissolution of the monetary system, because the euro helps drive German exports. Germany also shoulders the most significant costs— including bailouts, Eurobonds, and deposit insurance—in holding the system together. Given the stake it has in the eurozone, Germany's interest in forging a sustainable solution has always been clear.

The crisis was precipitated by Greece, which for years underreported its debt. Thus Germany has good reason to force sharp concessions from Greece, but the burden has fallen heavily on Greek citizens, who don't enjoy the same standard of living as Germans and who, as a result of budget austerity and debilitating unemployment, are seeing their economy collapse. Help given to Greece—or Spain or Italy or Ireland or Portugal—comes out of the equity built up by the EU's powerful and fiscally stable nations: principally Germany but also the Netherlands and Finland.

Thus, the European crisis has undermined the relationship between voters and elected politicians in many countries. The problem is exacerbated by European leaders' central-command style of governance, which makes little pretense of building popular support. This widening gap between the electorate and the elites threatens any constructive political solution. The Continent's "democracy deficit" is a real-world handicap in managing its budget and trade deficits.

Amartya Sen, economist and Nobel laureate, argues that the Continent's austerity measures were implemented so crudely and undemocratically that they threaten public cohesion and have sparked extremism. He believes that, at its heart, the Continent's fiscal and economic crisis is ultimately a political one that involves issues of civic participation and, yes, trust:

> Europe cannot revive itself without addressing two areas of political legitimacy. First, Europe cannot hand itself over to the unilateral views—or good intentions—of experts without public reasoning and informed consent of its citizens. Given the transparent disdain for the public, it is no surprise that in election after election the public has shown its dissatisfaction by voting out incumbents.
>
> Second, both democracy and the chance of creating good policy are undermined when ineffective and blatantly unjust policies are dictated by leaders. The obvious failure of the austerity mandates imposed so far has undermined not only public participation—a value in itself—but also the possibility of arriving at a sensible, and sensibly timed, solution.[3]

European populations have lost trust both in their own governments and in European institutions. Figure 4.2, taken from the Edelman survey, shows significant declines in trust over the last year. According to Martin Porter, managing director at Edelman, "The overwhelmingly significant finding of this year's survey, exemplified above all in Europe, was a decline in trust of governments at any level—the biggest decline in the survey's history. European countries are now defined as distrusting of government."[4] Indeed, most of the Continent has seen street protests against everything from government corruption to the EU's proposed austerity measures, along with increased public distrust.

As Porter sees it, people blame the harsh austerity measures on the failure of the various governing bodies that make up the European

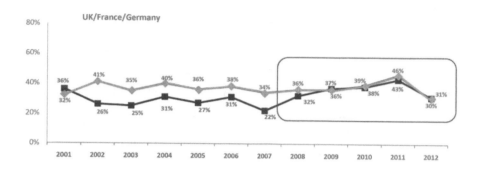

Figure 4.2. Trust in Business and Government (light gray is business).
(© Edelman, 2012. All rights reserved.)

Union: "While the austerity drive has been driven above all, if not exclusively, by individual Member States, EU institutions are being immediately associated with these unpopular austerity measures."[5] In fact, for all of the anger at bankers and Wall Street, and the international reach of the Occupy movement, the European public largely sees the crisis as a failure not of capitalism but of government. Writing in the *Financial Times*, Philip Stephens cites an opinion poll from Policy Network, a progressive, international think tank, which shows that voters have come to see the crisis "as one of public borrowing and debt as well as of bankers' greed. Voters do not think the answer to spiraling deficits is more government borrowing," Stephens writes. "Put another way, if capitalism needs fixing, Europeans have decided to leave the task to the politicians who best understand the marketplace."[6]

The backlash against the EU, the failure of multinational cooperation, and the rising tide of not just popular discontent but also political extremism in many European countries all make clear how serious the crisis has become.

The remarkable success of the European Continent in the postwar period is probably the greatest single example of the efficacy of determined, far-reaching multinational cooperation. From the ashes of the greatest war the world has ever known rose a peaceful, multiethnic, economic powerhouse—one that has not seen a single military conflict between its members since 1945. All of this now stands threatened, and, in large part, the situation was precipitated by the betrayal of authority and the resulting loss of legitimacy and broken public trust.

CONSEQUENCES OF BROKEN TRUST: RUSSIA

Vladimir Putin's long rule in Russia has seemed to follow a cyclical pattern: distrust in government leads to public unrest, which prompts a government crackdown and more repressive measures, thus exacerbating public grievances. Putin wielded an iron hand over various regions of Russia, giving himself sweeping powers and abolishing elections in some areas. He smothered independent media and established tight control over the nation's three main TV networks, all essentially state-controlled and run by Kremlin loyalists—not much different from Soviet days.[7]

Public anger came to a head in March 2012, when parliamentary elections returned Putin to the president's office amid widespread reports of fraud and other illegalities. Adding to the discontent was the ease with which President Medvedev and Prime Minister Putin discussed their intent to swap roles within the government, as if it were a mere private transaction. The French foreign minister, Alain Juppe, criticized Putin's plan, suggesting that it toyed with the democratic process: "To say that I am prime minister and you can have the presidency, and vice versa, that is something that ends up angering the people." The apparent corruption of the elections angered people even more.[8]

Election observers saw a range of illegalities, some old and time tested—like ballot stuffing—and some newer and more innovative.[9] Other methods used include:

1. *Vote-count fraud.* When Russian polling-station officials inflate or round up the numbers after election monitors leave a polling station. Monitors from the Organization for Security and Cooperation in Europe (OSCE) claimed the numbers were inaccurate in almost one-third of the observed polling stations.
2. *Carousel voting.* In which busloads of voters are driven around to cast ballots multiple times. Russian anticorruption blogger and opposition activist Aleksei Navalny called the scale of carousel voting "absolutely unprecedented."
3. *Fake monitors.* When bogus election observers are posted at polling stations to prevent the real volunteer monitors from observ-

ing the voting. Such fraud was alleged in St. Petersburg and Nizhny Novgorod.

4. *Corporate voting.* Wherein people employed in companies that operate around the clock can cast ballots at polling stations closest to their workplace. Allegations surfaced that some employers may have bused workers to multiple polling stations.

5. *Vote theft.* When a voter arrives at a polling station only to find out that someone else has already voted in his or her place. The Russian media reported that at least one victim of such fraud in Moscow received a threatening call on her cell phone just minutes after telling polling station officials of the irregularity.[10]

6. *Voter intimidation.* In a *New York Times* interview, an anonymous Russian official who heads a key regional election committee for United Russia, Putin's party, alleged that bureaucrats, doctors, teachers, and other state-paid workers were being asked to follow a "one-for-ten formula." He said, "This means that each one of us has to get ten people to vote for United Russia and we have to provide our superiors with a list of the names of these people." The official said that bureaucrats had been warned that their lists would be checked against the names of people who voted, and they could face sanctions such as blocked promotions if they failed to deliver as expected.[11]

As a consequence of voter-fraud allegations and the widespread demonstrations around the country, Medvedev and Putin ordered an investigation. Surveys showed that most protesters were doubtful that the investigations would be genuine.

In response to the massive demonstrations, authorities have arrested thousands, including opposition leaders. Protests during Putin's inauguration turned violent when an estimated twenty thousand people clashed with police.[12] The Russian Duma in June 2012 passed a law intended to smother dissent by raising fines for those who participate in demonstrations that threaten public order.[13] Thus far, neither protesters nor the Russian government show any signs of backing down.

The courageous Russian protest movement is the firmest evidence of the nation's enduring breakdown in public trust. According to Reporters Without Borders, "The Web has played a key role in the political debate prompted by legislative and presidential elections and in the postelection mobilization of the opposition and civil society. These developments provoked a strong official response. The blogosphere has grown stronger and better organized in the face of state attacks." As with the Arab Spring, Green Revolution, and other social-media-driven uprisings, protests in Russia are largely led by young people using Twitter and Facebook. After the December 2011 parliamentary elections, more than seventeen thousand people signed up on a Facebook page calling for a demonstration at Revolution Square in Moscow. State resistance remains potent, however: the Kremlin has jailed bloggers, maintains a list of banned topics, and has conducted cyber attacks against opponents. [14]

CONSEQUENCES OF BROKEN TRUST: CHINA

One could write books about China on the question of trust alone and whether its citizens, increasingly enjoying the fruits of a free-market economy, truly embrace a regime that sees no contradiction between capitalist economics and Communist politics. As I've noted, the dominant media argument is that China's model is "working"—that its citizens accept the trade-offs of oppression in exchange for a rising standard of living. I've never accepted this argument, and I think I have good grounds for my skepticism.

For some context, consider the views of Guy Sorman, an economist and French public intellectual who has traveled widely in China and authored the powerful 2008 book *The Empire of Lies*. Sorman sees China's rise as benefitting only a comparative few of the nation's 1.2 billion people, and he sees even these gains as ill gotten, coming at the cost of inordinate oppression and misery:

> China's success is, at least in part, a mirage. True, two hundred million of her subjects, fortunate to be working for an expanding global market, increasingly enjoy a middle-class standard of living. The remaining one billion, however, remain among the poorest and most exploited people in the world, lacking even minimal rights and public services. Popular discontent simmers, especially in the countryside, where it often flares into violent confrontation with Communist Party authorities. China's economic "miracle" is rotting from within.

> The Party's primary concern is not improving the lives of the downtrodden; it seeks power more than it seeks social development. It expends extraordinary energy in suppressing Chinese freedoms— the media operate under suffocating censorship, and political opposition can result in expulsion or prison—even as it tries to seduce the West, which has conferred greater legitimacy on it than do the Chinese themselves.[15]

The party's efforts at control obscure a humanitarian crisis in the country's vast interior, home to nearly one billion people. An AIDS epidemic ravages the province of Henan—a crisis largely caused by the practice of peasants selling their blood plasma, a trade the party controls. Hundreds of thousands are dying with little or no government assistance. The government's brutal one-child policy has led to forced abortions and murders of girl infants. The government has even prepared maps of the country that don't show Henan!

Writing in 2007, Sorman referred to "an explosion of peasant revolts in the Chinese countryside," where residents live entirely apart from the supposed Chinese miracle that has benefited some large cities. As Sorman described it then, "the uprisings are really mutinies, sporadic and unpremeditated. They express peasant families' despair over the bleak future that awaits them and their children."[16]

The underlying desperation of Chinese citizens—and even some party members—can be glimpsed in news stories. Twice in 2012, Chinese citizens sought the protection of U.S. diplomats. In February 2012, the former policy chief of Chongqing fled to the U.S. consulate out of fear of Bo Xilai, the powerful Communist Party secretary for the municipality.[17] And in April, Chinese dissident Chen Guangcheng fled to the U.S. embassy after escaping house arrest.[18] These individuals clearly trusted the United States more than their own government.

The case of Bo Xilai demonstrates that a severe culture of distrust exists among senior government leaders and upper echelons of Chinese society. Bo was removed from his post in March 2012 and expelled from the Politburo the following month after a subordinate revealed that Bo's wife was involved in the murder of a British business associate. The origins of this incident lie in anticorruption and anticrime initiatives Bo used to cement his power in the municipality, creating a culture of pervasive surveillance. In 2010, Bo had the former Chongqing deputy police chief executed on corruption charges, resulting in his subordinate's subsequent flight to the U.S. consulate. Even more notably, Bo used his surveillance apparatus to spy on fellow officials, including China's top leader, Hu Jintao. According to the *New York Times*, "The story of how China's president was monitored also shows the level of mistrust among leaders in the one-party state. To maintain control over society, leaders have embraced enhanced surveillance technology. But some have turned it on one another—repeating patterns of intrigue that go back to the beginnings of Communist rule."[19]

Bo has since disappeared into an extreme, shadowy criminal-justice system, known as *shuanggui*, that the Communist Party uses to enforce discipline and in which it punished nearly one million party members from 2003 to 2008. The system employs sleep deprivation and torture techniques, elicits forced confessions, and features suicides and deaths under mysterious circumstances, according to the *Times*.[20] Bo is now facing serious legal challenges as he prepares for trial—his brothers and sisters have been instructed by the CCP not to find him lawyers.[21] Although his mother-in-law has retained counsel for him, his chances of getting a fair trial are extremely slim.

China ranked seventy-fifth out of 182 countries in Transparency International's 2011 Corruption Trust Index, scoring a 3.6 on a scale from one (highly corrupt) to ten (very clean).[22] Yet abuses of power remain a safe activity for government officials. According to research from the Carnegie Endowment for International Peace, corrupt officials stand only a 3 percent chance of going to jail.[23] But the Chinese public seems broadly aware of the corruption of public officials while also claiming to trust the government. What explains this disparity?

To some extent, the government rules more through ignorance than fear—resulting in genuine, if misplaced, trust. The *shuanggui* system, while creating a system of fear to keep party members in line, also seeks to keep corruption from coming to light. Another way in which China ensures public ignorance is through a vast and superaggressive censorship regime. Certain topics—Tibet, Tiananmen Square, corruption, wealth disparity, among a host of others—are simply banned from discussion in the media.[24] The country censors TV, print, radio, and the Internet. Multiple rankings by NGOs suggest that China has one of the most repressive censorship regimes in the world.

This gets to the crux of the widely accepted argument that the Chinese people trust and approve of their government: we shouldn't be nearly so impressed that a country that ranks almost last in terms of press freedom ranks first in terms of trust. We should be surprised if this *weren't* the case.

China is ranked 174 out of 179—just above Syria, Iran, and North Korea—in the Reporters Without Borders Press Freedoms Index.[25] Freedom House in 2005 listed Chinese media as "Not Free"—its lowest designation—ranking it 177 out of 194 countries, and noted the use of propaganda circulars, "documents produced and disseminated by the CCP that contain specific instructions for the media nationwide. The primary function of these circulars is to identify stories that should not appear in news reports and provide guidance for treatment of certain sensitive stories."[26] China has aggressively cracked down on Internet use, building what is called the "Great Firewall."[27] According to *Bloomberg Businessweek*, "Beijing has a vast infrastructure of technology to keep an eye on any potential online dissent. It also applies lots of human eyeballs to monitoring. The agencies that watch over the Net employ more than thirty thousand people to prowl Web sites, blogs, and chat rooms on the lookout for offensive content as well as scammers."[28]

All of this diligence on the part of the government to repress free expression has operated until now with a powerful advantage: the ongoing Chinese economic miracle. In the future, however, the regime will likely face more daunting challenges in maintaining this economic growth. China may be finishing its first great stage of market-based growth and moving closer to parity with Western nations. It may soon shift from an economy driven by export-led manufacturing to one driven by a more innovative, consumer middle class. Its current model of development is increasingly regarded as unsustainable, with large trade imbalances resulting in asset bubbles and inflationary pressures. Furthermore, foreign investment is likely to drop as labor costs rise and foreign companies move their operations elsewhere. China must soon look beyond manufacturing to fuel its growth.

It is one thing to become a market power through authoritarian political structures by capitalizing on low labor costs (and lack of human rights) to dominate manufacturing; it is another to sustain one's place in a competitive, knowledge-based economy once this earlier advantage has played itself out. Innovation and entrepreneurship require free exchange of ideas without concerns of censorship. These things simply don't exist in China, no matter what its apologists say. When the old model has run its course, China will face the challenge of political adaptability—a challenge it cannot meet successfully without some form of democratization and cultivation of public trust.

Reaching the next stage of economic development will also require some reckoning with the epic scale of Chinese corruption. Like its problems with democracy and openness, the problem of corruption in China has largely been papered over by the powerful tide of economic development and GDP growth. But as the pace of Chinese economic growth begins to stabilize and even slow, corruption will be harder to ignore—especially since it is directly responsible for taking job opportunities from ordinary Chinese and lavishing such positions on party officials or those connected with them. As jobs become scarcer, this kind of favoritism—call it crony Communism—will provoke more and more public discontent. (I examine Chinese corruption in chapter 7.)

In the end, of course, China is too vast and complex to venture sweeping prognostications about—and the West has a long history of poorly assessing Chinese politics and culture. But we should also be skeptical about the long-running media story about China's successful model. The country may enjoy strong economic indicators and apparent public approval, but poke a bit under the surface and you find that the Chinese juggernaut stands on shaky ground—most of all, with its own people.

CONSEQUENCES OF BROKEN TRUST: EGYPT

Unlike the Chinese, the Egyptians didn't bother with the pretense of telling pollsters that they trusted their government—and the protest movement that ultimately swept Hosni Mubarak from power was rooted in total rejection of the regime as a legitimate authority. Egyptians reacted to decades of broken government promises and ineffective, illegitimate authority.

For example, in the 1990s Egypt received a series of loans contingent on the country's compliance with IMF restructuring programs. The conditions required that Egypt cut government services, liberalize interest rates, and increase privatization. In effect, what the IMF program required was that Mubarak break what was known as "Nasser's bargain"—a promise to provide social services, employment, subsidies, education, and health care in exchange for political control. Egypt saw some boost in its macroeconomic prosperity after implementing the reforms, but many Egyptians lost their jobs, took pay cuts, lost benefits, or were forced into early retirement.

Similarly, the country's entry into the WTO, while cheered by the nation's business elite, brought hardships to ordinary workers. Free-trade rules reduced tariff protections and exposed many labor-intensive sectors to more job cuts—especially Egyptian textiles, which took a beating from Chinese and Southeast Asian producers. And the small number of Egyptian firms that did prosper in the new climate were owned by families with close ties to Mubarak (crony capitalism is as bad in Egypt as it is anywhere). This provided some of the fuel for the protests that would eventually ignite the Arab Spring.

Not long after Mubarak's ouster, the Danish-Egyptian Dialogue Institute released a fascinating study of Egyptian political culture. Most strikingly, it shows the extent of political participation: more than 6 million Egyptians, or 8 percent of a population of 81 million, took part in the revolution in some form—the equivalent of 24 million Americans taking to the streets or practicing some other form of protest (figure 4.3).

Most fascinating, however, as reflected in figure 4.3, is the centrality of the issue of trust. By far the most prevalent reason for protesting was to resist corruption. Egyptians no longer trusted the Mubarak regime to administer the nation's affairs or to deal fairly with individuals, especially those who might lack social or familial connections to the regime.

The trust issue in Egypt is dramatized also by the survey's findings about those citizens who chose to stay home rather than protest. When asked why they didn't participate in the political movement, 35 percent of respondents answered that they were "not interested in politics." This was the most popular survey response. We don't always allow for the possibility of political apathy in authoritarian regimes, or of people being so demoralized that they can tell themselves that they are not interested in politics—even when, to adapt a phrase, politics is always interested in them. But apathy can also be a cover for another emotion: fear. A nearly equal proportion of respondents said that they avoided political activity because of "fear for personal safety" (figure 4.4).

Finally, to demonstrate the corrosive influence of authoritarianism on political trust as well as personal and social trust, consider the sur-

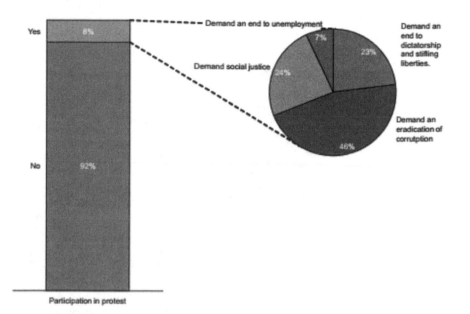

Figure 4.3.   Political Participation—Informal (Participation in Protest); Participation in Demonstrations between January 25 and February 11? *Source:* Jakob Erle, Jakob Mathias Wichmann, and Alexander Kjaerum, "Political Culture in Egypt," Danish-Egyptian Dialogue Institute, 2012, http://dedi.org.eg/wp-content/uploads/Political-Culture-in-Egypt.pdf.

vey's findings on whether Egyptians trust *one another*. The "social capital" graph, figure 4.5, shows levels of trust that Egyptians expressed for other people.

Here the insular circle of social interaction in authoritarian societies is made clear. The boundary of trust for most Egyptians apparently extends not much further than their own home or closest friends: they expressed high degrees of trust for family, neighbors, and coworkers. But by an overwhelming margin (89 percent), they expressed little trust in strangers. I won't attempt a psychological analysis of these responses, but I think it's safe to say that they are broadly consistent with the kinds of interpersonal dynamics we find in most authoritarian societies: governments that rule by fear instill in their citizens suspicion of nearly everything and everyone.

The Egyptian case, then, reveals the effects of broken trust in autocratic states. All of the characteristics we might expect to find are here: low trust for outsiders or anyone beyond one's close-knit circle of family

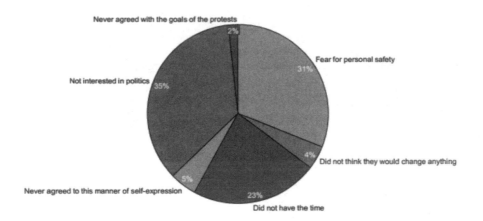

Figure 4.4. Political Participation—Informal (Participation in Protest); Motivation for Nonparticipation *Source:* **Erle, Wichmann, and Kjaerum, "Political Culture in Egypt."**

and friends; desire to see an end to the political regime coexisting with fear for one's own safety if one expresses such wishes; utter rejection of the regime's legitimacy coexisting with a pervasive sense of demoralization, apathy, and disgust.

CONCLUSION

The autocracies we have looked at in this chapter have at least two things in common: broken or fragile trust with their citizens and the potential for even more explosive developments as citizens pose challenges to these governments. Faced with a persistent and swelling protest movement, Putin might become an out-and-out strongman, like his Soviet forbears. As its economic growth slows, China might begin to hear complaints about openness and democracy not just from its dissidents but also from its business elites. And as this book went to press, Egypt was perched on the brink of chaos after the military responded to mass protests by ousting President Mohamed Morsi and installing an interim government—indicating that the country's democratic revolution remains very much a work in progress.

Democracies, too, face a reckoning. If the last decade has made anything clear, it is that both democratic and autocratic regimes have

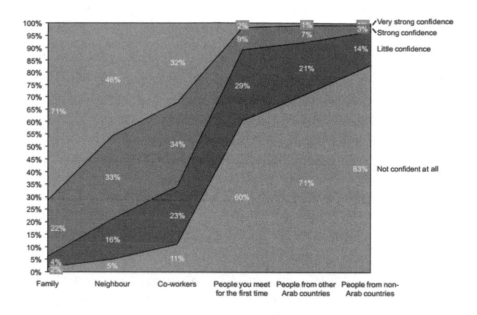

Figure 4.5. Social Capital—Trust (Interpersonal Trust); Confidence in Different Groups of People. *Source*: Erle, Wichmann, and Kjaerum, "Political Culture in Egypt."

frequently failed when faced with major disasters or emergencies. The United States can't seem to come to terms with its exploding entitlements and debt, and the last several years have made it clear that neither Washington nor the EU can solve their crippling problems through partisan warfare or top-down dictates from political elites. Beyond the West, multiple African nations have ineffectively or incompetently dealt with widespread famine, and disastrous floods in India, Pakistan, and Russia killed untold numbers of civilians while their governments failed to perform their basic task of protection and information-sharing.

What both democracies and autocracies increasingly lack is the confidence of their constituents. This can only come by restoring citizens' sense that they have a partner in government—whatever kind of government that may be. But for the West, in particular, the need is enormously pressing: only through restoration of authority and legitimacy can democratic governments enable their citizens to flourish again in the ways that once made Western democracy the envy of the world. Given the multilayered meaning of trust in democratic societies, the stakes for democracies may be highest of all.

NOTES

The epigraphs in this chapter are drawn from the following sources: Martin Porter, "Trust in Government during a Time in Crisis" (London: UCL European Institute, 2012), http://www.ucl.ac.uk/european-institute/events-view/reviews/porter/Martin_Porter_FINAL.pdf; and Jonathan Ansfield, "Ousted Chinese Leader Is Said to Have Spied on Other Top Officials," *New York Times*, April 25, 2012, http://www.nytimes.com/2012/04/26/world/asia/boxilai-said-to-have-spied-on-top-china-officials.html.

1. Rudolph Penner, "The Greenspan Commission and the Social Security Reform Act of 1983," in David Abshire, *Triumphs and Tragedies of the Modern Presidency* (Westport, CT: Praeger Publishers, 2001), 129–31.

2. Ibid.

3. Amartya Sen, "The Crisis of European Democracy," *New York Times*, May 22, 2012, http://www.nytimes.com/2012/05/23/opinion/the-crisis-of-european-democracy.html.

4. Porter, "Trust in Government."

5. Ibid.

6. Philip Stephens, "Leaders Who Generate Diminishing Returns," *Financial Times*, January 18, 2012, http://www.ft.com/intl/cms/s/0/36297676-413f-11e1-8c33-00144feab49a.html.

7. Sebastian Smith, "How Putin Has Remade the Media to Suit His Needs," *U.S. News & World Report*, July 9, 2006, http://www.usnews.com/usnews/news/articles/060709/17russia.htm.

8. "Medvedev Orders Probe of Russian Election Fraud Allegations," Voice of America, December 10, 2011, http://www.voanews.com/content/medvedev-russia-to-probe-election-fraud-allegations-135404443/149423.html.

9. Francesca Mereu, "Russian Election Insider Outlines Fraud," *New York Times*, November 27, 2007, http://www.nytimes.com/2007/11/27/world/europe/27iht-27fraud.8495486.html.

10. "Russian Election-Fraud Tactics—Something Old, Something New," Radio Free Europe Radio Liberty, March 5, 2012, http://www.rferl.org/content/russia_election_fraud_tactics_putin/24505805.html.

11. "Russia Election: Fraud Violations Listed by Observers on Putin's Vote," Huffington Post, March 5, 2012, http://www.huffingtonpost.com/2012/03/05/russia-elections-fraud_n_1320834.html.

12. "Editorial: Authorized Riots," Gazeta.ru, July 5, 2012, http://en.gazeta.ru/opinions/2012/05/07/a_4576657.shtml.

13. "Russia Bill Aims to Smother Dissent," Reuters, June 6, 2012, http://www.stuff.co.nz/world/europe/7048890/Russian-bill-aims-to-smother-dissent.

14. "Russia," Reporters Without Borders, March 12, 2012, http://en.rsf.org/russia-russia-12-03-2012,42075.html.

15. Guy Sorman, "The Empire of Lies," *City Journal* (Spring 2007), http://www.city-journal.org/html/17_2_china.html.

16. Ibid.

17. "Bo Xilai," *New York Times*, accessed July 5, 2013, http://topics.nytimes.com/top/reference/timestopics/people/b/bo_xilai/index.html.

18. "China Dissident Chen Guangcheng 'in US Embassy,'" BBC News, April 28, 2012, http://www.bbc.co.uk/news/world-asia-china-17877005.

19. Jonathan Ansfield and Ian Johnson, "Ousted Chinese Leader Is Said to Have Spied on Other Top Officials," *New York Times*, April 25, 2012, http://www.nytimes.com/2012/04/26/world/asia/bo-xilai-said-to-have-spied-on-top-china-officials.html.

20. Andrew Jacobs, "Accused Chinese Party Members Face Harsh Discipline," *New York Times*, June 14, 2012, http://www.nytimes.com/2012/06/15/world/asia/accused-chinese-party-members-face-harsh-discipline.html.

21. William Wan, "Bo Xilai's Family Complains of Chinese Government Obstacles to His Defense," *Washington Post*, October 24, 2012, http://www.washingtonpost.com/world/asia_pacific/bo-xilais-family-complains-of-chinese-government-obstacles-to-his-defense/2012/10/24/c9c7bd82-1de6-11e2-9cd5-b55c38388962_story.html.

22. "Corruption Perceptions Index 2011," Transparency International, accessed July 5, 2013, http://cpi.transparency.org/cpi2011/results/.

23. Minxin Pei, "Corruption Threatens China's Future," Carnegie Endowment for International Peace, *Policy Brief* 55 (October 2007), http://www.carnegieendowment.org/files/pb55_pei_china_corruption_final.pdf.

24. Kenji Minemura, "China Bans Reporting on 18 Subjects," *Asahi Shimbun Digital*, March 26, 2010, http://www.asahi.com/english/TKY201003250329.html.

25. "Press Freedom Index 2011–2012," Reporters Without Borders, January 25, 2012, http://en.rsf.org/press-freedom-index-2011-2012,1043.html.

26. "Freedom House: New Report Details China Censorship Mechanisms," Freedom House, February 2006, http://www.freedomhouse.org/article/freedom-house-new-report-details-china-censorship-mechanisms.

27. Jonathan Watts, "China's Secret Internet Police Target Critics with Web of Propaganda," *Guardian*, June 13, 2005, http://www.guardian.co.uk/technology/2005/jun/14/newmedia.china.

28. Ben Elgin and Bruce Einhorn, "The Great Firewall of China," *Bloomberg Businessweek*, January 22, 2006, http://www.businessweek.com/stories/2006-01-22/the-great-firewall-of-china.

5

INCOME INEQUALITY AND
THE CRISIS OF CAPITALISM

What disturbs me most is the fact that America has ceased to be a land of opportunity, with the chances of those at the bottom making it to the middle or top being much lower even than in old Europe; in fact, it is worse here than in any of the other advanced industrial countries for which there is data.

—Joseph Stiglitz

If Americans want to live the American dream, they should go to Denmark.

—Richard Wilkinson

The social contract is starting to unravel in many countries. This study dispels the assumptions that the benefits of economic growth will automatically trickle down to the disadvantaged and that greater inequality fosters greater social mobility. Without a comprehensive strategy for inclusive growth, inequality will continue to rise.

—OECD Secretary-General Angel Gurría

If the financial crisis is the nerve center of the trust breakdown, then income inequality is its beating heart. The vast and growing disparity between society's wealthiest and poorest members, which has widened dramatically since the 1970s, seems emblematic, in a more ongoing and slow-building way, of the failure of governments to provide for their citizens. Societies like the United States, in which a superclass has captured nearly all of the income gains in recent years, seem to confirm for many that economic and political systems are rigged in favor of the wealthy, connected, and powerful.

Even more important, the vast wealth disparities in nations around the world represent an existential threat to our international system. Massive inequality threatens to destabilize governments everywhere, of every kind—poor and despotic, economically ascending but authoritarian, wealthy and democratic. No government is safe from the corrosive effects of inequality on their populations and ultimately on their economies and their political systems.

Libertarian economists like to say that the market "works," but the fact is that income inequality at the levels we're seeing *doesn't* work: it represents a breakdown in the functioning as well as the promise of free-market systems. For decades, the market economy made a strong case as the best hope for raising standards of living around the world. Empirical evidence lent much support to these claims.

Now, all bets are off: when so many within a society see their incomes fall, when the underclass has no clear route upward amid fleeing manufacturing jobs and declining jobs, and when oligarchs like Russia's Boris Berezovsky, crony capitalists like Royal Bank of Scotland chief Stephen Hester, and outright criminals like Bernard Madoff seem to call the shots, we face nothing less than an international crisis of free-market capitalism.

∽

"I grew up going to Hawaii every summer. Now I'm here, applying for assistance because it's hard to make ends meet. It's very hard to adjust," said Laura Fritz, twenty-seven, of Wheat Ridge, Colorado, describing her slide from rich to poor as she filled out aid forms at a county center. Fritz had grown up wealthy, but her parents lost their fortune in the 2007 housing bust and soon began living off food stamps. So much for her college money: she joined the army instead, but she was injured in basic training and had to be discharged. Now she lives on disability.

Fritz's plight, and those of millions of Americans like her, played out against news that U.S. poverty ranks were about to reach their worst statistical point since the 1960s, before the start of the War on Poverty. The official poverty rate in the United States was set to rise, according to the AP, "from 15.1 percent in 2010, climbing as high as 15.7 percent." And while some economists predicted only a modest spike, "even a 0.1 percentage point increase would put poverty at the highest level since 1965."[1]

Meanwhile, consider the "plight" of Gregg L. Engles, CEO of Dean Foods, a Texas-based food and beverage company. Engles owns a $6 million home in a posh Dallas suburb, sixty-four acres in Vail, Colorado, and belongs to at least four golf clubs in the two states. His "office" at the company headquarters occupies *nine floors*, and when he needs to travel he does so in the company's $10 million Challenger 604 jet.[2]

Yet while American examples tend to get the most coverage, the truth is that around the world, everyday citizens are struggling mightily to make ends meet—while very much aware that for a select few, the good times just keep on rolling.

"Every day I have to do the sums and make sure my budget is balanced. I have been teaching for thirty-three years, so I hope I am not going to lose my job, but every school is being forced to cut posts, and it will keep happening," says Olga Cornejo, a schoolteacher in Burgos, Spain.[3]

Amid so much economic hardship, there is more talk of the inadequacies of capitalism than has been heard in generations.

"We need a socially responsible capitalism that doesn't make the poorest pay the most," says Dany, in Madrid. "I am afraid that change will only happen in a violent way, like in the French Revolution."[4]

In Greece, ground zero of the European debt crisis, families are struggling so severely to care for their children that record numbers are asking for foster support, at least temporarily. SOS Children, an orphan charity, reported a 70 percent increase in requests for support from Greek parents unable to support their families.[5] In addition to high unemployment, Greeks also must contend with reduced social services from a federal government struggling to remain solvent. Before the financial crisis, most referrals to SOS were because of child abuse; now, almost 100 percent of new referrals are coming from families with financial needs.

Greek economist Theodore Pelagidis sees a two-tiered society on the horizon. "You are going to see a part of the population, the middle class, comprising say 30 to 50 percent, involved in some kind of resurgence. . . . But another part of the population will be living on 300 or

400 euros [$400 to $500] a month. This part of Greek society won't be living a Western European lifestyle. It will be more like Bulgaria."[6]

Millions around the world are already living the scenario Pelagidis describes: a steady, inexorable widening of the gaps between those very well-off—especially the stupendously rich—and everyone else, from the middle class to the poor. It's a phenomenon confirmed by a wealth of empirical evidence.

According to a May 2011 report from the Organisation for Economic Co-operation and Development—which comprises thirty-four democratic, market-oriented countries—"The gap between rich and poor in OECD countries has reached its highest level for over thirty years." The report found that across OECD countries the average income of the wealthiest 10 percent was about nine times that of the poorest 10 percent.[7] Some countries are worse off than others, but the problem poses a threat to every major democracy.

Even the so-called superelites—some, anyway—recognize this. In January 2012, at the World Economic Forum's annual meeting in Davos, Switzerland, income inequality was a leading topic of discussion. A sample:

From Azim Premji, chairman of Wipro Ltd., India's third-largest software exporter: "We have seen in 2011 what ignoring this aspect can result in. If we don't take cognizance of it and try to solve this problem, it can create a chaotic upheaval globally."[8]

From Ukraine's Victor Pinchuk, founder of steel-pipe maker Interpipe: "The global social-economic order will change, if we want it or not." Pinchuk also said that businesses needed to combine profitability with ensuring "a more just distribution of wealth."[9]

From billionaire Rahul Bajaj, chairman of Mumbai-based Bajaj Group: "These growing inequalities are not acceptable. The rich have done much better than the poor, and that creates problems."[10]

Unless we find a way to put these concerns into action and address the spiraling wealth inequities around the globe, we will face an increasingly ungovernable international situation—one that promotes instability, anger, and antisystemic political efforts.

Ironically, though the problems of income inequality began deepening a generation ago, they were for the most part ignored in our political

conversation until recently. In part, that's because of the relatively robust economies the West, and particularly the United States, enjoyed
from the early 1980s until 2007. Liberal Democrats would sometimes
raise the issue, but for the most part their warnings weren't heeded.
The financial crisis and Great Recession made income inequality more
prominent in public debate, but what really put the issue front and
center was the Occupy Wall Street movement, which began in New
York in the fall of 2011.

If Occupy Wall Street has accomplished anything, it is putting income inequality on the political agenda, in terms of both policy and,
perhaps more important, rhetoric. The movement's ingenious "99 percent" versus "1 percent" formulation did what all great political slogans
do: distill complexity into an easily memorable and evocative phrase. In
a very short time, the 99 percent and the 1 percent have become part of
our political vocabulary. President Obama has used the terms, and so
did Mitt Romney during the 2012 presidential campaign. Moreover, the
Occupy movement has resonated with people around the world facing
similar issues of wealth disparity and lack of opportunity.

While inequities in most OECD nations have grown over the last
several decades, the huge gap in the United States makes it nearly
unique among the world's rich nations. According to the CIA's World
Factbook, income inequality in the United States is far more severe
than in the EU member countries. America's income inequality put us
in the ranks of such developing nations as Cameroon, Ivory Coast,
Uganda, and Jamaica.[11]

America, writes Nobel laureate Joseph Stiglitz in his new book *The
Price of Inequality*, is "no longer the land of opportunity." In fact, Stiglitz now believes that the "American dream is a myth."[12] Stiglitz is
hopeful that the United States can still create a more dynamic economy
and a fairer society, but the outlook is uncertain at best. Journalist Chris
Hayes echoes Stiglitz's sentiment, arguing in *Twilight of the Elites:
America after Meritocracy* that "extreme inequality produces elites that
are less competent . . . than a more egalitarian social order would."[13]
Indeed, as elites grow further removed from the life experiences and
challenges of ordinary people, the "leadership" they provide has become ill conceived, self-aggrandizing, and ineffective.

But beyond the problem of good governance is the broader damage
that income inequality does to democracy itself. The fading idea that

one can rise as high as one's abilities can carry one, the generally shared sense that the economy and political system are fair, and the core issue of trust, both in government and in social interactions, all have been casualties of the income-inequality explosion. Because of the way inequality tends to feed on itself and self-replicate, it is a problem whose effects compound over time. Indeed, as the OECD report points out, income mobility—the ability to move up the economic ladder—suffers in countries with steep inequality: "Intergenerational earnings mobility is low in countries with high inequality such as Italy, the United Kingdom, and the United States, and much higher in the Nordic countries, where income is distributed more evenly."[14]

The growing concentration of wealth into the hands of fewer and fewer people perpetuates their advantages, allowing them to insulate their children from many social institutions, such as the public schools, which continue to deteriorate. This helps ensure that those with less will remain disadvantaged in a meaner, leaner public environment from which the superrich increasingly withdraw their dollars, support, and attention.

If solving the problem of governance is central to resolving the loss of trust, then finding a sustainable, equitable, and practical solution to the massive wealth inequities bedeviling the globe is no less vital. "A nation cannot prosper long when it favors only the prosperous," President Obama said in his first inaugural address. Whether the president has the right policy answers for the United States is a matter of opinion; what shouldn't be at issue is his diagnosis of the problem.

Let's take a look at some of the numbers, both in the United States and internationally.

INCOME INEQUALITY BY THE NUMBERS

The nations with the highest rates of inequality in the May 2011 OECD report were Chile and Mexico, where the incomes of the richest are still more than twenty-five times those of the poorest, though these rates have begun to drop somewhat. As the report makes clear, nations outside of the OECD have much higher rates of inequality: Brazil, for instance, has an income gap of fifty to one between its richest and poorest citizens.

Even more striking, the report found that the income gap rose in countries known for their egalitarian economic policies, like Germany, Denmark, and Sweden; the income gap had risen from five to one in the 1980s to six to one today. The gap is ten to one in Italy, Japan, Korea, and the United Kingdom and fourteen to one in Israel, Turkey, and the United States (figure 5.1).[15]

Another way of looking at wealth disparities is through the well-known Gini coefficient, which rates countries from zero to one, where zero indicates perfect income equality and one indicates a country in which a single person holds all of its wealth (sometimes the index is represented from zero to one hundred, but it comes out the same—.35, for example, would correspond to thirty-five, one to one hundred, and so on). The OECD study showed which countries are experiencing the worst gaps between the richest and the poorest. Between the mid-1980s and the late 2000s, the average Gini coefficient for all OECD countries has risen annually by an average of 0.3 percent and stands now at 0.31.[16]

The following is a list of the OECD countries with the top ten Gini coefficients:[17]

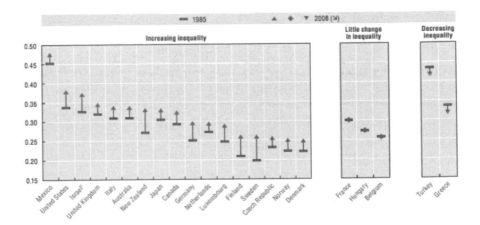

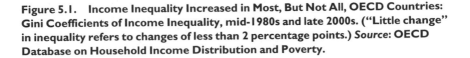

Figure 5.1. Income Inequality Increased in Most, But Not All, OECD Countries: Gini Coefficients of Income Inequality, mid-1980s and late 2000s. ("Little change" in inequality refers to changes of less than 2 percentage points.) *Source:* **OECD Database on Household Income Distribution and Poverty.**

1. Chile: .50
2. Mexico: .48
3. Turkey: .41
4. United States: .38
5. Israel: .37
6. Portugal: .36
7. Australia: .34
8. Italy: .34
9. United Kingdom: .34
10. New Zealand: .33

These growing disparities coexist with an enormous increase in overall global wealth over the last decade. An October 2010 report by Credit Suisse, for example, showed that of the world's 4.4 billion adults, wealth had grown 72 percent, to $195 trillion, since 2000. That figure was expected to increase another 60 percent, to $315 trillion, by 2015.[18]

The problem is that this wealth is so unevenly distributed. The same Credit Suisse report showed that people with a net worth of more than $1 million, while making up just 0.5 percent of the world's population, hold approximately 35.6 percent of the world's wealth. At the same time, those with a net worth of under $10,000—comprising a staggering 68.4 percent of the world's population—hold just 4.2 percent of the world's wealth. Credit Suisse's "wealth pyramid" maps out the dynamic, as shown in figure 5.2.

While the United States is far from the most unequal society in the world, it is the most powerful and economically prosperous country with such high inequality. And because so much of what the United States does affects the rest of the world—from foreign policy to economic policy—it is worth taking a closer look at the United States, where, as of 2012, the top 1 percent of wage earners take home about 21 percent of the nation's income, while accounting for 35 percent of its overall wealth.[19]

In the United States

The growing wealth gap in the United States indicates a society in which the distance between winners and losers, always fairly substantial in American life, has become a chasm. In a reversal of trends that

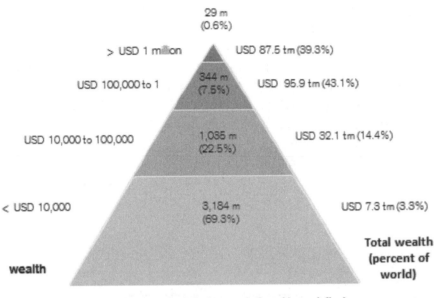

29 m
(0.6%)

> USD 1 million   USD 87.5 tm (39.3%)

USD 100,000 to 1   344 m
                          (7.5%)   USD 95.9 tm (43.1%)

USD 10,000 to 100,000   1,035 m
                               (22.5%)   USD 32.1 tm (14.4%)

< USD 10,000   3,184 m   USD 7.3 tm (3.3%)
                      (69.3%)

wealth   Total wealth
                (percent of
                world)

Number of adults (percent of world population)

Figure 5.2.

prevailed in the mid-twentieth century, America's wealthiest are cap-
turing almost all income gains.

In a major study at Slate called "The United States of Income Inequality" (later a book, *The Great Divergence*), Timothy Noah pointed
out how income inequality had always been a part of American life but
never to such a dramatic degree. In 1915, when University of Wisconsin
statistician Willford I. King published *The Wealth and Income of the
People of the United States*, the nation's richest 1 percent possessed
about 15 percent (some said it was 18 percent) of the nation's income—
a proportion that King found alarming. Nearly one hundred years later,
however, as Noah reports, the richest 1 percent account for 24 percent
of U.S. income. Things are that much worse, then, but, as Noah notes,
they didn't get to this point by following a straight line: in between, the
United States experienced what economic historians have termed the
Great Compression, in which incomes became dramatically more equal
across economic groups.

The Great Compression corresponded with America's celebrated
postwar period, when the nation developed the largest and most pros-

perous middle class in history while also enjoying rapid economic growth. But it ended in the economically troubled 1970s, when wage growth stagnated, inflation ate away at incomes and savings, and higher unemployment bedeviled the U.S. economy. Income inequality began growing again, spiking in the 1980s, slowing briefly in the 1990s, and resuming "with a vengeance" over the last decade.[20] This past generation of increasing disparity is what economist Paul Krugman calls the Great Divergence. Its trajectory is mapped in figure 5.3.

The truly frightening thing about the Great Divergence is that it took place during a period that included two of the greatest economic booms in American history—1983 to 1989, and the early 1990s to about 2007, the so-called "long boom." Yet from 1980 to 2005, as Noah chron-

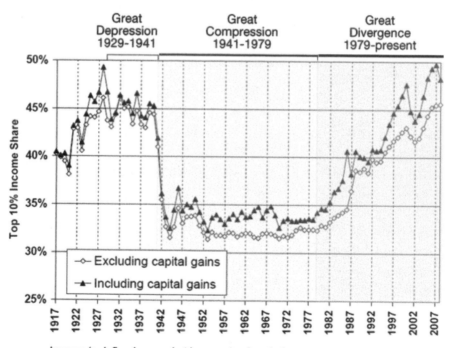

Income is defined as market income (and excludes government transfers). In 2008, top decile includes all families with annual income above $109,000.

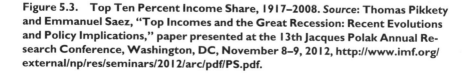

Figure 5.3. Top Ten Percent Income Share, 1917–2008. *Source:* Thomas Pikkety and Emmanuel Saez, "Top Incomes and the Great Recession: Recent Evolutions and Policy Implications," paper presented at the 13th Jacques Polak Annual Research Conference, Washington, DC, November 8–9, 2012, http://www.imf.org/external/np/res/seminars/2012/arc/pdf/PS.pdf.

icles, "more than 80 percent of total increase in Americans' income went to the top 1 percent." Even over the last decade, when economic growth was more uneven, U.S. productivity growth improved by a robust 20 percent—yet it sparked little or no income gains for the middle class or those below.[21]

The Great Recession, while it hit the rich as well, only magnified these disparities. According to recent studies by Emmanuel Saez, an economist at the University of California, Berkeley, on the eve of the Great Recession income gaps had reached extremes last seen in the 1920s. Initially, the rich took a much larger hit from the economic downturn: between 2007 and 2009, the top 1 percent saw a staggering 36 percent decline in income, compared with a 11.6 percent drop for the bottom 99 percent.

Of course, those numbers need to be kept in perspective. Losing 36 percent of one's income is certainly serious, but when one is starting from such a place as the 1 percent, it is bearable, whereas an 11.6 percent drop in income for millions of Americans is the difference between staying in their home and foreclosure. In fact, the 11.6 percent drop was the largest decline since the Great Depression.

And the rich rebounded quickly, even in the "Obama economy" often derided by Republican critics. From 2009 to 2010, the top 1 percent was back in the driver's seat: they captured an astounding 93 *percent of the income growth*,[22] enjoying income gains of more than 11 percent, while everyone else gained just 0.2 percent.[23] Indeed, a June 2011 Pew poll found that over the past year, between a quarter and a third of those earning less than $75,000 had trouble paying for medical care or paying a mortgage or rent and feared either being laid off or suffering a pay cut in the next year.[24]

Studies now show that the explosion in executive pay, which has nearly quadrupled in real dollars since the 1970s, has played a key role in widening the income gap. According to a study cited in the *Washington Post*, the largest chunk of today's highest-income earners, nearly 60 percent, are "executives and other managers in firms."[25] They're not just in finance, either, but also in traditional industries like the dairy business. The next largest groups were lawyers and real-estate professionals. The crucial fact is not only that these groups make up such a disproportionate percentage of the top earners but also that their earnings so far outstrip everyone else's.

It hasn't always been this way.

Remember Gregg Engles, the Dean Foods CEO? The company he now leads was headed a generation ago by Kenneth J. Douglas, who by any standard lived a comfortable life. He earned what today would equal about $1 million annually. He had a nice four-bedroom home, a company car, and a country-club membership. That was CEO life in 1970, and, then as now, it put men like Douglas at the top of the economic pyramid. The difference was that they didn't stand twenty thousand fathoms above everyone else. Douglas was wealthy, but he wasn't what we call today "superrich." In fact, Douglas was known to turn down raises occasionally, saying they were bad for company morale.[26] It's hard to imagine a CEO doing that today.

The two-tiered society represented by Engles and others has created the genuine danger that, as Noah writes, the United States could become something like a "banana republic." This is especially true when the top 1 percent—or perhaps top 5 or even 10 percent—seems increasingly able to insulate itself from the rest of the country and live as a kind of separate class.

It was this so-called superclass that the *Atlantic*'s Chrystia Freeland wrote about so powerfully in 2011: a group of people of such overwhelming wealth that they have essentially become a separate culture. As Freeland wrote, this new class of "jet-setting meritocrats" believe themselves, in Ayn Rand–like fashion, to be "deserving winners of a tough, worldwide economic competition," and they're often dismissive of those less successful—which is basically everyone else. They have become, Freeland writes, "a transglobal community of peers who have more in common with one another than with their countrymen back home."[27]

Beyond the United States

Although the United States tends to get the most attention, the truth is that income inequality has been on the rise worldwide.

In Russia, income inequality has widened since the fall of the Soviet Union—as would be expected in a nation making the transition to a market economy. According to Moscow's Higher School of Economics, income inequality between the mid-1980s and the mid-2000s has increased eight times more in Russia than in Hungary and five times more in Russia than in the Czech Republic. In fact, the number of Russians who made the *Forbes* list of the world's billionaires jumped from none in 2000 to 101 in 2010. Moscow has become the billionaire capital of the world, while the average monthly salary in Russia was only 21,000 rubles ($670) in 2010.[28]

As Reuters reported, "Russia qualifies as a middle-income country as a whole, but the average pay in three-quarters of more than eighty regions is below the national level."[29] According to an April 2011 article in the *Guardian*, the richest third of the Russian population has doubled its wealth since 1990; the other two-thirds have seen no gain, while the poor are barely *half* as wealthy as when the Soviet Union fell.[30]

Since 1990, the general decline of agriculture, education, and health in all regions of Russia and the rise of industrial production (energy), construction, transport, and finance in just a few regions has greatly contributed to rising income inequality. What's really striking, though, is the huge spike in inequality just since 2005, showing that economic gains in Russia are becoming even more unevenly distributed. Russia's Gini figure, according to the World Bank, went from 37.5 in 2005 to 42 in 2010.

Or consider Israel, one of the wealthiest countries in the world, now facing sustained "tent-city" protests about income inequality. Those tens of thousands of protesters weren't merely venting temporary frustrations: statistics justify their anger. According to the CIA World Factbook (which uses the one to one hundred scale), Israel's Gini coefficient went from 35.5 in 2001 to 39.2 in 2008;[31] at the same time, Israel's poverty rate, the highest in the OECD, is *double the average* of other developed nations.[32] Like the United States, rising inequality in Israel has led to a hollowing out of the middle class, which has declined from roughly one-third of the nation's population to roughly one-quarter since 1988.[33]

According to the OECD, income inequality has grown faster in the United Kingdom than in any other "rich country" since the mid-1970s. The OECD found that the average annual income of the United Kingdom's top 10 percent of earners was about twelve times that of the bottom 10 percent—up from a ratio of eight to one in the 1980s.[34] And—evidence that Occupy Wall Street's "1 percent" mantra applies internationally—the top 1 percent's total share of income doubled, going from 7.1 percent in 1970 to 14.3 percent in 2005.

In non-OECD member nation India, meanwhile, income inequality has doubled over the last two decades—"making it the worst performer on this count of all emerging economies," according to the *Times of India*. India's top 10 percent of wage earners now earn twelve times what the bottom 10 percent does. The top 10 percent also far out-earns the median 10 percent, meaning that there are huge gaps not just between the rich and the poor but also between the rich and the middle class.

As for the nations that make up the infamous Top Three of the OECD's income-inequality list—Chile, Mexico, and Turkey—all show the kinds of gaping wealth disparities frequently typical in developing nations. In fact, some observers find it unfair that such nations are included in comparisons with more developed OECD countries, and perhaps rightly so. But regardless, the numbers don't lie. Chile's developing economy is often lauded by free-market economists in the West, but nearly 19 percent of the nation's citizens live in poverty, a figure almost double the OECD average. Chile's Gini score of .5 is much higher than the OECD average of .31, and Chile has more people living in poverty than any other OECD nation except for Israel and Mexico.[35]

As for Mexico, the nation's income-inequality gap actually narrowed somewhat in the last twenty years, surrendering the top spot to Chile. But the average income of the top 10 percent of Mexican income earners was twenty-six times higher than the average income of the bottom 10 percent. In Turkey, meanwhile, the top 20 percent make nearly half of the nation's income; the bottom 20 percent make just 5.8 percent.

What this quick survey makes clear, then, is that inequality is growing and pervasive internationally. The United States might get most of the ink, but the problem of wealth disparity afflicts most countries, and for many it is only getting worse. Only an understanding of its causes and consequences can allow us to take the steps necessary to address it. These concerns will be the subject of the following chapter.

NOTES

The epigraphs in this chapter are drawn from the following sources: Cullen Murphy, "Q&A: Joseph Stiglitz on the Fallacy That the Top 1 Percent Drives Innovation, and Why the Reagan Administration Was America's Inequality Turning Point," *Vanity Fair*, June 5, 2012, www.vanityfair.com/online/daily/2012/06/joseph-stiglitz-innovation-fallacy-reagan; "Speakers Richard Wilkinson: Public Health Researcher," TED, July 2011, http://www.ted.com/

speakers/richard_wilkinson.html; and "Society: Government Must Tackle Record Gap between Rich and Poor, Says OECD," OECD, May 12, 2011, http://www.oecd.org/document/40/0,3746,en_21571361_44315115_49166760_1_1_1_1,00.html.

1. Hope Yen, "US Poverty on Track to Rise to Highest since 1960s," Yahoo! News, July 23, 2012, http://news.yahoo.com/us-poverty-track-rise-highest-since-1960s-112946547--finance.html.

2. Peter Whoriskey, "With Executive Pay, Rich Pull Away from Rest of America," *Washington Post*, June 18, 2011, http://www.washingtonpost.com/business/economy/with-executive-pay-rich-pull-away-from-rest-of-america/2011/06/13/AGKG9jaH_print.html.

3. "Spain Economic Crisis: Your Stories," BBC News, June 13, 2012, http://www.bbc.co.uk/news/world-europe-18422565.

4. Ibid.

5. "Greek Financial Crisis: Families Turn to SOS Children for Help," SOS Children's Villages, May 31, 2012, http://www.soschildrensvillages.org.uk/about-our-charity/archive/2012/05/greek-financial-crisis-families-turn-to-sos-children-for-help.

6. Russel Shorto, "The Way Greeks Live Now," *New York Times*, February 13, 2012, http://www.nytimes.com/2012/02/19/magazine/the-way-greeks-live-now.html.

7. "Society: Governments Must Tackle Record Gap."

8. Matthew Miller, "Mega-Rich Occupy Davos as 0.01 percent Decry Income Gap," Bloomberg, January 25, 2012, http://www.bloomberg.com/news/2012-01-24/billionaires-occupy-davos-as-0-01-bemoan-economic-inequalities.html.

9. Ibid.

10. Ibid.

11. Whoriskey, "With Executive Pay."

12. "Columbia Professor Joseph Stiglitz: The 'American Dream' Is a Myth," *Atlanta Blackstar*, June 11, 2012, http://atlantablackstar.com/2012/06/11/columbia-professor-the-american-dream-is-a-myth-joseph-stiglitz/.

13. Christopher Hayes, *Twilight of the Elites: America after Meritocracy* (New York: Crown Publishers, 2012).

14. "An Overview of Growing Income Inequalities in OECD Countries: Main Findings" (Paris: OECD, 2011), http://www.oecd.org/dataoecd/40/12/49499779.pdf.

15. "Society: Governments Must Tackle Record Gap."

16. Harry Bradford, "10 Countries with the Worst Income Inequality," Huffington Post, May 24, 2011, http://www.huffingtonpost.com/2011/05/23/10-countries-with-worst-income-inequality_n_865869.html#s278244&title=1_Chile.

17. Ibid.

18. "Credit Suisse: Global Wealth Is Expected to Increase 61 percent by 2015; Middle Segment of Wealth Pyramid Holds One-Sixth of Global Wealth, to Become Emerging Consumers and Drive Economic Growth," Credit Suisse, October 8, 2012, https://www.credit-suisse.com/news/en/media_release.jsp?ns=41610.

19. Rana Foroohar, "What Ever Happened to Upward Mobility?" *Time*, November 14, 2011, http://www.time.com/time/magazine/article/0,9171,2098584,00.html.

20. Timothy Noah, "The United States of Inequality," Slate, September 3, 2010, http://www.slate.com/articles/news_and_politics/the_great_divergence/features/2010/the_united_states_of_inequality/introducing_the_great_divergence.html.

21. Ibid.

22. Murphy, "Q&A: Joseph Stiglitz."

23. "The Gap Widens, Again," *Economist*, March 10, 2012, http://www.economist.com/node/21549944.

24. "Pessimism about National Economy Rises, Personal Financial Views Hold Steady," Pew Research Center, June 23, 2011, http://people-press.org/2011/06/23/section-2-views-of-personal-finances/.

25. Whoriskey, "With Executive Pay."

26. Ibid.

27. Chrystia Freeland, "The Rise of the New Global Elite," *Atlantic*, January 4, 2011, http://www.theatlantic.com/magazine/archive/2011/01/the-rise-of-the-new-global-elite/8343/.

28. Lidia Kelly and Maya Dyakina, "Analysis: Russia's Wealth Gap Wounds Putin," Reuters, December 20, 2011, http://www.reuters.com/article/2011/12/20/us-russia-inequality-idUSTRE7BJ19Z20111220.

29. Ibid.

30. Tom Parfitt, "Russia's Rich Double Their Wealth, but Poor were Better Off in 1990s," *Guardian*, April 11, 2011, http://www.guardian.co.uk/world/2011/apr/11/russia-rich-richer-poor-poorer.

31. "Distribution of Family Income," CIA World Factbook, accessed July 5, 2013, https://www.cia.gov/library/publications/the-world-factbook/fields/2172.html.

32. Eyal Press, "Rising Up in Israel," *New York Review of Books*, November 24, 2011, http://www.nybooks.com/articles/archives/2011/nov/24/rising-israel/.

33. "Israel, a Social Report," Adva Center, December 25, 2010, http://www.adva.org/default.asp?PageID=1002&ItmID=626.

34. Randeep Ramesh, "Income Inequality Growing Faster in UK than Any Rich Country, Says OECD," *Guardian*, December 5, 2011, http://www.guardian.co.uk/society/2011/dec/05/income-inequality-growing-faster-uk.

35. Adrián Martínez, "Chile: Economy, Income Inequality Growing," Infosur Hoy, April 26, 2011, http://infosurhoy.com/cocoon/saii/xhtml/en_GB/features/saii/features/economy/2011/04/26/feature-02.

6

INCOME INEQUALITY

What's Causing It, Why It Matters, and What to Do

Societies that manage a narrower gap between rich and poor enjoy longer economic expansions.
——David J. Lynch, *Bloomberg Businessweek*

Our country has been good to us. It provided a foundation through which we could succeed. Now, we want to do our part to keep that foundation strong so that others can succeed as we have. Please do the right thing for our country. Raise our taxes.
——Patriotic Millionaires for Fiscal Strength

Explanations for growing income inequality vary widely, depending on where you are. In Israel, for example, many believe that the economic reforms that transformed the nation from a socialist to a capitalist state have left wealth concentrated in fewer hands. According to a 2011 Reuters story, a report from the Israeli parliament found that "ten large business groups control 30 percent of the market value of public companies, while sixteen control half the money in the entire country."[1] Israel's sell-off of many of its state assets, a process said to have been rife with cronyism, enabled certain families to make these purchases at bargain prices and become incredibly wealthy.[2]

In Great Britain, many blame the trend on policy choices by recent administrations. The creation of a new British "superrich class" can be traced, according to several scholars, to policies that helped London's financial district, The City, become a Wall Street–like empire of financial wizardry. Successive governments cut taxes on the wealthy substantially, and tax policy in Britain became much less redistributive. Although taxes on the wealthy in Britain recently have risen, the go-go 2000s saw the top marginal rate drop to 40 percent—down from 60 percent in the 1980s.[3]

India, too, has seen intensified concentration of wealth among an elite, but the causes might be more particular to that country's unique dynamics. The OECD blames an "increase in wage inequality between regular wage earners—contractual employees hired over a period of time. By contrast, inequality in the casual wage sector—workers employed on a day-to-day basis—has remained more stable." India has a vast number of "informal workers," and their wages have not seen any uptick, while those in more professional sectors have raced ahead.[4]

But national differences aside, certain broad trends can be identified. Globalization has clearly played a role in widening income gaps. In many, if not most, OECD countries productivity gains have largely enriched those with more education and more specialized job skills. Advances in information and communication technology have also exacerbated the income gaps between those with more and less education—especially since technology has played a crucial role in the offshoring of jobs. Finally, policy choices make a difference as well.

Considering the nation's centrality to the global economy, understanding the causes of inequality in the United States has been a source of great interest for critics and scholars. The United States is something like the ground zero of the income-inequality debate. After spending the better part of the twentieth century fostering the largest and most prosperous middle class the world has ever seen, the United States has now watched for at least a generation as the wealthiest pull further and further away from the poorest while the middle class struggles to tread water economically. America remains the world's essential economy, but its productivity has increasingly benefited those at the upper echelons of the income pyramid. What happened, many now ask, to the American Dream?

UNEQUAL AMERICA

Two leading U.S. economists, Joseph Stiglitz and Paul Krugman, tend to identify specific federal-policy choices as the drivers. Stiglitz, author of *The Price of Inequality*, identifies Ronald Reagan's presidency as the "fork-in-the-road moment" at which U.S. policies began to exacerbate inequality. He argues that before Reagan the United States had enjoyed decades of economic growth in which people broadly shared—and, in fact, those at the bottom did better, proportionally, than those at the top. But with the Reagan years came financial deregulation and enormous tax cuts for upper-income payers, reducing the tax system's progressivity. As Stiglitz writes,

> Deregulation led to the excessive financialization of the economy—to the point that, before the crisis, 40 percent of all corporate profits went to the financial sector. And the financial sector has been marked by extremes in compensation at the top and has made its profits partly by exploiting those at the bottom and middle, with, for instance, predatory lending and abusive credit-card practices. Reagan's successors, unfortunately, continued down the path of deregulation. They also extended the policy of lowering taxes at the top, to the point where today the richest 1 percent of Americans pay only around 15 percent of their income in taxes, far lower than those with more moderate incomes.[5]

In his groundbreaking study at Slate, Timothy Noah examines pretty much every theory about the causes for income inequality and finds that most of them don't explain what has occurred. Rather, Noah finds, in the end, that government policies, broadly considered, have created the Great Divergence—and government, he says, is *us*. Here is his breakdown of causality:

- He attributes 30 percent to Wall Street and corporate boards' pampering of the wealthy—such as CEOs.
- He finds the failures of the U.S. education system responsible for another 30 percent.
- The decline of labor unions is responsible for 20 percent.
- Trade policies are responsible for 10 percent.
- Tax policy is responsible for 5 percent.

- Immigration is responsible for 5 percent.
- He attributes zero causality to race and gender, single parenthood, or "the imagined uniqueness of computers as a transformative technology."

"Most of these factors reflect at least in part things the federal government either did or failed to do," Noah concludes. "In a broad sense, then, we all created the Great Divergence, because in a democracy, the government is us."[6]

So Noah concludes that the key forces driving U.S. inequality are government policies favoring the wealthy and the financial sector; the growing importance of a college degree in the economy; America's increased trade with lower-wage nations, which has the effect of depressing wages here; and the precipitous decline in membership and power of labor unions, which during their heyday were able to ensure relatively robust wages for the American worker.

These forces have also created an economy whose internal processes are very different than any other we have seen before. Namely, what we've seen over the last decade is the phenomenon of GDP growth and productivity increases, without corresponding job growth. This is what Thomas B. Edsall calls the "hollowing out of the employment marketplace,"[7] a process that has produced a U.S. unemployment rate of more than 8 percent for four years running now, with millions out of work for longer than six months. Technological efficiency delivers the productivity gains and the bottom-line profits that executives and managers need without necessarily generating lots of middle-class jobs.

Erik Brynjolfsson and Andrew McAfee, both of MIT, have studied the phenomenon closely and come to a stark conclusion: this "hollowing out" will only continue as technological progress marches on. They argue that our "current labor-force woes are not because the economy isn't growing, and they're not because companies aren't making money or spending money on equipment. They're because these trends have become increasingly decoupled from hiring—from needing more human workers."[8] If they're right, the U.S. economy has a bleak future. Whether or not one accepts this argument (and many economists don't), economists have yet to offer convincing explanations for the coexistence of high productivity and high unemployment.

For his part, Paul Krugman disputes structural arguments of this kind. The way he sees it, the real "structural" problem the United States faces is not economic but political: our system, he writes, "has been warped and paralyzed by the power of a small, wealthy minority. And the key to economic recovery lies in finding a way to get past that minority's malign influence."[9] He argues that a tiny minority of super-wealthy patrons has essentially bought out the Republican Party, skewing its policy priorities entirely toward the rich. Because almost all income gains have accrued to the 1 percent, he argues, their efforts have been pretty successful.

Obviously, the scope of all of these arguments is beyond my purposes here. The fact remains that as long as such economic trends continue, income-inequality rates will continue to spiral.

SOCIETY, DEMOCRACY, AND ECONOMY: WHY INCOME INEQUALITY MATTERS

By now, most observers agree that income inequality is a serious issue and that widening gaps between those at the bottom and those at the very top are not healthy. Some, especially on the libertarian right in the United States, argue that income inequality is not a cause for concern. They contend that rising income inequality reflects an opportunity economy—that those with the most talent and the most initiative are getting ahead, so the system is working as designed. But unless one is a devotee of Ayn Rand (which some of these commentators are), one is not likely to see rising income inequality as a sign of systemic health.

The other argument some libertarians make is that income inequality is relative—that even people on the bottom today, especially in the West, live better than they did one hundred years ago. This is true materially, but it's basically meaningless to how people live in the present. As Noah puts it, "people do not experience life as an interesting moment in the evolution of human societies."[10] The simple fact remains that in a society in which opportunity is not widely shared, those at the top wield disproportionate influence, authority, and wealth.

Besides, there are at least three core grounds on which we should lament rising income inequality: the health and well-being of society, the effect on democracy and democratic values, and the impact on economies.

British public-health researcher Richard Wilkinson has done pioneering work on a range of social indicators in various nations. His 2009 book, *The Spirit Level*, written with Kate Pickett, identified sweeping differences between societies with huge income gaps and those with much more narrow divisions between rich and poor. Their book became a blockbuster in the United Kingdom and has been cited across the political spectrum, from Prime Minister David Cameron to liberal opposition parties.

Generally, Wilkinson and Pickett found that the more equal the society, the happier and healthier were its members. They worked with vast data sets and found that almost every modern social malady—from poor heath to mental illness, from violence to teen pregnancy, from obesity to drug use—was worse in less equal countries (and within the United States, they were worse in less equal states). The United States does not match up well, for instance, against Scandinavian countries when it comes to the whole range of health and well-being indicators.

Some studies that Wilkinson cites show staggering increases in homicide rates, teenage birth rates, and prison populations, all related to inequality.

Beyond health and well-being, inequality also has corrosive effects on people's feelings about their governments, and about democracy itself. In other words, high inequality correlates closely with the subject of this book: the end of authority and the loss of trust.

Across societies, Wilkinson and Pickett found that the quality of democracy itself deteriorated with greater inequality. Again referring to America, they note that the political divide increases with greater income differences and that there was much more political overlap in previous times—Democrats voting for Republicans, and vice versa—when incomes were less unequal. Such wealth disparity inevitably affects that precious resource for a democratic government—legitimacy and trust. As Wilkinson has said, "Compare attitudes toward government action in the States with attitudes in the Scandinavian countries, for instance. The Swedes tend to regard their government as the instrument through which they do what they need to do together—as indeed we in Britain used to do when income differences were smaller."[11]

Social trust has plummeted most severely among the poorest third of Americans, as David Brooks pointed out in a 2012 *New York Times* column. He cites sociologist Robert Putnam's provocative statement at the Aspen Ideas Festival: "It's perfectly understandable that kids from working-class backgrounds have become cynical and even paranoid, for virtually all our major social institutions have failed them—family, friends, church, school, and community."[12] In every sense, poorer kids in the United States face more constrained opportunities than they have in a generation. The impact on trust is self-evident.

All of this endangers not only our democratic system but also our market economy. As Wilkinson sees it, "even if you're just interested in preserving the free market and democracy, you should be interested in greater equality." Indeed, this argument dates back at least as far as Franklin Roosevelt, whom some credit with "saving capitalism" from its excesses in the Great Depression. If this is to be done again, we had better get started.

In Europe, in particular, the crisis of capitalism and market economics has even led to a resurgence of interest in Marxism among the young. Sales of Marx's *Das Kapital* have surged in Germany since 2008,[13] and in Britain, a twenty-seven-year-old socialist, Owen Jones, authored a political bestseller about the "demonization of the working class."[14]

Fortunately, Jones and most of his ilk don't seem interested in calling for bloody revolution, but their new popularity clearly indicates the troubled shoals on which capitalism finds itself. It shouldn't be surprising that income inequality fosters these sentiments—with massive wealth disparities amid high unemployment, how can the younger generation regard market capitalism with anything other than suspicion?

For decades, amid rising income inequality in the United States especially, many commentators have argued that these costs are necessary as part of a functioning and successful economy. That so many on the bottom were struggling was bad news, they argued, and we should work on redressing these imbalances—yet we must also acknowledge that this is just how capitalism works. But more recently others have shown that such extremes of income inequality aren't even justifiable in economic terms—in fact, high disparities like that in the United States are holding economies back.

"Societies that manage a narrower gap between rich and poor enjoy longer economic expansions," wrote David J. Lynch in *Bloomberg Businessweek*, citing research from the International Monetary Fund. Given how income disparities are increasing in the United States, we may face much shorter economic booms. With fewer people possessing the disposable income necessary to fuel consumer spending, it's a pretty logical hypothesis.[15]

Inequality may even affect equity markets over the long term. As some economists have pointed out, even the wealthy see massive inequalities as a negative—to the extent that they might abandon their investments, concluding that "the market is a rigged game for insiders," according to Fusion IQ CEO Barry Ritholtz. "You're going to lose a generation of investors," says Ritholtz. "And that's how you end up with a twenty-five-year bear market. That's the risk if people start to think there is no economic justice."[16]

WHAT TO DO?

It should be clear that the current trends of widening income inequality are not sustainable. We should understand that what we have right now doesn't work and that ignoring it—let alone defending it—will only worsen the problem.

I believe very strongly that we need a global acknowledgment of income inequality and efforts, both nationally and internationally, to address it. Fortunately, awareness has grown, even in unlikely places. In the United States, for example, a group called Patriotic Millionaires for Fiscal Strength has organized to advocate higher taxes on the wealthy to help pay down the nation's deficit and support greater equity among income groups. Elsewhere, there are some good policy ideas, but more are needed.

In the United States, while some don't make this connection, I think there is a strong connection between campaign-finance reform and income-inequality issues. The reason comes back to what Stiglitz calls "rent seeking": when we have a political system dominated by Super PACs and other instruments of the super wealthy, it only stands to reason that the wealthy—whether individuals or institutions that serve them, like hedge funds and investment banks—will exert their influence over policymakers to ensure that their goals are met. Those goals generally don't include raising taxes on themselves or otherwise making our system more transparent and more equitable.

Both Stiglitz and Krugman propose a range of what would be considered progressive policy proposals. I don't agree with all of them; Krugman, in particular, believes that the government should resume massive, Keynesian-style stimulus spending to generate employment. This strikes me as fiscally reckless, though I concede his premise that, in times of austerity, government spending can help. Where I agree with both economists is on the question of taxation: not only should the rich pay a higher marginal income-tax rate—President Obama's "Buffett Rule"—but they should also pay more on investment income. The very low capital-gains tax rate is biased in favor of the rich, allowing the wealthy—who often make all or most of their income from investments—to pay much less of it in taxes than do the middle class or the poor. Mitt Romney, for example, paid just 14 percent of his income in taxes in 2011. That's because most of his earnings came from capital gains, taxed at just 15 percent. The imbalance of our current tax structure might also distort the economy by increasing speculative behavior and decreasing the fund of tax dollars by which government can invest in infrastructure, schools, health care, or national defense.

I also agree with Stiglitz that we need corporate-governance reforms in order to increase the accountability of leadership and, in particular, to rein in the almost unbelievable lavishness of CEO compensation and perks. Suggestions for how to do this vary, ranging from putting employee representatives on company boards—a no-brainer—to changing companies themselves into more cooperative-type structures. The more transformative structural changes, naturally, would likely prove more controversial and meet more resistance. But we can see where the present arrangements have gotten us.

Timothy Noah offers a range of policy proposals—most of them comfortably on the liberal side of the fence. Noah points to research showing that, since 1948, Democratic presidents have presided over income gains that diminish as you move up the income scale, while Republican presidents have overseen income gains that diminish on the way down. Be that as it may, many of Noah's ideas—which range from a federal jobs program modeled on FDR's Works Progress Administration to imposing price controls on colleges and universities—don't stand much chance of being enacted. His call for greater competition in the banking sector, however, makes good sense and would help tame the out-of-control compensation packages of banking executives.

There might be some more modest but substantive things we can do for the less fortunate, and even some ideas that could attract bipartisan support. One good idea is what are called "social-impact bonds," which allow private investors to help fund low-income people with jobs, education, and the like. A government agency evaluates the results and, if the program succeeds, reimburses investors. If not, the investors eat their investment. This policy obviously wouldn't change the world, but it is directed at taking tangible action to assist those at the bottom of the economic ladder.[17] The Obama administration has endorsed social-impact bonds, and the idea is being tested in Britain.

Internationally, unless policy steps are taken to strike some balance between equity and economic growth, the disparities in wealth will only increase. Writing for UNICEF, Isabel Ortiz and Matthew Cummins contrast past policies in many nations that emphasized employment and social insurance with today's dominant policy model, which tends to emphasize growth only—a focus that almost invariably rewards the highest earners.[18] Their main point is that we have lost sight of how more equitable income distribution can reduce poverty.

More recently, economic growth has been emphasized as a way out of poverty, but, as they point out, equitable distribution (through favorable tax policies and the like) can also drive economic growth on its own, by producing more secure, prosperous consumers: "While exclusively focusing on distribution can lead to stagnation and leave populations worse-off, which has been the fate of countries under some 'populist' governments, exclusively focusing on growth can lead to large inequalities, as many countries have experienced in recent decades."[19]

In short, we must find a way back to a policy balance.

The bottom line, according to UNICEF, is that financing a more equitable global economic system will require "a degree of transfer from the wealthy to the poor across three levels": North-South transfers, South-South transfers, and national transfers. If the UN's Jeffrey Sachs is right, it would require just 1 percent of the combined GDP of the OECD nations to eradicate extreme poverty worldwide. South-South transfers would include regional development banks and organizations, as well as bilateral transfers between sovereign nations. National transfers would involve changes to policy within nations, whether through taxation, debt relief, or alternative financing, to fund more socially equitable policies that could lessen inequality.

The OECD report calls for a range of policy reforms, including more robust "income-support" and government-transfer policies for those at the bottom of the wage scale. (In the United States, at least, such policies don't usually enjoy majority support.) To its credit, the OECD report acknowledges that most of its member nations face serious policy and fiscal constraints, and, especially in the United States, raising taxes, even on the wealthiest earners, is extraordinarily difficult politically. The report also recognizes that all the income transfers in the world cannot compete with the best remedy for income inequality: growing economies that generate plentiful and well-paying jobs.

To this end, the OECD offers some solid ideas: reforms that would address the disparities between standard and nonstandard forms of employment; more job access for underrepresented groups, including youths and the elderly; and, most of all, human-capital investments to promote the "up-skilling of the workforce." By this, it means better job training and education for the less skilled, as well as access to ongoing educational opportunities over one's working life. This latter idea may sound a bit pie-in-the-sky, but given the competitiveness of the global economy and the growing global population, can anyone below the CEO level afford to stop educating himself?

One of the most encouraging signs internationally is Richard Wilkinson's UK-based organization, the Equality Trust, a nonprofit that works to educate the public on inequality issues and build political support for remedies. The organization has inspired more than a dozen local Equality Groups around the country. A number of municipal governments in England, some in major cities—including Liverpool, Newcastle, and Nottingham—have set up Fairness Commissions to address local inequality issues.[20] Wilkinson, who has spoken at some of the meetings, believes the world is full of "closet egalitarians" who understand that current income disparities are unsustainable and dangerous.

Whatever form it takes, we desperately need a concerted, multinational effort to redress imbalances in income, education, and health care. Governments must encourage social mobility and renew the middle class through greater investment in education and community development. Low-income earners, as we have seen, have been hardest hit, and they require the most immediate attention.

At the same time, we can't lose sight of the next generation of earners. With the costs of education skyrocketing, we must take concrete steps to make education more affordable. One idea that seems worth exploring is the use of organized apprenticeship programs as a viable alternative to a university education. Such programs could save many young people from a lifetime of debt while providing them with improved skills for their chosen professions.

CONCLUSION

Perhaps the wisest words I've read on the income-inequality problem come from David Brooks. In a 2012 column about inequality in the United States, called "The Opportunity Gap," he wrote that "people are going to have to make some pretty uncomfortable decisions" if we hope to reclaim the identity of America as a land of opportunity:

> Liberals are going to have to be willing to champion norms that say marriage should come before childrearing and be morally tough about it. Conservatives are going to have to be willing to accept tax increases or benefit cuts so that more can be spent on the earned-income tax credit and other programs that benefit the working class.
>
> Political candidates will have to spend less time trying to exploit class divisions and more time trying to remedy them—less time calling their opponents out-of-touch elitists and more time coming up with agendas that comprehensively address the problem. It's politically tough to do that, but the alternative is national suicide.[21]

The stakes are every bit as high as Brooks warns, not just for America but also for the international community more generally and especially the Western democracies. Our future depends on finding a way to turn around the current trends.

But aside from specific policy proposals, on which people disagree, tackling income inequality, as Brooks notes, will take political courage: we are going to have to make decisions that make powerful people angry and arouse resistance from entrenched interests. Do we have the will to do this, or are we content to fiddle while so much of the promise of Western democracy burns before our eyes?

If democracy and market capitalism are to remain history's best hope for a fair, free, and prosperous way of life, then the Western democracies, in particular, must find a way to solve the problem of income inequality.

NOTES

The epigraphs in this chapter are drawn from the following sources: David J. Lynch, "How Inequality Hurts the Economy," *Bloomberg Businessweek*, November 16, 2011, http://www. businessweek.com/magazine/how-inequality-hurts-the-economy-11162011.html; and "The Official Patriotic Millionaires Letter," Patriotic Millionaires, accessed July 5, 2013, http:// patrioticmillionaires.org/#letter.

1. Tova Cohen and Ari Rabinovitch, "Special Report: Is Israel Inc. Too Powerful?" Reuters, July 29, 2011, http://www.reuters.com/article/2011/07/29/ us-israel-concentration-idUSTRE76S1NP20110729.

2. Eyal Press, "Rising Up in Israel," *New York Review of Books*, November 24, 2011, http://www.nybooks.com/articles/archives/2011/nov/24/rising-israel/.

3. Randeep Ramesh, "Income Inequality Growing Faster in UK than Any Other Rich Country, Says OECD," *Guardian*, December 5, 2011, http://www. guardian.co.uk/society/2011/dec/05/income-inequality-growing faster-uk.

4. "India's Income Inequality Has Doubled in 20 Years," *Times of India*, December 7, 2011, http://timesofindia.indiatimes.com/india/Indias-income-inequality-has-doubled-in-20-years/articleshow/11012855.cms.

5. Cullen Murphy, "Q&A: Joseph Stiglitz on the Fallacy that the Top 1 Percent Drives Innovation, and Why the Reagan Administration Was America's Inequality Turning Point," *Vanity Fair*, June 5, 2012, http://www. vanityfair.com/online/daily/2012/06/joseph-stiglitz-innovation-fallacy reagan.

6. Timothy Noah, "The United States of Inequality: Entry 9," Slate, September 15, 2010, http://www.slate.com/articles/news_and_politics/the_great_ divergence/features/2010/the_united_states_of_inequality/how_the_decline_ in_k12_education_enriches_college_graduates.html.

7. Thomas B. Edsall, "The Hollowing Out," *New York Times*, July 8, 2012, http://campaignstops.blogs.nytimes.com/2012/07/08/the-future-of-joblessness/.

8. Andrew McAfee, "The Rebound that Stayed Flat," Race Against the Machine, January 5, 2012, http://raceagainstthemachine.com/2012/01/05/the-rebound-that-stayed-flat/.

9. Paul Krugman, "Plutocracy, Paralysis, Perplexity," *New York Times*, May 3, 2012, http://www.nytimes.com/2012/05/04/opinion/krugman-plutocracy-paralysis-perplexity.html.

10. Timothy Noah, "The United States of Inequality: Entry 10," Slate.com, September 16, 2010, http://www.slate.com/articles/news_and_politics/the_great_divergence/features/2010/the_united_states_of_inequality/why_we_cant_ignore_growing_income_inequality.html.

11. Emily McManus, "'We Quite Suddenly Realized that We Were Looking at a General Pattern': Q&A with Richard Wilkinson," TED, October 26, 2011, http://blog.ted.com/2011/10/26/we-quite-suddenly-realized-that-what-we-were-looking-at-was-a-general-pattern-qa-with-richard-wilkinson/.

12. David Brooks, "The Opportunity Gap," *New York Times*, July 9, 2012, http://www.nytimes.com/2012/07/10/opinion/brooks-the-opportunity-gap.html.

13. Kate Connolly, "Booklovers Turn to Karl Marx as Financial Crisis Bites in Germany," *Guardian*, October 15, 2008, http://www.guardian.co.uk/books/2008/oct/15/marx-germany-popularity-financial-crisis.

14. Stuart Jeffries, "Why Marxism Is on the Rise Again," *Guardian*, July 4, 2012, http://www.guardian.co.uk/world/2012/jul/04/the-return-of-marxism.

15. Lynch, "How Inequality Hurts the Economy."

16. Ibid.

17. James Wilson, "Angry about Inequality? Don't Blame the Rich," *Washington Post*, January 26, 2012, http://www.washingtonpost.com/opinions/angry-about-inequality-dont-blame-the-rich/2012/01/03/gIQA9S2fTQ_print.html.

18. Isabel Ortiz and Matthew Cummins, *Global Poverty: Beyond the Bottom Billion* (New York: UNICEF, 2011), http://www.unicef.org/socialpolicy/files/Global_Inequality.pdf.

19. Ibid.

20. McManus, "We Quite Suddenly Realized."

21. Brooks, "The Opportunity Gap."

7

POLITICAL CORRUPTION AND CRONY CAPITALISM

For years, mayors and governors anxious about local jobs had agreed to G.M.'s demands for cash rewards, free buildings, worker training, and lucrative tax breaks. As late as 2007, the company was telling local officials that these sorts of incentives would "further G.M.'s strong relationship" with them and be a "win/win situation," according to town council notes from one Michigan community.

Yet at least fifty properties on the 2009 liquidation list were in towns and states that had awarded incentives, adding up to billions in taxpayer dollars . . . their overtures were to no avail. G.M. walked away and, thanks to a federal bailout, is once again profitable. The towns have not been so fortunate, having spent scarce funds in exchange for thousands of jobs that no longer exist.

New York Times, December 1, 2012

Putin's system is dependent on corruption as a form of management and a guarantee of loyalty from officials. They will not kick out from under themselves the stool that they are standing on.

—Aleksei Navalny

For the United States, the moment to act is now, before the cancer of crony capitalism metastasizes. . . . It is not too late for the United States, but the clock is ticking. We have already begun to look like Italy. If we don't do something to stop that soon, we will end up like Greece.

—Luigi Zingales

The level of corruption in China would make a Chicago alderman
blush.

—Steven Cortes, CNBC

In the previous two chapters I examined the global phenomenon of
rising income inequality, driven in part by policies that have generally
benefited the wealthiest at the expense of everyone else. I've suggested
that income inequality has reached such a point of severity that it
threatens the future of the free-market system itself.

It's not the only condition that poses such a threat. Over the last few
decades that free-market system has increasingly become captured by a
nexus of both government and private interests that have manipulated
and distorted market outcomes, gained special privileges for insiders,
and suppressed opportunity for upstarts and others lacking connections
and insider relationships. This system has come to be called *crony capitalism*. Along with failures of government performance and the huge
gaps in income bedeviling most countries, crony capitalism has played a
key role in the crisis of authority and the loss of trust.

Of course, political corruption has been around forever; crony capitalism is only a recent variation. Whether it's election fraud, crooked
justice systems, or broad-ranging insiderism, attempts to game political
systems are as old as government itself. But protesters around the
world, whether in Moscow or the Middle East, have run out of patience
with governments showing such blatant disregard for fair play and
transparency. Governance itself has become so corrupt, so captive to
insider practices and different sets of rules for those in power and
everyone else, that people in countries as different as Russia and the
United States look at their political leaders with mounting disgust.

Like political corruption, crony capitalism—a system in which business success depends on government connections and favors, and in
which the government plays a leading role in choosing market winners
and losers—has always existed in some form. But over the last two
decades it has become rampant around the world, undermining and
even destroying the legitimacy of governments of all types—authoritarian, quasi-democratic, and democratic. It comes in two main forms.

The first is what we generally see in advanced Western countries like
the United States and some of the more affluent countries in Europe: a
political system that increasingly works on behalf of wealthy elites at the

expense of ordinary people. Elites in the private sector collaborate with politicians and interest groups to ensure favorable laws, special exemptions and financial breaks, and lenient, if any, punishment for wrongdoing. Crony capitalism in the United States and elsewhere is increasingly destabilizing and destructive, but it remains subject, however imperfectly, to political constraints: powerful elites may game the system, but they do not control it.

The second brand of crony capitalism is more virulent, an all-encompassing systemic phenomenon in which what some call superelites really do control and manipulate governments; in some cases, they are the government, or at least they're hard to distinguish from it. Examples here include the Russian oligarchs, the Chinese "princelings," African oligarchs like Congo president Joseph Kabila or those associated with the African National Congress in South Africa, and well-connected business elites in Syria and Pakistan. In these and other countries, crony capitalism operates at an entirely different level: it is a kind of quasi-government.

Though it operates differently in different societies, crony capitalism tends to produce similar outcomes: economic benefits overwhelmingly accruing to the business leaders and shareholders of favored companies, at the expense of ordinary taxpayers, localities, and employees; public services made less efficient and effective as taxpayer dollars are directed to the enrichment of private interests; and a stifling of economic growth and opportunity, as the market's ability to weed out worthy from unworthy competitors is overruled by government policy. The more virulent form of crony capitalism tends to produce these outcomes more severely.

The inequities of crony capitalism have helped fuel a deep distrust of both government and financial elites, leading to much less public willingness to back government policies—particularly austerity programs, as we've seen in Europe. Citizens in these countries consider austerity the direct result of their governments' giveaways to cronies who use government to enrich themselves at public expense. It's difficult to blame them for feeling that way. Meanwhile, in a 2012 poll, 70 percent of Americans said that their elected officials mainly reflect the values of the wealthy, not the values of the middle or working classes. [1]

As if loss of trust in government weren't enough, the pervasiveness of crony capitalism has also produced a significant weakening in public confidence in the institutions and practices that make up the free market. This loss of faith in the economic system that has produced more wealth and human advancement than any other is a major threat to our future. It makes clear how destructive the insiders' game of crony capitalism has become. It has played a leading role, worldwide, in the broad erosion of any respect for institutional authority.

The idea that America's political leaders are corrupt, or at least compromised, lay at the heart of the 2012 U.S. presidential campaign, one of the most negative in history. Both President Obama and GOP nominee Mitt Romney accused each other of practices amounting to crony capitalism, with merit to the charges on both sides. The campaign was the first one in the United States in which neither candidate observed federal-election spending limits. A Supreme Court decision in 2010, *Citizens United*, freed up corporate and union political spending to levels never previously imagined through the new independent political groups known as Super PACs.

One of the Romney-supporting Super PACs was run by the Koch brothers, who have vast oil, gas, and logging interests. Not surprisingly, Romney refused to support the proposed elimination of federal subsidies to the oil and gas industries. He also urged the federal government to sell national and forest park land to the logging industry. Obama was no better. His administration loaned $535 million to alternative-energy firm Solyndra just before it went bankrupt, a loan that became the subject of a criminal investigation. In July 2012, Obama spokeswoman Lis Smith said that Solyndra was "widely praised as successful and innovative,"[2] opening the door to further attacks from Republicans.

The 2012 election returned most of the same people to power in Washington, offering little prospect for changing the dysfunctional politics that have left so many Americans baffled, angry, and disillusioned. Autocratic governments in China and Russia vacillate between condemning political corruption and practicing it in plain view. Middle East governments, fresh from popular revolutions, must prove that they will be able to resist the worst temptations of power. So far, the evidence is not terribly encouraging.

With such continued failures of political leadership, it is no wonder that the many popular movements that have arisen around the world doubt that current regimes can reform themselves without outside pressure. But in the case of political corruption, and especially electoral fraud, popular movements face a high hurdle: How do you change the system if you can't get the votes counted first?

POLITICAL CORRUPTION

According to Transparency International's 2011 Global Corruption Barometer, survey respondents from the United States, Western and Eastern Europe, Brazil, India, Japan, and South Korea, among others, see political corruption as more serious than corruption in policing, the courts, or the media.[3] Seventy-two percent of Americans said that corruption had increased over the last three years, while 53 percent of respondents in Russia and 46 percent of those surveyed in China said the same. In the Czech Republic, one in three managers of small- and medium-sized businesses thinks that firms like theirs cannot win a public contract without resorting to bribery or kickbacks.[4] It's becoming difficult to identify a nation in which corruption—or at least the perception of it—hasn't worsened.

Although political corruption tends to manifest itself differently in democracies and autocracies, in both kinds of societies it has compromised government's primary responsibility to serve the citizenry (however that responsibility is understood). Political corruption has eroded the relationship between the governors and the governed. The problem starts on the ground floor of political practice—with elections, which have been stalked by the specter of fraud.

Electoral Fraud

The failure of many governments to properly regulate elections—and, in the worst cases, their willingness to rig them—is an essential component of the trust collapse. Consider the words of an anonymous commentator on Mexico's latest election, after which tens of thousands protested across twenty-three Mexican cities against the president-elect, Enrique Peña Nieto:

> This is a message from the Global revolution to politicians, dictators, and plutocrats all over the planet. Surprised by the global disobedience? . . . Here, in Mexico, we are marching against electoral fraud,

committed on the 1st of July 2012 by the PRI party and Enrique
Peña. Mexico needs your help now. Remember, the change is happening, with or without you. The people shouldn't fear the government. The government should fear the people. We are the people.[5]

Mexican protesters alleged voter fraud, claiming that Peña, his Institutional Revolutionary Party (PRI), and the electoral authority had
bought votes and paid off TV networks for support. Signs carried at the
protests, which officials estimated brought fifty thousand participants to
central Zocalo Plaza, read, "Mexico, you pawned your future for 500
pesos" and "Peña, how much did it cost to become President?"[6]

Accusations of vote buying surfaced in June, a month before the
election, when people rushed to grocery stores on the outskirts of Mexico City to redeem prepaid gift cards worth about 100 pesos ($7.50).
Many said that they got the cards from PRI supporters before the
election, a clear attempt at vote buying. The Mexican case illustrates
that it is not just autocracies robbing the citizenry of their right to an
accountable government; through coercion and illegal electioneering,
politicians in democracies are also getting away with all manner of ques-
tionable and even criminal behavior.

On the streets of Moscow, protestors clutched white balloons and
banners with the slogan "For Free Elections" after Vladimir Putin's
December 2011 electoral "win." Blogger Aleksei Navalny, a prominent
figure in the protests, called March's presidential election a "procedure
and not really an election."[7] Putin challenger and oligarch Mikhail
Prokhorov was "indignant over the use of force against people who
came to express their civic position."

In the United States, we have seen elections corrupted by the campaign-finance system and special-interest groups—as well as, over the
last decade or so, politically traumatic presidential recounts and allegations of voter fraud. During the 2012 presidential campaign, some lib-
erals argued that Romney could win only through Republican-spon-
sored voter-suppression efforts such as voter ID laws; on the right,
some suggested that Obama could win only if Democrats succeeded in
enrolling illegal voters or in perpetrating other forms of voter fraud.
Such widely held sentiments don't speak well for public confidence in
our election system.

Even London, with one of the world's oldest representative governments, has seen its share of fraud. In the 2008 mayoral election, the

Labour Party's incumbent, Ken Livingstone, enjoyed strong support from the extremist Muslim leader of the poor borough of Tower Hamlets, a man widely believed to have overseen the coercion of voters and falsification of ballots on Livingstone's behalf. In 2008, the Labour vote rose 23 percent, and turnout increased by 35 percent in the borough, all during a time of growing voter apathy. In the 2012 election, when Livingstone contested the mayoralty again, records in Tower Hamlets showed that sixty-four properties in the borough housed 550 registered voters, an average of three people per bedroom.

In far too many countries, elections have become symbols of corruption and instability. More than 1.5 million votes were deemed "suspect" in the August 2009 Afghan presidential elections, up to a third of which were cast for President Hamid Karzai. Peter Galbraith, who served as deputy head of the UN mission in Kabul until he was removed from his post for disagreeing with Kai Eide, the head of the mission, over fraud in the presidential election,[8] said of the vote, "I was not prepared to be complicit in a cover-up or in an effort to downplay the fraud that took place. I felt we had to face squarely the fraud that took place. Kai downplayed the fraud."[9] In Galbraith's case, protecting the notion of a fair election was more important than ensuring that an election actually happened. After all, a rigged election isn't worth holding.

Afghanistan's Independent Elections Commission (IEC) was ultimately held responsible for the fraudulent result, but a committee consisting of a seven-member board of Karzai appointees was never likely to be independent. An elaborate system of "ghost" polling stations produced hundreds of thousands of fraudulent votes for Karzai while the UN stood by and supported the IEC's "free and fair elections." This dishonest plebiscite wasted more than $300 million of the United States' and other Western countries' money. Things didn't improve in the 2010 parliamentary elections, in which the IEC invalidated thousands of votes, sparking protests in Kabul.

The term *rigged election* has become familiar around the world. Iran's 2009 presidential election was clearly one: in the only poll before the election, Mir-Hossein Mousavi was leading President Ahmadinejad 54–39. He went on to lose 63–34, an unheard-of turnaround. Furthermore, according to official results, Mousavi managed to lose his home district. Before the election, the Iranian Revolutionary Guard warned that it would crush Mousavi's people if they complained about a rigged election. Even so, Mousavi declared that the "people won't respect those who take power through fraud," [10] and he was proved right: demonstrators flooded the streets in Tehran, shouting "Death to the Dictator!" [11] as they hurled rocks at riot squads.

These are just a few examples of a global problem that shows no signs of abating. It comes as no surprise that elections across Africa—in DRC, Darfur, Kenya, and Nigeria, among others—have been plagued by violence and corruption as well. While this kind of behavior has a history in many of these countries, the public response over the last few years represents an important shift in attitude, away from acquiescence and toward confrontation. Whether because governments no longer deliver the benefits that long defined such implicit acceptance—we'll provide stability if you stay quiet, in other words—or because the idea of genuine democracy has become more desirable, citizens, especially the young, are no longer willing to tolerate such abuses.

In the end, though, it's not the people's job to serve as the election watchdog—political leaders must make sure that the ballots are counted honestly. If they continue to make a mockery of that responsibility, they shouldn't be surprised if large numbers of people take to the streets.

Insiderism

In China, where dissidence is harshly punished and loyalty to the Communist Party remains generally high, political corruption has bred cynicism. In the Beishi district of Baoding in October 2011, a drunk driver ran into two female university students, killing one. When guards stopped the driver, Li Qiming, all he told them was "My father is Li Gang"—the deputy police chief of the district. Li was free to go, but his story spread rapidly around China, triggering anger and protests. There were contests on the Internet for people to incorporate the phrase "My father is Li Gang" into Chinese poetry. Today, people throughout China use the phrase "My father is Li Gang" as an excuse to shirk responsibility.

In late 2011, a leaked government document exposed extraordinary corruption in China. Beijing had identified 225 corrupt officials, 58 of them at the high political level and above, who had embezzled more than $392 million. The document named 1,640 corrupt officials in

Guangdong Province—170 of them high-level cadres—who had stolen more than $18 billion. According to Bao Tong, a former director of the Chinese Communist Party's Office of Political Reform, one-party rule makes stamping out corruption impossible. "Everyone helps each other out," he said. "If you are in trouble, I'll help you out, and if I'm in trouble you help me out." He added, "If I were in the current system, I'd be corrupt too."[12] Indeed, Bao's twisted version of a golden rule has become far too commonplace in China and elsewhere.

So much so, in fact, that even Communist Party head Xi Jinping, in his first speech to the Politburo, warned that pervasive corruption could "doom the party and the state."[13] Xi clearly was responding to the concerns of ordinary Chinese, who have cited corruption—including patronage and nepotism—as one of their biggest concerns. That these concerns could penetrate the often-insular party leadership shows how real and pervasive they are.

Xi's comments indicated his awareness of how corruption has motivated political protest movements elsewhere: "In recent years," he said, "the long-pent-up problems in some countries have led to the venting of public outrage, to social turmoil and to the fall of governments, and corruption and graft have been an important reason. A mass of facts tells us that if corruption becomes increasingly serious, it will inevitably doom the party and the state. We must be vigilant. In recent years, there have been cases of grave violations of disciplinary rules and laws within the party that have been extremely malign in nature and utterly destructive politically, shocking people to the core."[14]

Though Xi did not mention them by name, surely two of the scandals in people's minds involved Bo Xilai—the party official facing criminal trial for his wife's involvement in the murder of a British business associate—and Prime Minister Wen Jiabo. A Bloomberg news story reported that Bo's family held hundreds of millions of dollars in investments and other assets, while the *New York Times* reported that Wen's family was worth at least $2.7 billion.[15] When Xi used an old Chinese aphorism—"worms come only after matter decays"—he had lots of matter to which to refer. But it remains to be seen whether his remarks constitute a genuine attempt to crack down on self-dealing.

In Russia, too, public disgust with insider political dealing has forced even the Putin regime to take notice. Recent scandals include hundreds of millions of misallocated construction funds, missing millions from the nation's space agency, and about $31.5 billion, or one-fourteenth of the national budget, squandered in corrupt state-procurement practices. The procurement scam has been perpetrated, in part, by Defense Ministry officials who purchase low-quality coal at low prices and sell it back to the ministry at a tenfold increase.[16]

Opposition campaigns and political protests have taken some toll on the government, which announced an anticorruption drive. "A tough, uncompromising battle with corruption has begun," said a progovernment television host introducing a documentary on the subject.[17] The newspaper *Vedomosti* even announced that the "cleansing of the elite" in Russia was at hand.[18] But others were more skeptical. Putin has never shown much willingness to prosecute, or even fire, his top officials. Russian deputy prime minister Igor Shuvalov, for example, made $200 million co-investing with Russian tycoons while he served in high government positions. Putin's hands-off instinct seems to have been confirmed again by the news that former defense minister Anatoly E. Serdyukov, the highest-ranking official to be implicated in wrongdoing, had been offered a lucrative position with a high-tech manufacturing company.

As anticorruption activist Aleksei Navalny put it, "Putin's system is dependent on corruption as a form of management and a guarantee of loyalty from officials. They will not kick out from under themselves the stool that they are standing on."[19]

A SURVEY OF CRONY CAPITALISM

In democracies and autocracies across the globe—in Russia, China, the Arab nations, Western European countries, India, and even the United States—governments are threatened from within by their enmeshment with private financial interests, relationships that are based on self-dealing and even outright theft. As David Stockman, the former budget director for President Reagan, describes this dynamic, "we have neither capitalism nor democracy [anymore]. We have crony capitalism."[20]

Crony capitalism—when companies seek political favors, subsidies, and preferential treatment from government, often after their directors have contributed large sums to officeholders' campaigns—distorts the economy by pushing capital toward companies that the market would not otherwise reward. The market is thus prevented from functioning efficiently and maximizing value. Worse, when the market produces backlash against these companies, it is most often taxpayers, rather than shareholders or executives, who pay the price—through publicly financed bailouts, for example. Partly as a result of these practices, public confidence in major economic and financial institutions has plummeted from the highs of the 1990s.

Consider the Chicago Booth/Kellogg School Financial Trust Index, which has tracked American attitudes toward banks and other financial institutions since 2008. Here's how a press release announced the survey's October 2012 results: "As the economy continues to be a top issue for voters in the final days of the presidential campaign, a new report finds that 23 percent of Americans say they trust the country's financial system. According to the latest Chicago Booth/Kellogg School Financial Trust Index issued today, this is an increase of two percentage points since the last issue of the Index in June 2012 and reflects a rebound of trust in the banking sector."[21]

So not even one-quarter of Americans trust the nation's financial system—and this represents an increase!

That skepticism pervades other surveys examining the question of corruption more generally. Transparency International's 2011 Corruption Perceptions Index, surveying 183 countries, found the vast majority scoring below five on a scale of zero (highly corrupt) to ten (very clean). New Zealand, Denmark, and Finland ranked at the top, while North Korea and Somalia were at the bottom.[22] The United States ranked twenty-fourth, below Qatar, the Bahamas, and Barbados. France ranked twenty-fifth. Italy shared the sixty-ninth spot on the list—below even Saudi Arabia, Oman, Cuba, and Latvia. As for Russia, it ranked 143rd, with a score of just 2.5.

It's no wonder that Russia ranks so low. Few countries have such an entrenched system of crony capitalism. By some estimates, the corruption market is equivalent to 20 percent of Russia's GDP. Eighty percent of Russian businesses pay bribes, according to INDEM, a think tank that studies corruption. The Kremlin itself estimates that the country loses over $35 billion a year through state-rigged tenders.[23] As summarized in the *Economist*:

Russia may not have democratic elections or the rule of law, but it does have one long-standing institution that works: corruption. This has penetrated the political, economic, judicial, and social systems so thoroughly that it has ceased to be a deviation from the norm and become the norm itself. A corruption index compiled by Transparency International gives Russia 2.1 points out of ten, its worst performance for eight years and on a par with Kenya and Bangladesh. Ordinary Russians are well aware of this, with three-quarters of them describing the level of corruption in their country as "high" or "very high."[24]

In China, members of the Chinese Communist Party run all the banks and all of the biggest firms outside the banking sector. Often, relatives of high-level party officials get in on the riches. They have been dubbed China's "princelings," and they increasingly operate with impunity, enabled by very weak conflict-of-interest laws and effective censorship of any media scrutiny of elite families' financial dealings. China's leading political families often hold shares in highly profitable companies secretly; the princelings have expanded this reach into private equity and, most recently, into the movie business. As a May 2012 *New York Times* article put it, "the Communist Party has effectively institutionalized an entire ecosystem of crony capitalism."[25]

There may be no better example of this than the story of the giant insurer Ping An, which, like many other financial-services companies, ran into serious trouble during the 1997–1998 Asian financial crisis. Concerned about the stability of the financial system, the Chinese government forced three of the nation's state-run insurers and many of its biggest banks to break up—but it allowed Ping An to stay together after the direct appeal of the company's chairman to then–vice premier Wen Jiabao.

"I humbly request that the vice premier lead and coordinate the matter from a higher level," Ping An's chairman, Ma Mingzhe, wrote. His wish was granted: Ping An was not broken up. The company was permitted to hold onto all of its businesses—not just property and life insurance but also its brokerage and a trust company, while additionally obtaining a banking license. Ping An survived the financial crisis and went on to become a company with $40 billion in 2011 revenue and a net worth greater than that of AIG, MetLife, or Prudential.[26]

A major report from the *New York Times* illustrated the likely reasons why Wen and the Chinese government intervened on Ping An's behalf. I mentioned earlier that Wen's family was said to be worth more than $2 billion. They earned that wealth in no small part through the shares they held in Ping An through an investment company, Taihong, that they eventually controlled. They bought Ping An shares at a steep discount—one-quarter of the price HSBC Holdings paid for its shares a few months before. The shares quadrupled in value within a few years, turning a $65 million investment into shares worth $3.7 billion.[27] Wen's family's involvement in the holdings was well concealed, the *Times* reported, "behind layers of obscure partnerships rather than being held directly in their names."

I've questioned whether the trust in government that Chinese citizens seem to possess, as reflected in the Edelman survey, is really all that it seems. With the Ping An scandal in mind, it's worth noting that in Transparency International's survey, China ranked seventieth, with a transparency rating of just 3.6. The two surveys don't measure precisely the same things, but it's telling that Chinese citizens have such a dim view of the openness and integrity of their government.

While the financial crimes of Russian oligarchs or high Chinese officials may get more international press, crony capitalism is also deep and pervasive in the United States and has exacerbated key national problems like unemployment, rising prices, and income inequality. The Occupy Wall Street movement sprang up in part as a reaction to the insider abuses of crony capitalism.

As the *New York Times*'s Nicholas Kristof noted, "So, yes, we face a threat to our capitalist system. But it's not coming from half-naked anarchists manning the barricades at Occupy Wall Street protests. Rather, it comes from pinstriped apologists for a financial system that glides along without enough of the discipline of failure and that produces soaring inequality, socialist bank bailouts, and unaccountable executives."[28]

Crony capitalism's large contribution to the financial collapse is beyond the scope of this book; the definitive treatment of its depredations has yet to be written. Certainly books like George Stiglitz's *Freefall*, Andrew Ross Sorkin's *Too Big to Fail*, and Nouriel Roubini's *Crisis Economics* contain pieces of the puzzle. But without question, crony capitalism has played a major role in eroding authority and trust.

Crony capitalism lies at the heart of the U.S. housing debacle. The mortgage giants Fannie Mae and Freddie Mac leveraged their quasi-public, quasi-private status to keep oversight at an absolute minimum. They exploited their close government connections, taking a hand in writing legislation meant to regulate their activities and enriching their senior executives. And, of course, they were assisted and joined in this effort by Washington politicians and regulators as well as Wall Street insiders.

The 2008 financial crisis became so enormous that even the government had to point the finger, eventually, at Kristof's "pinstriped apologists." Consider the report from the House Oversight and Government Reform Committee, which found that Countrywide Financial Corporation used its discounted VIP mortgage program to aid its lobbying efforts in Washington and strengthen its relationship with taxpayer-funded Fannie Mae, the mortgage giant. Committee chair Darrell Issa stated, "Countrywide lobbyists . . . used discounted loans as a tool to ingratiate itself with policymakers in an effort to benefit the company's business interests . . . [these relationships helped Countrywide increase profits] while dumping the risk of bad loans on taxpayers."[29]

Unfortunately, it appears that President Obama has learned little from this history. Witness a major crony-capitalist initiative of his administration: the half-billion-dollar Solyndra debacle. In 2011, the federal government granted a $535 million loan commitment to Solyndra, a solar-panel manufacturer, in a bid to advance green jobs. Within months, Solyndra went belly-up.

The links between Solyndra and the Obama administration are now clear and represent an obvious conflict of interest. Steven Spiner, an elite Obama fundraiser, oversaw the loan program and pushed the Department of Energy to approve the loan quickly. Spiner's wife's law firm represented Solyndra. Oklahoma billionaire George Kaiser was a major Solyndra investor and raised between $50,000 and $100,000 for Obama's 2008 campaign. In fact, Kaiser visited White House aides sixteen times between the time that Obama took office and Solyndra declared bankruptcy.[30] Steve Westley, another Obama fundraiser, was also linked to Solyndra. As Republican presidential nominee Mitt Romney told supporters while standing outside Solyndra's California headquarters, "It's the taxpayers that get stuck."[31]

American courts also have learned little from such disasters. Favoritism for insiders is now codified into law, thanks to the Supreme Court ruling in *Citizens United*, entitling corporations and unions, as "persons," to unlimited political expenditures as a form of free speech under the First Amendment. As I argue in my 2012 book *American Casino: The Rigged Game that's Killing Democracy*, political money of such unprecedented volume is eroding the foundations of our political system. Because of the increasing, even determinative, role of money in our elections, unfettered spending by campaigns, and seemingly unlimited wealthy donors, we are losing the very essence of our democracy— one man, one vote. In such an environment, in which the highest court in the land grants corporations a larger political voice than individuals, why would the public have any trust of those in power?

Jack Abramoff, a.k.a. "The Man Who Bought Washington,"[32] has opened up about the underbelly of the Washington scene since his release from prison in 2010 over the American Indian lobbying scandal. Abramoff is explicit: congressional votes are for sale to the highest bidder. The use of money to buy electoral outcomes is now a known hallmark of the U.S. legislative system: "You can be completely contemptible, frankly, within the system and be completely legal, and that is part of the problem of Washington," he writes. "Basically what it comes down to is making a relationship with a senator, congressman, or his staff and then availing oneself of the relationship and going into your friend and seeing if that friend would reasonably agree to the thing you are asking for. And that, by the way, is all fine, except for the money part."[33]

The underbelly of American crony capitalism isn't even in Washington. It's not found in the big financial scandals or the Abramoff exposés. Rather, it exists at the city and state level in the form of a dizzying range of tax subsidies, exemptions, and giveaways from state and local governments to private companies in exchange for those firms locating their offices or plants there—or promising not to move them. In a major *New York Times* series in late 2012, "The United States of Subsidies," the paper reported that states, counties, and cities gave more than $80 billion each year to private companies. "The beneficiaries," the paper reported, "come from virtually every corner of the corporate world, encompassing oil and coal conglomerates, technology and entertain-

ment companies, banks and big-box retail chains."[34] The report went on
to say,

> Far and away the most incentive money is spent on manufacturing,
> about $25.5 billion a year, followed by agriculture. The oil, gas, and
> mining industries come in third, and the film business fourth. Tech-
> nology is not far behind, as companies like Twitter and Facebook
> increasingly seek tax breaks and many localities bet on the industry's
> long-term viability.
>
> Those hopes were once more focused on automakers, which for
> decades have pushed cities and states to set up incentive programs,
> blazing a trail that companies of all sorts followed. Even today, G.M.
> is the top beneficiary, public records indicate. It received at least
> $1.7 billion in local incentives in the last five years, followed closely
> by Ford and Chrysler.[35]

Aided by a whole industry of tax consultants that advise them on
strategy for pressuring governments, the companies have become adept
at threatening to move their plants overseas, and governors and mayors,
desperate to protect jobs, are often willing to pay a high price to keep
them—or to win bidding wars with neighboring states or localities. This
occurs even though the companies often don't deliver on their promises
to stay put and preserve jobs. G.M., for example, having received billions in taxpayer dollars before its bailout in 2009, nonetheless pulled
up stakes in dozens of communities in Michigan and Ohio that had
helped keep the company afloat in leaner times.

These government subsidies not only thwart free-market principles,
allowing companies to game governments for special advantages, but
also have a crippling effect on already-cash-strapped local and state
governments. According to the Center on Budget and Policy Priorities,
in 2011 states cut public services and raised taxes by a collective $156
billion. More specifically, the awards have crippled school budgets, particularly in states like Texas, which gives out more awards—$19 billion
annually—than any other state. Texas offers generous corporate exemptions from school taxes to companies like Dow Chemical and Texas
Instruments. The results? High-rise office towers and manufacturing
plants for high-technology companies overlooking impoverished and
understaffed local schools.[36] As Dale Craymer, president of Texas Taxpayers and Research Association, puts it, "While economic develop-

ment is the mantra of most officials, there's a question of when does economic development end and corporate welfare begin."[37]

At the very heart of that question is the critique of crony capitalism by University of Chicago economist Luigi Zingales, author of *A Capitalism for the People*. The way Zingales sees it, the essence of crony capitalism—which has become a distressingly bipartisan practice in Washington—is what he calls "probusiness" policies. Sounds good, right? Wrong: what Zingales means by *probusiness* is policies that favor individual companies instead of upholding the broader principles that allow economic innovation and growth (such as permitting failed companies to go out of business). The alternative, he says, is "promarket" policies, which would advance free-market principles, foster competition, and put an end to, or at least greatly curtail, the special favors and advantages that allow favored companies to flourish at the expense of smaller, more innovative competitors.

Zingales warned that the United States risks deteriorating into a Berlusconi-style, crony-capitalist system. (I wonder if we're already there.) When Zingales suggests that the United States has already begun to resemble Italy, he speaks from firsthand experience about the nation in which he grew up. "In Italy today, even emergency-room doctors gain promotions on the basis of political affiliation," he writes. "Instead of being told to study, young people are urged to 'carry the bag' for powerful people in the hope of winning favors. Mothers push their daughters into the arms of the rich and powerful, seeing it as the only avenue of social promotion. The nation's talent-selection process is broken: One routinely finds highly intelligent people employed in menial jobs while mediocre people often hold distinguished positions."[38]

Italy's prime minister until April 2013, Mario Monti, probably worked as hard on his anticorruption laws as on his economic policies. The damage left behind by his predecessor, Silvio Berlusconi, could take decades to repair. Berlusconi is estimated to have passed as many as eighteen laws specifically designed to meet his personal needs. As recently as 2009, he picked several dozen TV showgirls to be groomed as candidates for the European Parliament. Silvio Berlusconi owned three of Italy's seven media stations, one of which refused to cover any news relating to his sex scandals, declaring that the stories were merely gossip. The channel had never before shirked the covering of sex scandals.

In India, meanwhile, a booming economy in commodities and tele-communications has allowed officials to make windfalls by controlling zoning and mining permits and extracting bribes. Dozens of officials have been jailed for allocating wireless spectrum to friends and associates and illicitly selling iron ore to China for higher prices. B. S. Yeddyurappa of India's main opposition party, Bharatiya Janata, quit as chief minister of Karnataka in July 2011 after he was indicted in a mining scandal. The scam cost more than $3 billion from 2006 to 2010, with Janata taking payoffs from mining companies and helping executives become politicians themselves. The scandal unfolded while the nation's rate of income inequality spiraled.

A protest movement emerged: Anna Hazare's India Against Corruption movement gained millions of followers and is considered by some to be India's "second struggle for independence." In 2011, Hazare conducted a four-day hunger strike in support of the Jan Lokpal Bill, which would have protected whistleblowers and deterred corruption. The Indian parliament's lower house eventually passed a watered-down version of the bill, which died in the upper house. Despite deteriorating health, Hazare began another hunger strike in late July 2012 to protest government corruption and call for an independent investigation of government ministers. "Even if I die, I will die for my country," he said before it began.[39]

The Arab Spring revolutions across the Middle East and Northern Africa show that this trade—one's life in exchange for political reform—is one some protesters are willing to make. In a single act, Mohamed Bouazizi, the Tunisian street vendor who kicked off the Arab Spring in early 2011, sent a clear message to Tunisia and the rest of the world that the Arab development model was a failure. The state-centered Arab paradigm purports to guarantee the essentials of life for all citizens—food, jobs, shelter, and public services, courtesy of the government. Relying on strict economic controls and noncompetitive practices, it's a system that brings benefits only to those who control it—the ruling elites and those whose interests they protect. The result has delivered little in the way of prosperity or social justice—and these are the overarching grievances of the Arab Spring.

A weak private sector dependent on the state is a recipe for unabashed crony capitalism. If the state functions through a system of bribes and kickbacks, the average citizen has almost no chance. As

Bouazizi's sister told the press, "What kind of repression do you imagine it takes for a young man to do this? A man who has to feed his family by buying goods on credit when they fine him . . . and take his goods . . . those with no connections and no money for bribes are humiliated and insulted and not allowed to live."[40]

Sadly, this description fits not only the Tunisian case but also many others, including that of Egypt. Hosni Mubarak ran Egypt as if it were his own private estate. A tiny economic elite controlled production and imports, seized assets, and held monopoly positions in key commodities markets. Studies from before Mubarak's demise show that approximately one thousand families controlled a majority of the economy.[41] Indeed, in Egypt, national wealth was consolidated into a few private hands. The rest of the population was protesting in favor of an increase in the minimum monthly wage during a time of mass privatization and rising living costs.

Recently convicted and sentenced to ten years in prison, former Egyptian agriculture minister Yousef Wali is being punished for a deal he made with a private businessman close to Mubarak. The arrangement saw thousands of hectares of public land, valued at more than $34 million, sold for less than $1.5 million. In fact, Egypt's food security is in danger today because of deals that Wali brokered with business leaders. He sold valuable farmland so that these men could plant high-profit strawberries, mangos, and guavas for European supermarkets instead of seeding the desert with wheat and other affordable crops. Filling the coffers of the wealthy before feeding the public is a trademark of crony capitalism. And as Thomas Friedman argues, though Mubarak has been deposed, many of his cronies still hold on to power. "This sordid business makes one weep and wonder how Egypt will ever turn the corner," Friedman writes.[42]

Pakistani president Asif Ali Zardari is so associated with corruption allegations ranging over several decades that he is known as Mr. Ten Percent. The widower of the murdered Benazir Bhutto, Zardari gets the nickname from his alleged practice of using his wife's position to charge 10 percent commissions to anyone asking for help to set up projects or obtain loans.

Another Mr. Ten Percent is Syrian businessman Rami Maklouf, who has gained accolades from some for his commercial acumen but is despised by most Syrians for the way he built his fortune. Earning his nickname for his skill at getting a cut of any business deal in the country, Maklouf is the CEO of Syriatel, a firm that controls 55 percent of the country's mobile-telecommunication services. He also happens to be a first cousin of President Bashar al-Assad and a vital part of Assad's web of crony capitalists. Under the guise of liberalizing the economy, the Syrian government has enriched its cronies. These insiders, in turn, have become a prime target of the uprising.

As late as summer 2012, the good times continued to flow for Syria's elite and Assad's wealthy supporters. Since then, however, the battle between the government and the opposition has intensified. "I feel there is no secure district or suburb in the whole of Damascus. We can see the Republican Palace, and I am sure that Bashar al-Assad is hearing his elite forces attack us," said a forty-year-old Qudsaya resident. "He will not feel happy and sleep well if the fighting is next to his palace."[43] But the Syrian elite try to carry on as if things haven't changed, continuing to live lavishly even as gruesome violence takes place in the streets below. Indeed, as Janine di Giovanni reports, Syria "has become a schizophrenic place, a place where people's realities no longer connect."[44] Those at the top remain in powerful positions, though they are increasingly haunted by the prospect of what will happen when Assad finally goes.[45]

In short, no nation is exempt from the corrosive impact of crony capitalism. British MP Jesse Norman argues that over the last few decades the United Kingdom, like many other countries, has drifted away from genuine, market-based capitalism, in which "real people take real risk, invest real time in real work and reap real rewards for their efforts." What he calls simply "a day's work for a day's pay" has devolved into a system in which the elite use other people's money to play with the financial markets, keeping the profits for themselves.[46]

Norman's analysis has far-reaching implications for the United Kingdom, as well as for other governments that seemingly have forgotten what their role in the market should be. Rather than acting as the best friend of business, government should regulate, protect, and administrate in the best interest of the citizenry. Under current arrangements, average citizens will always lose out. They have neither the money nor the connections to participate in a system run by insiders.

BANK BAILOUTS AND SCANDAL

Other than government, perhaps no institution has suffered more damage to its reputation than the financial-services industry. As Merryn Webb writes in the *Financial Times*, "Here's a good statistic for you: 36 percent of Americans believe in UFOs, but only 22 percent feel they can trust their banks. So there you have it. More U.S. citizens expect their country to be invaded by aliens than expect fair treatment by the global financial system."[47] The financial-services industry hasn't always been held in such low repute. Beginning in 2008, with the $700 billion bailout package in response to the subprime-mortgage crisis, however, public confidence in finance and banking has plunged. The impetus behind the bailout seemed correct.

Let me be clear: We did need to stabilize the economy, improve liquidity, and restore investor confidence. But from the start, the connections between the U.S. Treasury department and Wall Street didn't sit right with the public.

Hank Paulson was a former CEO of Goldman Sachs, a firm that stood to benefit from the bailout. Senator Judd Gregg, the lead Republican author of the TARP program, had a multimillion-dollar investment in Bank of America.[48] In an open letter to Congress, more than one hundred university economists expressed concern over Paulson's bailout plan, citing its lack of fairness, its ambiguities, and potential long-term effects as issues worthy of further consideration before its implementation. Paul Krugman argued that Paulson's plan was "a combination of sheer giveaway and mystic faith that a slap in the market's face will make everything okay" and that it was "a bad solution (and probably no solution at all)."[49] The public agreed: protests sprang up in more than one hundred cities, and representatives were flooded with complaints about the package.

Like millions around the world, ordinary Americans asked: Why do governments bail out the banks and not ordinary people? From the United States to Spain to Greece and beyond, people have wondered why they aren't protected as fiercely as financial institutions are. On the subject of Europe's bailouts, Krugman writes, "You get a picture of a European policy elite always ready to spring into action to defend the banks but otherwise completely unwilling to admit that its policies are failing the people the economy is supposed to serve."[50]

In America, the 2008 bank bailout represented a turning point in the public's perception of the government. The bailout outraged millions because it appeared to benefit one particular group—the same group that had sunk the economy in the first place. As Luigi Zingales points out, "The bailout made the system suddenly look fundamentally unfair. Why should outsourced workers, whose only fault was to have entered the wrong sector, bear the burden of market discipline while rich bankers were offered a government safety net?"[51]

Surveys examining confidence in financial institutions reflect this sentiment: trust is in absolute free fall. In July 2012, only 19 percent of Spanish poll respondents said they were confident in the country's banking sector, down from 52 percent in 2008.[52] Appointees to the boards of Spanish banks have been only slightly more qualified than Berlusconi's showgirl candidates for the European Parliament, so this result isn't surprising. A board member of one of Spain's largest banks, Caja de Ahorros del Mediterraneo, confessed, "I didn't have sufficient financial, legal, or accountancy skill . . . board members were not legally required to have any sort of qualifications or experience."[53] It's hard to trust a group like that with the financial future of the fourth-largest economy in the eurozone.

The more recent Libor scandal has done little to persuade citizens that politicians and bankers have mended their ways. The London Interbank Offered Rate is an average interest rate calculated through submissions of interest rates by major banks in London. It was revealed that, at several points during the market volatility of the financial crisis, certain banks had inflated or deflated their rates so as to appear more solvent and prevent runs on themselves. The scandal—which broke only two months after the disastrous trading losses of J. P. Morgan's infamous "London Whale"—showed that financial shenanigans weren't confined to a few "bad apples." The financial-services profession itself, apparently deeply riddled with corruption, has justifiably lost most of its former prestige.

By all accounts, Libor was a failure on the part of the economic-leadership class to keep its house in order. As Jeremy Warner writes in the *Telegraph*, "To believe that finance operates best when it is un-supervised is seriously to misunderstand the nature of free-market economics, as daft as thinking you can have law and order without police."[54] Yet even when banking is supervised, mistakes and misjudgments abound.

As I watched Ben Bernanke testify to Congress that Libor was "structurally flawed"[55] and that the U.S. Federal Reserve began to realize this back in 2007, it was hard for me to believe that the United States was the only nation to notice the rate rigging. Some bankers, such as Stephen Hester, the controversial head of the Royal Bank of Scotland, have apologized for the mess. As Hester told the *Guardian*, banks have fallen down on the job: "An element of banks became detached from society around it, an element was for traders making money for themselves or the banks, and customers [were] the means of making money. We have to be sure that banks do it the other way around."[56]

But haven't bankers been saying the same thing since the subprime-mortgage crisis? Why should ordinary citizens believe that bankers suddenly get it and that they can now be relied on to police themselves? Public mea culpas can't redeem the financial industry's reputation. If and when we ever put a stop to rate rigging, rogue trading, and even, in one of the most outlandish cases, laundering money for drug cartels and pariah states (as HSBC did),[57] then credibility may begin to recover. As it stands, there's a long road ahead. I'm not convinced that we've made much of a start.

THE CASE FOR REFORM

Capitalism remains "the greatest force for economic development and wealth creation" that has ever been conceived, as Jesse Norman made clear in his analysis of the British economy. The problem, as he and others, such as Luigi Zingales, point out, is that we are losing our grip on a genuinely capitalist, free-market system. Crony capitalism now predominates, lining the pockets of the wealthy and well connected and their political facilitators. Something has to be done. Organizations like Transparency International and other civil society groups have done a stellar job in highlighting these issues, but the institutionalization of corruption and crony capitalism will be difficult to dislodge.

There is an obvious need for more transparency and access to information. In autocracies, where this process cannot be managed easily, we need a strong global-regulatory framework that protects whistle-blowers and holds nations to higher international standards. Support for civil-society organizations and governments making efforts in this arena is also crucial. Too many are underfunded and often ignored.

Luigi Zingales offers a number of broad-stroke ideas: "We need to demand simple regulations that we can understand. We need a simpler tax code. The differences in [the] tax code are horrendous and facilitate dishonesty. The code favors people trying to hide money rather than favoring hard-working America. I think the need for simplicity and transparency is crucial." He also suggests more support for whistleblowing as a form of popular control and even governance—perhaps eliminating some government agencies—wherein "we could have very simple rules enforced by ordinary people rather than government agencies that don't have the political will to go after the powerful." Finally, he calls for an end to government subsidies, which "distort markets and take away the incentive to achieve."[58]

We should also link the fight against corruption with the fight against poverty. Corruption often affects disadvantaged communities disproportionately, derailing efforts to improve citizens' lives. Efforts to address these two major areas should be understood as fundamentally connected.

Equal access and equal rights is what democracy is all about, but the world's democracies aren't doing a very good job of this at the moment. Until people believe that their leaders will treat them with some semblance of fairness and priority, and that the rule of law applies equally to everyone, they will have little reason to trust the institutions of government or business. Simply imploring them to do so makes little sense in the absence of tangible reform. Trust, in public as in private life, must be earned.

NOTES

The epigraphs in this chapter are drawn from the following sources: Louise Story, "As Companies Seek Tax Deals, Governments Pay High Price," *New York Times*, December 1, 2012, http://www.nytimes.com/2012/12/02/us/how-local-taxpayers-bankroll-corporations. html; Ellen Barry, "Russia Looks Askance at Anticorruption Drive Even as New Scandals Arise," *New York Times*, November 17, 2012, http://www.nytimes.com/2012/11/18/world/europe/russia-looks-askance-at-corruption-drive.html; Luigi Zingales, "Crony Capitalism and the Crisis of the West," *Wall Street Journal*, June 6, 2012, http://online.wsj.com/article/SB10001424052702303366590457745007188471212152.html; and Jim Meyers, "LIGNET:

China's Coming Crash Threatens U.S. Economy, Security," Newsmax, December 3, 2012, http://www.newsmax.com/Newsfront/lignet-china-briefing-huntsman/2012/12/03/id/466242.

1. Mark Penn, "Americans Are Losing Confidence in the Nation but Still Believe in Themselves," *Atlantic*, June 27, 2012, http://www.theatlantic.com/national/archive/2012/06/americans-are-losing-confidence-in-the-nation-but-still-believe-in-themselves/259039/.

2. Daniel Halper, "Obama Spokesman on Solyndra: Widely Praised as Successful and Innovative," *Weekly Standard*, July 18, 2012, http://www.weeklystandard.com/blogs/obama-spokesman-solyndra-widely-praised-successful-and-innovative_648716.html.

3. "Visualizing the 2010/11 Global Corruption Barometer," Transparency International, 2012, http://gcb.transparency.org/gcb201011/infographic/.

4. Brian Kenety, "'Money, Politics, and Power' Report Points to Czech Crony Capitalism," CzechPosition, July 6, 2012, http://www.ceskapozice.cz/en/news/politics-policy/%E2%80%98money-politics-and-power%E2%80%99-report-points-czech-crony-capitalism.

5. Diane Sweet, "Mexico: World's Largest Protest against Electoral Fraud," Occupy America, July 22, 2012, http://occupyamerica.crooksandliars.com/diane-sweet/mexico-worlds-largest-protest-against-.

6. "Tens of Thousands Protest in Mexico against President-Elect, Alleging Vote Fraud," MSNBC News, July 8, 2012, http://worldnews.nbcnews.com/_news/2012/07/08/12622028-tens-of-thousands-protest-in-mexico-against-president-elect-alleging-vote-fraud.

7. Ellen Barry and Michael Schwartz, "After Election, Putin Faces Challenges to Legitimacy," *New York Times*, March 5, 2012, http://www.nytimes.com/2012/03/06/world/europe/observers-detail-flaws-in-russian-election.html.

8. Peter Galbraith, "How the Afghan Election Was Rigged," *Time*, October 19, 2009, http://www.time.com/time/magazine/article/0,9171,1929210-2,00.html.

9. "Dismissed Afghan Envoy Speaks Out," Takeaway, October 1, 2009, http://www.thetakeaway.org/2009/oct/01/dismissed-afghan-envoy-speaks-out/transcript/.

10. Colin Freeman, "Iran Elections: Revolt as Crowds Protest at Mahmoud Ahmadinejad's 'Rigged' Victory," *Telegraph*, June 13, 2009, http://www.telegraph.co.uk/news/worldnews/middleeast/iran/5526721/Iran-elections-revolt-as-crowds-protest-at-Mahmoud-Ahmadinejads-rigged-victory.html.

11. Ibid.

12. Albert Ding and Angela Wang, "Leaked China Documents Show Massive Corruption, Officials Fleeing Country," *Epoch Times*, last updated July 25, 2012, http://www.theepochtimes.com/n2/china-news/leaked-china-documents-show-massive-corruption-268395.html.

13. Edward Wong, "New Communist Party Chief in China Denounces Corruption in Speech," *New York Times*, November 19, 2012, http://www.nytimes.com/2012/11/20/world/asia/new-communist-party-chief-in-china-denounces-corruption.html.

14. Ibid.

15. Ibid.

16. Barry, "Russia Looks Askance."

17. Ibid.

18. Ibid.

19. Ibid.

20. Bill Moyers, "David Stockman on Crony Capitalism," Moyers and Company, March 9, 2012, http://billmoyers.com/segment/david-stockman-on-crony-capitalism/.

21. "Trust Rises to 23 Percent in Chicago Booth/Kellogg School Financial Trust Index," Chicago Booth, October 30, 2012, http://www.chicagobooth.edu/about/newsroom/press-releases/2012/2012-10-30.

22. "Corruption Perceptions Index 2011," Transparency International, accessed July 8, 2013, http://cpi.transparency.org/cpi2011/results/.

23. Anthony Homer, "Crony Capitalism: A Global Malaise Not Just Restricted to Emerging Economies," Oriental Xpress, March 28, 2011, http://orientalxpress.com/crony-capitalism-a-global-malaise-not-just-restricted-to-emerging-economies-moneylife/.

24. "Grease My Palm," *Economist*, November 27, 2008, http://www.economist.com/node/12628030?story_id=12628030.

25. David Barboza and Sharon LaFraniere, "'Princelings' in China Use Family Ties to Gain Riches," *New York Times*, May 17, 2012, http://www.nytimes.com/2012/05/18/world/asia/china-princelings-using-family-ties-to-gain-riches.html.

26. David Barboza, "Lobbying, a Windfall and a Leader's Family," *New York Times*, November 24, 2012, http://www.nytimes.com/2012/11/25/business/chinese-insurers-regulatory-win-benefits-a-leaders-family.html.

27. Ibid.

28. Nicholas D. Kristof, "Crony Capitalism Comes Home," *New York Times*, October 26, 2011, http://www.nytimes.com/2011/10/27/opinion/kristof-crony-capitalism-comes-homes.html.

29. Peter Roff, "Darrell Issa Takes On Countrywide Financial's Crony Capitalism," *U.S. News & World Report*, July 6, 2012, http://www.usnews.com/opinion/blogs/peter-roff/2012/07/06/corrupt-mortgage-market-responsible-for-economy.

30. Jim Snyder, "FBI Raid on Solyndra May Herald Escalation of Watchdog Probe," Bloomberg, September 8, 2011, http://www.bloomberg.com/news/

2011-09-08/solyndra-s-california-headquarters-raided-by-fbi-agency-spokeswoman-says.html.

31. Seth McLaughlin, "Romney: Obama Didn't Risk Much in Solyndra —Taxpayers Did," *Washington Times*, May 31, 2012, http://www.washingtontimes.com/news/2012/may/31/romney-obama-had-little-to-lose-in-solyndra/.

32. Karen Tumulty, "Jack Abramoff: The Man Who Bought Washington," *Time Magazine*, January 8, 2006, http://www.time.com/time/magazine/article/0,9171,1147156,00.html.

33. Stacy Curtin, "Jack Abramoff: Hell Yes Washington Is Corrupt—It's Legalized Bribery!" Business Insider, February 23, 2012, http://www.businessinsider.com/jack-abramoff-washington-is-corrupt-2012-2.

34. Story, "As Companies Seek Tax Deals."

35. Ibid.

36. Louise Story, "Lines Blur as Texas Gives Industries a Bonanza," *New York Times*, December 2, 2012, http://www.nytimes.com/2012/12/03/us/winners-and-losers-in-texas.html.

37. Ibid.

38. Zingales, "Crony Capitalism."

39. "Team Anna Back on the 'Fast Track' Against Corruption," IBN Live, July 25, 2012, http://ibnlive.in.com/news/team-anna-back-on-the-fast-track/274191-37.html.

40. Lin Nouihed, "FEATURE: Peddler's Martyrdom Launched Tunisia's Revolution," Reuters, January 19, 2011, http://af.reuters.com/article/libyaNews/idAFLDE70G18J20110119.

41. Salwa Ismail, "A Private Estate Called Egypt," *Guardian*, February 6, 2011, http://www.guardian.co.uk/commentisfree/2011/feb/06/private-estate-egypt-mubarak-cronies.

42. Thomas Friedman, "Egypt's Step Backward," *New York Times*, February 21, 2012, http://www.nytimes.com/2012/02/22/opinion/friedman-fayzas-last-dance.html.

43. Anne Barnard, "Syrian Forces Attack Rebel Stronghold Near Palace," *New York Times*, October 5, 2012, http://www.nytimes.com/2012/10/06/world/middleeast/syria.html.

44. Janine di Giovanni, "Champagne Flows while Syria Burns," Daily Beast, July 9, 2012, http://www.thedailybeast.com/newsweek/2012/07/08/champagne-flows-while-syria-burns.html.

45. Fareed Zakaria, "Syria's Detached and Deluded Elite?" CNN World, July 11, 2012, http://globalpublicsquare.blogs.cnn.com/2012/07/11/syrias-detached-and-deluded-elite/.

46. Jesse Norman, "The Case for Real Capitalism," Free Enterprise Group, http://www.jesse4hereford.com/pdf/The_Case_for_Real_Capitalism.pdf.

47. Merryn Somerset Webb, "Trust Index Sinks to an All-Time Low," *Financial Times*, June 29, 2012, http://www.ft.com/intl/cms/s/0/1e2d197c-c1de-11e1-b76a-00144feabdc0.html.

48. Judd Gregg, 2007 Financial Disclosure Report of Judd Gregg, May 15, 2008, http://pfds.opensecrets.org/N00000444_2007.pdf.

49. Paul Krugman, "The Good, the Bad, and the Ugly," *New York Times*, September 28, 2008, http://krugman.blogs.nytimes.com/2008/09/28/the-good-the-bad-and-the-ugly/.

50. Paul Krugman, "Another Bank Bailout," *New York Times*, June 10, 2012, http://www.nytimes.com/2012/06/11/opinion/krugman-another-bank-bailout.html.

51. Luigi Zingales, "Who Killed Horatio Alger?" *City Journal* 21, no. 4 (Autumn 2011), http://www.city-journal.org/2011/21_4_meritocracy.html.

52. Steve Crabtree, "Snapshot: Faith in Spanish Banks in Free Fall," Gallup World, July 20, 2012, http://www.gallup.com/poll/155894/snapshot-confidence-spanish-banks-free-fall.aspx.

53. Giles Tremlett, "Spain's Savings Banks' Culture of Greed, Cronyism, and Political Meddling," *Guardian*, June 8, 2012, http://www.guardian.co.uk/world/2012/jun/08/spain-savings-banks-corruption.

54. Jeremy Warner, "Britain Unleashed: Why Britain Needs Adam Smith More Than Ever," *Telegraph*, July 26, 2012, http://www.telegraph.co.uk/finance/financialcrisis/9429122/Britain-Unleashed-Why-Britain-needs-Adam-Smith-more-than-ever.html.

55. Brooke Masters and Chris Giles, "Libor 'Structurally Flawed,' Says Fed," *Financial Times*, July 17, 2012, http://www.ft.com/intl/cms/s/0/8f7fa84c-d02f-11e1-bcaa-00144feabdc0.html.

56. Jill Treanor, "RBS Faces Huge Fine over Libor Scandal, Says Stephen Hester," *Guardian*, July 29, 2012, http://www.guardian.co.uk/business/2012/jul/29/rbs-libor-scandal-stephen-hester.

57. Steve Slater, Matt Scufhamm, and Aruna Viswanatha, "HSBC Fears U.S. Money Laundering Fines to Top $1.5 Billion," Reuters, November 5, 2012, http://www.reuters.com/article/2012/11/05/us-hsbc-earnings-idUSBRE8A400920121105.

58. Nicole Coulter, "Interview with My Favorite Economist," RIA Central, March 21, 2012, http://riacentral.com/2012/03/21/interview-favorite-economist/.

8

THE RISE OF ANTISYSTEMIC POLITICS

Europe and the United States

Berlusconi is so dead he doesn't even wear his makeup anymore.
—Beppe Grillo, Five Star Movement, Italy

We offer what people want. People are really angry at all the other parties because they don't do what politicians should do. We offer transparency, we offer participation. We offer basic democracy.
—Matthias Schrade, Pirate Party, Germany

Their positions may be extreme, but the situation is extreme as well. So we need extreme measures.
—Maria Chandraki, unemployed Greek citizen, speaking of Golden Dawn

On July 22, 2011, just as much of the international community was focusing on the debt-ceiling standoff in Washington and the threat of a U.S. credit downgrade, the world's attention shifted to the unlikely venue of Oslo, Norway—where one of the worst cases of mass murder in recorded annals took place.

On that day, Anders Breivik, the son of an economist and a nurse, bombed several government buildings in Oslo—killing eight people—before taking a boat to Utoya Island, where the Norwegian Labour Party was conducting its annual youth camp for children of party officials. There, Breivik, dressed as a police officer, opened fire on everyone in his path, even chasing some youths into the water, pursuing them and killing them with no feeling whatsoever. The attacks lasted nearly an hour and killed sixty-nine people, resulting in a final total of seventy-seven victims.

Peaceful Norway hadn't seen a death toll like this since World War II, and it came as a shock beyond words. Breivik's motive, he said after being apprehended, was to make Norway and the Labour Party "pay the price" for surrendering the nation's well-being to multiculturalism and, in particular, Islamic immigration.

Though he no longer belonged to it, Breivik had spent much of his youth in Norway's Progress Party, which advocated restrictions on immigration and especially warned against allowing Muslims into the country. Although the Progress Party immediately disassociated itself from Breivik's actions and reminded Norwegians that he hadn't been affiliated with it since 2004, its motivating sentiments were integral to his beliefs and, eventually, his actions.

The Breivik massacre made clear like nothing else the dangers of extremism in Europe and the growing influence of extremist parties there. The European police agency, Interpol, warned in 2012 that right-wing extremism on the Continent had "reached new levels" and that it "should not be underestimated."[1] While few of these movements have acted violently, many express sentiments nearly identical to what Breivik spelled out in his infamous manifesto, which was recovered after the attacks. Indeed, in Italy, Mario Borghezio of the far-right Northern League party praised Breivik's ideas.[2]

While Borghezio condemned Breivik's violence, he supported the proposal to ban Muslim immigration to Europe. Surveys show growing support on the Continent for that position.[3] The extremist presence may be at its most virulent in Greece, where the fascist Golden Dawn has become the nation's third most popular political party. "Parts of Athens feel like a war zone," wrote William Wheeler in a *New York Times* report. "Racist gangs cruise the streets at night in search of victims."[4]

Yet while right-wing, nationalist extremism is a growing concern, especially in Europe, it is only part of a broader undercurrent of protest roiling not just the European continent but also Russia, India, the Middle East, Africa, and even the United States. The predominant thread connecting dozens of diverse and sometimes conflicting antisystemic movements worldwide is not murder or even racial or ethnic hatreds—though there is some of this, too—but instead the sense that established governing systems, institutions, political parties, and economic arrangements have ceased working in ways that serve the people's needs.

It is this grievance—much more prevalent than racial or ethnic enmity—that has prompted such a surge worldwide in protest movements.

The more accurate term to use that subsumes all of these groups together is not *extremist* but *antisystemic*: whether it's an Italian comedian leading a party that is rapidly winning local mayoral races and threatening the political establishment or a loosely organized "Pirate" party in Germany challenging the political system itself with a revolutionary mode of decision-making, or Greek and Hungarian nativist parties practicing self-help and providing economic assistance to struggling citizens, or youth-led movements in African countries like Angola and Uganda, protesting against their governments' refusal to share economic prosperity and national wealth more broadly—movements against the status quo have sprung up in nations all around the world.

To be sure, a good number of these movements have extremist elements. In Japan, for instance, the conservative Restoration Party was poised to become the nation's second-largest party with its promise of devolving power from Tokyo to more localized governments. But the party made an alliance with the outspoken hardliner and nationalist Shintaro Ishihara, who advocates a nuclearized Japan, an abandonment of Japan's pacifistic constitution, and a hardline stance toward China—positions that alarm many.[5] The party paid the price in the December 2012 election, finishing third.[6]

Many in Europe and around the world are drawn to antisystemic politics because they have lost all faith in their countries' institutions—particularly the government and the political parties but also the media, the judicial system, and such transnational organizations as the European Union; anti-austerity protests in Greece, after all, were directed not only at the Greek government but also at EU leadership. The message was that elites had failed Greek citizens and destroyed hope for a decent future. Reaction against what is often called the European Project has also grown in places like the United Kingdom, where Nigel Farage's anti–EU United Kingdom Independence Party may soon become the nation's third-largest political party, behind Labour and the Conservatives.

In short, what we're seeing is far from being simply a global outbreak of nativism or nationalistic bigotry in response to adversity: those sentiments are part of it, but they aren't all of it by a long shot. As the old 1960s song goes, "Something's happening here"—and at its core is a rejection of elite consensus. The shocks to the system are coming from a multiplicity of groups and a multiplicity of directions.

Americans, too, have seen their political system all but break down and cease to function. The most prevalent response in the United States has not been nativism but the rebirth of populism on the left and the right. On the left, it's represented by Occupy Wall Street and the hard-left wing of the Democratic Party; on the right, it is represented by the Tea Party. Only a few years ago, neither group was remotely on the U.S. political horizon.

In this chapter, I'll add some brief comments on the American situation, but my focus here and in chapter 9 will mostly be elsewhere: on Europe, especially, but also on Russia, India, Africa, and the Middle East. The prevalence of so many antisystemic groups and parties and their growing impact on national politics stands as another sign of the institutional breakdown that is at the heart of this book—the end of authority and the loss of trust. Broken trust, after all, leads people to look for alternatives. That's what they're doing now around the world.

Without endorsing these parties' and groups' policies—and in some cases their views are deeply repugnant—I think it's important to understand who they are, where they came from, and what they want. Ignoring them, as elites in some countries would prefer to do, will only guarantee more of the same.

EVERYWHERE YOU LOOK IN EUROPE

Extreme political parties have been on the rise in Europe over the course of the last half-decade. Remarkably, most such parties have at least doubled their portion of the vote in parliamentary elections. No question, economic hardship and in some cases austerity measures have contributed to their growth. But as an important August 2012 article in the *Economist* argued, "culture matters more." The article pointed out that many of the far-right parties lack economic answers and that their appeal stems from issues of "national culture, identity, and a way of life."[7] In fact, when it comes to economics, many European right-wing parties have taken a page from the left, pledging more protectionist policies and shoring up social-welfare programs—all as part of protecting native-born citizens from the depredations of immigration and global capitalism.

European nativist and nationalist parties say they are determined to defend traditional values and ways of life associated with their countries. With greater political clout has come more ability to shape policies broadly aimed at tamping down multiculturalism. These range from explicit anti-immigrant policies to more targeted actions, such as the ban on burqas in France or on minarets in Switzerland.

Identity shapes the rhetoric of nationalists. In Italy, for example, the Northern League seeks to protect Christian traditions, while most Scandinavian nationalist parties concern themselves with preserving ethnic origins. But whatever the motive, in all cases these groups see what they cherish as being under threat, usually from outsiders and immigrant populations—especially Muslims—and from elite policies devoted to multiculturalism and globalist economics. They advocate, for the most part, strict immigration limits and more stringent requirements that immigrants assimilate into the mainstream culture. They tend to oppose any policies that they see as infringing on their national sovereignty, and, with few exceptions, they oppose greater integration into the European Union.

Resurgent Nationalism in France

In France—home to Europe's largest Muslim population—the National Front (FN) seeks to protect the secular traditions of the French Republic. Founded in 1972 by Jean-Marie Le Pen, the party is now headed by his daughter, Marine. Until the 1990s it was a fringe party at best, playing a minimal role in French politics. But it rose to greater power in the 1990s as concerns about national identity came to the fore. The FN's nationalist platform focused on three main planks: anti-immigration, protectionism, and law and order. Initially, anti-immigration rhetoric took a back seat to law and order, and the early FN was also pro–free trade and pro-EU. But with time came a heightened nationalist focus and a switch from market-oriented economics to advocacy of protectionism.

The FN began a resurgence in 2010, winning 12 percent of the vote in the French regional elections. This was a result of economic discontent over a year-long recession combined with the rise of anti-immigrant and anti-Muslim sentiments sweeping the country. French president Nicolas Sarkozy himself launched a debate about national identity, hoping to woo far-right conservatives, and the FN then took the lead on anti-immigrant positions and rhetoric.

In 2011, Le Pen handed party leadership over to his daughter, Marine. She has softened some of the edges of her father's public positions, being particularly more sensitive to allegations of anti-Semitism. Where her father was dismissive of the Holocaust, calling it "a detail of Second World War history," she called it "the summit of human barbarism."[8] In the 2012 French presidential elections, she polled third, with 18 percent of the vote, behind François Hollande and the defeated incumbent, Sarkozy.

Today's FN remains focused on goals shaped by nationalism, national identity, and opposition to multiculturalism. As José Zúquete, author and student of European right-wing movements, describes it, "In the philosophy of the National Front, the French nation is not a group of citizens detached from their respective ethnic or religious origins around a social contract or political project. To the contrary, the nation is a community bonded by a continuity of generations, all of which share the same language and belong to the same historical France."[9]

But as it tries to broaden its appeal, the FN under Marine Le Pen has tried to repackage itself. It has retained its focus on culture, but now it portrays itself as "the party of welfare"—that is, welfare for native-born French people, not immigrants. As Peter Davies, who authored a 2002 book on the FN, points out, "Where social aid and education are concerned, the FN is only interested in the welfare of French people, not immigrants."[10] Marine Le Pen has also tried to downplay the FN's anti-immigrant rhetoric in favor of economic and social issues and "prosecular" policies—like the policy that resulted in France's burqa ban. It is a subtle shift in emphasis from being overtly anti-immigrant or anti-outsider to being pro-France and pro–French culture.

Le Pen's efforts to bring the FN into the mainstream have been described as *dédiabolisation* (decontamination). She has had some success, especially with French working-class women, who have rallied to the party in substantial numbers in recent years. Expanding its share of the women's vote, as FN seems to be doing, could help it gain up to 20 percent of the national vote—not enough to gain power, but perhaps sufficient to make it a significant player in national politics.[11]

Pirates and Comedians: Antisystemic Movements in Germany and Italy

In Germany, meanwhile, the momentum is moving less in a nationalist direction and more toward a nonsectarian, youth-oriented, antisystemic politics exemplified by the rise of the Pirate Party. Originating as an advocacy group for open-source Internet policies—hence their name— the Pirates have become a party with real potential in German politics. It now has thirty thousand members in Germany, and in spring 2012 it won almost 8 percent of the vote in Germany's North Rhine-Westphalia province, earning parliamentary seats in a fourth regional legislature. The party has more than a dozen members in the Berlin legislature. In the 2013 elections, the Pirates look toward possible entry into the lower house of the national parliament, the Bundestag.

The Pirates have an undeniably hipster vibe. Members dress down, often sporting ponytails and wearing bandannas. Calling a recent party conference "a riot of colour and noise," the BBC described the political atmosphere:

> Some members were dressed as pirates, complete with three-cornered hats. Others played in a children's pool filled with plastic balls, diving in and bursting out from under the surface.
>
> Granted, there were formal speeches from the platform, but the hall was filled with people glued to their laptops on lines of trestle tables. They seemed to participate in the conference with one ear listening to the real world but two eyes staring into cyberspace, their brains flitting in between the two.
>
> They are unconventional in another way, too. They do not have the usual range of policies on all the usual—and important—issues, like the detail of tax rates or how to save the euro. But the unconventional approach is working.[12]

Internet freedom remains a key Pirate Party issue, but now the party has expanded its focus to call for universal health care and a guaranteed basic income for all citizens. Their positions, most of which remain aspirational, with few specifics, include the following:

- action against racism and right-wing extremism
- free education at all levels
- free local public transport
- abandoning nuclear power
- equal status for marriage and registered partnerships between two or more people
- legalization of drugs
- separation of state and church [13]

That vagueness has to some degree explained the Pirates' appeal, especially when combined with what the party calls "liquid feedback," in which Internet users use the Web to discuss policy and make suggestions. An alogorithm then sifts through the various proposals in order to create resolutions.

In a nation in which polls show barely 60 percent combined support for the two main political parties—Chancellor Angela Merkel's Christian Democrats and the leading opposition, the Social Democrats—there is a huge vacuum of allegiance among voters. Both the leading parties will need third-party coalition support to get anything done. Until recently, that third party looked to be the Greens, but now the Pirates are breaking into the Greens' support. No wonder one Green Party leader, Volker Beck, has dismissed the Pirate movement as politically derivative and artificial.

"The ridiculous truth about the Pirates is that they take our proposals from parliament and put it into their liquid feedback system to discuss about it. They are taking up our content and propose them as their own." Beck also—somewhat contradictorily—criticizes the Pirates for having no political coherence. "Are they on the left, are they on the right? Are they for saving the euro, or are they against? Are they for fiscal consolidation, or are they for more debts?" he asks. "They put out ideas [that] don't fit together to a program. It's more a collection of several points [that] have nothing to do with each other. On everything I have no clear idea what the party is standing for." [14]

So far, the Pirates' main appeal has been to young voters, so many of whom feel disgusted with conventional German and European politics. "We offer what people want," says Matthias Schrade, one of the party' leaders. "People are really angry at all the other parties because they don't do what politicians should do. We offer transparency. We offer participation. We offer basic democracy."[15]

"People don't want people to tell them how it should be," says tech entrepreneur Thorsten Fischer. "They have their own ideas about these things, and that is something that really resonates with many people, and not only of my generation but, if you have an open mind, for everyone."[16]

Those things all sound good, of course—but to Beck's point, they're not policy, and they're not specific. What the Pirate Party would actually *do* were it to gain substantive political power is anyone's guess. For now, the most important point to remember is that they are as clear a reflection as exists, in any country, of the vacuum of political authority—the loss, among a substantial portion of the electorate, of any trust in traditional political process or political institutions. "Politics is broken, the system is rotten, and it must change" is the basic message. Admittedly, that's pretty vague, but it's also a clear reflection of the desire for systemic change, whatever form that might take.

This kind of antisystemic impulse can also be found in Italy, where Beppe Grillo's Five Star Movement has elected four town mayors and put 163 councilors into local legislatures. "We are adding a percentage point in the polls every week as the mainstream parties die out," Grillo said. "I am not sure who will be left to face us in parliament."[17] Polls in spring 2012 showed Five Star commanding 18.5 percent of voter support, good for second place behind the center-left party of former prime minister Mario Monti.

Like the Pirates in Germany, Grillo embodies antiestablishment values, and he is in many ways the ultimate representative of Europe's antisystemic tide. He refuses media interviews, choosing to build his campaigns through blogging and his one-man stand-up comedy performances, in which he ridicules the Italian political establishment. His politics are left of center: he has pushed environmentalist measures like recycling and electric cars, and he has come out fiercely against austerity measures, attacking Monti's tax hikes. He'd also like to see Italy leave the euro and supports nationalizing the nation's banks.

Grillo is a sixty-three-year-old comedian with a long history of political criticism; he was thrown off Italian TV in the 1980s for his caustic political content. But before you write him off as another political-gimmick candidate, consider a few things: His blog is the most widely read in Italy and one of the most widely visited in the world. He first started it as a tool to solicit material for his stand-up act, digging for dirt on local politicians. It grew into a social network of concerned citizens, and he has used it to form a network of more than 250 like-minded groups in Italy to run political candidates. He also remarkably engineered a political rally attended by *two million* Italians in 2007, which he mischievously called Vaffanculo (Go fuck yourself) Day. The rally called for the resignations of dozens of corrupt Italian politicians who had criminal records and also called for repealing a 2005 law that took voters' rights to choose MPs away, giving it to party leaders instead. According to a 2012 profile of Grillo in the *Guardian*, that law, "more than any, may have fatally weakened Italy's loyalties to its traditional parties."[18]

The symbolism of a comedian becoming a serious political player in Italy probably doesn't need to be pointed out—and I do not say that to denigrate Grillo. His entry into the political arena, and the effect he has had, is inspiring for what it says about the ability of nonpoliticians to shake up the system but also sobering for how it illustrates the utter absence of political leadership in a troubled country.

Grillo, a progressive, is also notable for being an antisystemic figure completely removed from the older nativist groups. "Italy invented fascism," he told the *Guardian*, "yet it is us, boy scouts and students, filling the void. Everyone should thank us, because if we fail we will get the xenophobes."

In Italy, everyone knows who the xenophobes are: they tend to congregate around the Northern League.

The League was founded in 1991 as the merger of several northern regional parties and became a political force a year later, winning more than 8 percent of the vote in parliamentary elections and becoming the fourth-largest party in the Italian parliament. The League garnered enough political support to participate in the first Silvio Berlusconi government in 1994.[19] So far, the best the party has done politically was in 1996, when it got 10.1 percent of the vote in parliamentary elections.

However, since 2005, the party has seen major gains, roughly doubling its support.

Umberto Bossi, a former Communist, has led the Northern League since its founding. He served in Berlusconi's second cabinet as reform minister in 2004 and then as minister of institutional reforms in 2008, a position he held until November 2011, when the Northern League withdrew from the coalition government.

The League is devoted to preserving the traditional culture of northern Italy and what it sees as its Judeo-Christian heritage, and it tends to oppose anything that would threaten these values—whether that be encroachment by the government in the south, by the European Union, or by Muslim immigrants. It is, therefore, Euroskeptic and considered by some to be anti-Muslim. The anti-Islamic strain, however, does not dominate: although some party officials have expressed racist or anti-Muslim views, the party itself has largely disavowed racial politics—especially as compared with some parties in other countries, like Geert Wilders's Party for Freedom in Holland. More properly, the League should be thought of as aggressively pro-Christian rather than virulently anti-Muslim.

True, the League's pro-Christian heritage stance largely takes an anti-immigration form. As political scientist Lapo Salacci has documented, the League is "now the only openly anti-immigration Italian party." Its voters score highest in surveys when asked about hostile sentiments toward immigrants. Their scores put them well to the right of mainstream Italian voters and provide, as Salacci says, "another confirmation that the League is solidly in command of the xenophobic electorate in Italy."[20]

The League's political prospects are unclear, because it was the only party in the ruling coalition to leave the government after Berlusconi's ouster in 2011. But its twenty-year history has demonstrated that, even if it cannot broaden its base dramatically, it retains a core among the Italian electorate that is determined to resist what it sees as elite encroachments on its way of life and values. No doubt, it will continue to be heard.

Geert Wilders and the Party for Freedom

Italy's Northern League may be xenophobic, but the Netherlands' Party for Freedom (PVV) takes nationalism to new heights. The PVV, led by Dutch political firebrand Geert Wilders, is famous for its defiant criticism of Islam and aggressive stance on preserving Dutch national culture. Wilders is an international celebrity, notorious in some circles and celebrated in others for his outspoken and deeply controversial political stands. "I don't hate Muslims; I hate Islam," he said in 2008.[21] He compared the Quran to *Mein Kampf* and called for banning the Muslim holy book across the Netherlands.

His critics and admirers agree that he is brave: he has faced criminal trials and death threats, among other things, during his stormy career, and he lives under police protection. His views got him bounced out of the People's Party for Freedom and Democracy (VVD), in which he got his political start. He then started the PVV. Separating the PVV from Wilders himself isn't easy, so outsized is his reputation and role.

Wilders's PVV stands for economic liberalism and a conservative program on immigration and culture—which means, most of all, stopping the "Islamization of the Netherlands." More specifically, this outlook advocates policies including

- establishing Judeo-Christian and humanist traditions as the dominant culture of the Netherlands;
- halting immigration from non-Western countries (especially Muslim countries);
- recording the ethnicity of all Dutch citizens;
- deporting citizens with dual nationality back to their home countries;
- closing Islamic schools; and
- establishing Dutch-language proficiency requirements.[22]

Wilders has pushed for what he crudely calls a "head-rag tax" that would force Muslim women to obtain a permit for wearing headscarves. Wilders's main criticism of Islam is that the religion is, as he sees it, hostile to European humanistic traditions. Indeed, as if to emphasize his identification with European values of tolerance, the PVV has taken strong stands against gender discrimination, homophobia, and anti-Semitism. Wilders and other PVV leaders argue for harsher punishments for Muslim crimes against homosexuals and Jews, and they want to forbid gender discrimination within Islam.

"There is no equality between our culture and the retarded Islamic culture," he said in 2008. "Look at their views on homosexuality or women." But he has this in common with Grillo in Italy: he sees himself as a progressive, devoted to traditional Western notions of freedom, equality, and tolerance. "My allies are not Le Pen or Haider," he told the *Guardian* in 2008. "We'll never join up with the fascists and Mussolinis of Italy. I'm very afraid of being linked with the wrong rightist fascist groups."[23]

That hasn't happened. In 2010, the PVV became the third-largest political party in the Netherlands, and while it did not join the governing coalition, it did participate in policy negotiations—which was galling enough for Wilders's many adversaries and critics. The party's political future is uncertain, however: in April 2012 Wilders withdrew from this parliamentary arrangement in protest of the government's austerity policies. His opponents branded him a coward for refusing to face the nation's difficult fiscal choices, and, indeed, regarding economics—as is the case with many nativist parties—the PVV does not have a compelling, or even coherent, program. In the 2012 general elections, Wilders campaigned on harsh criticism of the EU bailout packages and even advocated taking the Netherlands out of the EU. This time, voters pulled back: Dutch voters gave the PVV just 10 percent of the vote and only fifteen seats in parliament, down from 15 percent and twenty-four seats in 2010.

Still, Wilders has had a major effect not just on the politics of Holland but also on the formation and ideology of nationalist groups around Europe. A quick look at some of Netherlands' northern neighbors illustrates this point.

Scandinavian Nationalism

In July 2011, the worst fears of critics of right-wing movements were confirmed by the Breivik massacres in Oslo. The one-man attack, so cold-bloodedly executed and calmly and painstakingly planned, may never be equaled for its carnage—at least, we can all hope so. In his manifesto, Breivik made it clear that he meant to stop the spread of Islam in Norway. Muslims, he wrote, "have transformed my beloved

Oslo into a multicultural shithole."[24] He called for the violent erasure of what he called "Eurabia" and for expelling all Muslims from Europe.

To what extent his motivations revolve around Christian fundamentalism is in some dispute. In his manifesto, Breivik declared himself a "cultural Christian," by which he meant preserving traditional European culture. He acknowledged that he was not personally religious himself, and that, in fact, he regarded religion as something of a crutch. But he also wrote that he considered himself a "modern-day crusader" and said that he would pray to God for strength before his attacks. Clearly, Breivik's massacres were motivated by an extreme identification with his own culture and hatred of outsiders, especially Muslims. Whether this makes him a "fundamentalist" in the religious sense is a matter for others to judge, but at minimum his identification with what men once called Christendom provided a central motivation.

Making the Breivik massacre even more chilling, it occurred in a country that has repudiated its Quisling past and is not known for neo-Nazi or extremist movements—illustrating how the dangers of extreme behavior can strike almost anywhere. "If you had asked me where this might have happened a week ago, Norway would have been at the bottom of our list of potential targets, because it just doesn't exist in Norway," said Magnus Norel, a terrorism expert at the Swedish Defense Research Agency. "Right-wing extremism in Norway is virtually nonexistent."[25]

But Norway does have a nationalist, right-wing party, one to which Breivik once belonged: the Progress Party, now the nation's second-largest in parliament, with forty-one seats. (Breivik earlier held positions in the party's youth chapter, FpU, but years before the massacre he left the party, disappointed with what he saw as a move toward political moderation.)

The Progress Party began as an antitax party in 1973 and has since become a full-fledged libertarian, right-wing party that emphasizes smaller government, lower taxes, and restrictions on immigration and immigrant welfare benefits. (Like many other nationalist parties in Europe, the Progress Party defends the welfare state for native-born citizens and wishes to strengthen these benefits.) Siv Jensen, the party's chairman since 2006 and its candidate for prime minister in the 2009 parliamentary elections, has been compared with Margaret Thatcher. She has warned against the Islamization of Norway and even stated that sharia (Islamic law) is replacing Norwegian law. However, she strongly disavowed Breivik's actions as "horrible and cowardly attacks," which she called "contrary to the principles and values underpinning Norwegian society."[26]

In Finland, meanwhile, the populist, nationalist party is known as the True Finns and, as its name suggests, concerns itself with preserving Finnish culture and restricting immigration. Like its nationalist counterparts in Europe, while the party is right-wing on culture and immigration, it veers leftward on economics, particularly in emphasizing strong welfare-state protections. But the True Finns' real source of recent momentum is its opposition to the EU and especially to the EU bailouts. The party has never been stronger: in 2011 parliamentary elections, it won 19 percent of the vote to become the third-largest party and the leading opposition party.[27] The party leader, Timo Soini, actually won the most votes of all individual candidates. The True Finns' victories stunned the Finnish political establishment and seem to indicate a larger role for the party in the country's future. Some even see Soini as a future prime minister.

Nationalism is surging in Denmark as well, where the Danish People's Party, or DF (for Dansk Folkeparti), has made steady gains over the last decade, becoming the third-largest party in the Danish parliament. It supports a nationalist/nativist platform, with its overriding goal stated as protecting the people and culture of Denmark. As with the True Finns, the DF combines support for the welfare state with nationalist positions on immigration and the European Union. It opposes multiculturalism and a multiethnic future; the party's leader, Pia Kjærsgaard, has said a multiethnic Denmark would be a disaster.

The party warns of Islamization and wants immigrant populations to assimilate into Danish culture. In 2010, the DF proposed cutting off immigration from non-Western countries. While it hasn't succeeded in doing that, it has made significant inroads in restricting immigration, resulting in what some call Europe's toughest immigration laws.[28] It has a charismatic spokesperson in Kjærsgaard, who is "often voted Denmark's most powerful woman, ahead of the queen."[29]

It's probably too early to say whether a similar surge is in the offing for the Sweden Democrats, which has the most extreme roots among European right-wing parties. The party began in the neo-Nazi swamps, arising out of a merger of several racist parties. Its members slowly began moving away from this identification and renounced Nazism in 1999. But it wasn't until 2011 that the party finally crossed the 4 percent threshold to win representation in the Swedish parliament. Again, the party's rise, such as it is, owes much to the current atmosphere of Euroskepticism, economic travail, and tensions over immigration. In the last election cycle, the party created an ad showing an old lady approaching a table to receive welfare benefits, where a crowd of bur-qa-clad women pushing baby carriages overwhelms her. The ad was banned, but its explosive quality illustrates why (so far, anyway) the Swedish Democrats have been unable to build coalitions with other parties.

In summary, the Scandinavian nationalist parties, though they differ in various respects, rally around some common themes. As a 2012 *Economist* profile summarized, "They share a loathing of Islam, decry the attrition of Nordic culture, and have strong views on law and order. Outsiders can be surprised by their growing appeal in a region that is famous for tolerance. Yet their plain-speaking and promises to care for the elderly, reduce taxes, and preserve indigenous traditions strike a chord with many."[30]

Right-Wing Nationalism in Hungary and Greece

Extremist nationalist parties are not always as marginal as the Sweden Democrats. In Hungary, Jobbik, the Movement for a Better Hungary, is a powerful player in the nation's politics. The party began in 2002 as a right-wing youth movement and then emerged as a weak political force in the 2006 national election, winning 2 percent of the vote. It began its true ascent by exploiting a series of antigovernment protests later that year. In the 2010 parliamentary elections, Jobbik won 12.26 percent of the vote, becoming the country's third-largest party in parliament.

Jobbik's slogan for the 2009 European parliamentary elections, "Hungary belongs to the Hungarians," summarizes its overarching agenda. This is old-fashioned, crude nationalism, pure and simple. The party opposes policies that it sees working to the detriment of the Hun-garian people and their traditional values. This approach takes two key forms: (1) opposition to "radical capitalism," globalization, and the free flow of capital; and (2) opposition to multiculturalism, especially as it pertains to the Roma, or Gypsy, people.

"The situation in certain parts of the country is akin to civil war," says Jobbik's young leader, Gábor Vona, who ran for prime minister in 2010 and leads its parliamentary bloc. "Now only drastic interventions are capable of helping . . . we must produce an environment in which gypsy people can return to a world of work, laws, and education. And for those unwilling to do so, two alternatives remain: they can either choose to take advantage of the right of free movement granted by the European Union, and leave the country, because we will simply no longer put up with lifestyles dedicated to freeloading or criminality, or there is always prison."[31]

The party hasn't confined its rhetoric to Gypsies. More recently, some party members have made incendiary anti-Semitic remarks that have drawn denunciations from mainstream Hungarian politicians. One Jobbik member gave a speech in parliament repeating the old "blood libel" against Jews; in addition, some Holocaust memorials were desecrated. The situation has gotten so tense that "some Jewish families are considering emigrating."[32]

Interestingly, Jobbik's economic program—in service of what it calls an "ecosocial national economy"—while generally consistent with the European nationalist parties' goals, is more developed and specific, spelling out how protectionist policies and aid to farmers and small businesses will revive the Hungarian economy. Unfortunately, as an *Economist* profile points out, most Jobbik voters seem more interested in the party's anti-immigrant, anti-multicultural pronouncements than in its economic vision:

> Most Jobbik voters show little interest in the finer points of the party's economic policy. Instead they harbour a sour resentment against what they call the "multis," or multinationals, even though foreign companies, unlike some Hungarian firms, pay their employees' tax and social security. A whole subculture of national-identity politics is flourishing in Hungary, with its own music, summer camps, bars, and even a national taxi service called nemzeti [after an old nationalist battle cry].[33]

So Jobbik may have an economic platform, but it's clear that the bulk of its support comes from its nativist ideology and willingness to target "outsiders." Will it modulate this focus and broaden its base, or will an unreformed Jobbik rally more Hungarians to its intense and angry na-

tionalism? "Jobbik is openly legitimising anti-Roma violence. It is openly anti-Semitic," says Austrian political scientist Anton Pelinka, who
lives in Budapest.[34]

This seems clearly true—yet Jobbik is surging.

In Greece, meanwhile, a similar movement has sprung up, dedicated
to serving the needs of Greek citizens—and only Greek citizens. Gold-
en Dawn has grown from a fringe organization to a major political
player in Greek society. In the May and June 2012 Greek parliamentary
elections, the party won 7 percent of the vote, entering the Greek
parliament for the first time with twenty-one seats. The party rejects
the fascist or neo-Nazi labels hung on it by some critics, though it has
used Nazi symbolism and has even praised some Nazi figures. The
party's symbol resembles a swastika, and party members deliver a Nazi-
like salute when its leader, Nikos Michaloliakos, gives speeches. But
with the kinds of hardships Greeks are facing today, a movement
pledged to help Greeks and only Greeks is bound to attract public
support.

"We are providing food produced in Greece for Greek citizens only,"
said Ilias Kassidiaris, a Golden Dawn spokesman, in August 2012. He
spoke as hundreds of Greek citizens, most of them elderly, were lining
up in Syntagma Square to receive food rations. Golden Dawn volunteers, young men and women clad in the party's signature black T-
shirts, checked identification before dispensing the food.[35]

For the moment, Golden Dawn's fortunes are on the upswing: in the
June 2012 Greek parliamentary elections, the party captured 6.9 percent of the vote and eighteen seats, mostly in Athens, at parliamentary
elections. It draws support from old and young—the young and disaf-
fected and the elderly, like those who came for food aid, either struggling to make ends meet or worried about crime in their neighborhoods. Greeks also worry about immigrants, both legal and illegal, as
the nation has long suffered from porous borders, making it a magnet
for newcomers from Africa and Asia.

Many blame illegal immigrants for taking jobs and hurting the already reeling Greek economy. Others point to the high crime rates in
neighborhoods with heavy proportions of outside migrants. Many look
to Golden Dawn, which pledges not only safety from violence but also
economic opportunity for Greeks. Unfortunately, Golden Dawn has
been linked with both Nazi and fascist symbols, as well as with violence.

Just a week after its parliamentary victories, several dozen members, riding motorbikes and "armed with heavy wooden poles," rode to the working-class suburb of Nikaia:

> As townspeople watched, several of them said in interviews, the men careened around the main square, some brandishing shields emblazoned with swastikalike symbols, and delivered an ultimatum to immigrants whose businesses have catered to Nikaia's Greeks for nearly a decade.
>
> "They said: 'You're the cause of Greece's problems. You have seven days to close or we'll burn your shop—and we'll burn you,'" said Mohammed Irfan, a legal Pakistani immigrant who owns a hair salon and two other stores. When he called the police for help, he said, the officer who answered said they did not have time to come to the aid of immigrants like him. [36]

While Golden Dawn members denied that their organization was involved in the incident, the *New York Times* cited "an abundance of anecdotal evidence" showing "a marked rise in violence and intimidation against immigrants by members of Golden Dawn and its sympathizers." [37] The *Times* also cited a Human Rights Watch report that xenophobic violence in Greece had reached "alarming levels."

It should not be surprising that a nation facing Greece's problems would see an uptick of this kind of political activity. Greece is the basket case of Europe: not just fiscally, but also economically and socially. The fear of immigrants and the desire to protect the Greek welfare state have made Golden Dawn much more appealing to ordinary citizens.

"They're doing what the politicians should be doing," says Nikos Katapodis, a sixty-nine-year-old funeral-home owner in Athens. "There's a hole, and they fill it." [38]

The rise of Golden Dawn makes clear that Greece's state of emergency is not simply fiscal: unless the government soon takes steps to restore political, economic, and social stability, a quasi-fascist, nationalist party apparently willing to take the law into its own hands may see its appeal grow.

A BRIEF WORD ON AMERICA

I've written extensively elsewhere on the growing antisystemic U.S. movements that perceive the nation's political system as fundamentally broken. While marginal groups on the left and right fringes compare with some European nativist groups, the main protest action in the United States comes from two prominent political movements: the Tea Party on the right and Occupy Wall Street on the left. Both arose within a few years of one another and in response, more or less, to the same sense that special interests had hijacked politics in America: that those special interests had bought and paid for both major parties, that the Constitution and the nation had become endangered by the rule of elites, and that only radical solutions could fix the situation.

Where they differ, of course, is in whom they blame and what they recommend.

The Tea Party arose in 2009 in response to President Obama's enormous, $787 billion stimulus package and mobilized even more energetically in opposition to his health-care-reform bill. Although comprised generously of independents, the Tea Party did eventually become closely aligned with the Republican Party, pushing a conservative vision of small government—including enormous, across-the-board spending cuts—and adherence to a strict reading of the Constitution. The Tea Party also differs from most movements in this chapter in being unabashedly devoted to working within the system—changing it, to be sure, but becoming part of it so as to effect those changes. It has enjoyed enormous success, as the 2010 congressional elections proved, and it has changed the Republican Party, moving it further right. But its long-term forecast, in the wake of President Obama's reelection, is unclear.

Occupy, meanwhile, is as unabashedly left-wing as the Tea Party is unabashedly conservative. It arose in the fall of 2011 as a mass protest movement in lower Manhattan's Zucotti Park, and its principal organizing idea was that the nation had become a land of haves and have-nots—the 1 percent versus the 99 percent. "We are the 99 percent!" the Occupiers declared, arguing that the nation's financiers and business elites had essentially hijacked the government and public policy in favor of the superwealthy. In another era—say, even ten years ago—the Occupy movement wouldn't have drawn more than a few hundred people and an appreciative chuckle from sympathetic columnists. But in a nation with high unemployment not seen in a generation, with millions of homes in foreclosure but a banking system that's humming along just fine, its protests became a movement.

Where Occupy falters in comparison with the Tea Party is that it lacks a coherent, concrete, reform agenda. Most of all, it has failed to make any inroads into the Democratic Party in terms of affecting policy. To some extent, its leaders are to blame, because, unlike the Tea Party's leaders, they seem almost to revel in their outsider status, as if it confers moral authority. Moreover, Occupy's rhetoric about capitalism and 1960s-style ethos of communitarianism are unlikely to appeal beyond a certain liberal base.

Still, Occupy has powerfully affected the national conversation: it has put the "99 percent" and the "1 percent" into the political vocabulary. If it hasn't influenced policy, it has at least influenced the conversation.

As a lifelong observer of the American political scene, I've rarely witnessed two more representative movements in terms of public mood, anger, and sense of betrayal. Regardless of what one thinks of either the Tea Party or Occupy Wall Street, they unmistakably reflect an era in U.S. politics in which the majority of Americans have lost nearly all faith in the political system. That's a frightening state of affairs, especially for the world's lone superpower—and it's not likely to change soon.

NOTES

The epigraphs in this chapter are drawn from the following sources: Tom Kington, "Italian Comedian Causing a Stir with String of Election Victories," *Guardian*, May 25, 2012, http://www.guardian.co.uk/world/2012/may/25/italian-comedian-election-victories; Stephan Evans, "Germany's Pirate Party Riding High," BBC News, May 11, 2012, http://www.bbc.co.uk/news/world-europe-18017064; and William Wheeler, "Europe's New Fascists," *New York Times*, November 17, 2012, http://www.nytimes.com/2012/11/18/opinion/sunday/europes-new-fascists.html.

1. "Analysis: Europe Far Right Shuns Breivik's Acts, Flirts with Ideas," *KyivPost*, August 26, 2012, http://www.kyivpost.com/content/world/analysis-europe-far-right-shuns-breiviks-acts-flirts-with-ideas-312064.html.
2. Ibid.
3. Ibid.

4. Wheeler, "Europe's New Fascists."

5. Mure Dickie, "Restoration Party Emerges as 'Third Force,'" *Financial Times*, December 16, 2012, http://www.ft.com/intl/cms/s/0/b3822b48-478f-11e2-8c34-00144feab49a.html.

6. Martin Fackler, "Japan Election Returns Power to Old Guard," *New York Times*, December 16, 2012, http://www.nytimes.com/2012/12/17/world/asia/conservative-liberal-democratic-party-nearing-a-return-to-power-in-japan.html.

7. "Dédiabolisation," *Economist*, August 9, 2012, http://www.economist.com/node/21560280.

8. Ibid.

9. José Zúquete, *Missionary Politics in Contemporary Europe* (Syracuse, NY: Syracuse University Press, 2007), 35.

10. Peter Davies, *The National Front in France: Ideology, Discourse, and Power* (London: Routledge, 1999), 5.

11. "Dédiabolisation."

12. Evans, "Germany's Pirate Party."

13. Georg Lentze, "German Media Skeptical of Pirate Party Momentum," BBC News, last updated June 1, 2012, http://www.bbc.co.uk/news/world-europe-18281445.

14. Eric Westervelt, "A Party on the Rise, Germany's Pirates Come Ashore," NPR, June 6, 2012, http://www.npr.org/2012/06/06/154388897/a-party-on-the-rise-germanys-pirates-come-ashore.

15. Evans, "Germany's Pirate Party."

16. Westervelt, "A Party on the Rise."

17. Kington, "Italian Comedian Causing a Stir."

18. Ibid.

19. Lapo Salucci, *Migration and Political Reaction in Italy: The Fortunes of the Northern League* (Boulder: University of Colorado Press, 2009).

20. Ibid.

21. Ian Traynor, "'I Don't Hate Muslims, I Hate Islam,' Says Holland's Rising Political Star," *Guardian*, February 16, 2008, http://www.guardian.co.uk/world/2008/feb/17/netherlands.islam.

22. "De Agenda Van Hoop En Optimiste," PVV, http://www.pvv.nl/images/stories/Webversie_VerkiezingsProgrammaPVV.pdf.

23. Traynor, "'I Don't Hate Muslims.'"

24. Ujala Sehgal, "The Rise of Right Wing Extremism in Europe," *Atlantic*, July 24, 2011, http://www.theatlanticwire.com/global/2011/07/rise-right-wing-extremism-europe/40330/.

25. Andrew Roth, "Norway Searches Political Soul on Immigration after Breivik Killings," RIA Novosti, July 27, 2011, http://en.rian.ru/analysis/20110727/165411613.html.

26. Ibid.

27. "The Far Right in Northern Europe: On the March," *Economist*, March 17, 2011, http://www.economist.com/node/18398641.

28. Ibid.

29. Ibid.

30. "Culture Matters More," *Economist*, August 19, 2012, http://www.economist.com/node/21560294.

31. Ian Traynor, "Hungary Party to Follow European Extremism's Move Away from Fringes," *Guardian*, April 8, 2010, http://www.guardian.co.uk/world/2010/apr/08/jobbik-hungary-move-from-fringes.

32. "Old and Nasty," *Economist*, July 26, 2012, http://www.economist.com/node/21559677.

33. "Culture Matters More."

34. Traynor, "Hungary Party to Follow European Extremism's Move."

35. "Culture Matters More."

36. Liz Alderman, "Greek Far Right Hangs a Target on Immigrants," *New York Times*, July 10, 2012, http://www.nytimes.com/2012/07/11/world/europe/as-golden-dawn-rises-in-greece-anti-immigrant-violence-follows.html?pagewanted=all.

37. Ibid.

38. Wheeler, "Europe's New Fascists."

9

THE RISE OF ANTISYSTEMIC POLITICS

Russia, India, the Middle East, and Africa

Everyone understands that the law no longer protects people. All business owners know that their companies can be taken away from them at any second, as can freedom and perhaps even their lives.
— Vladimir Pastukhov, Russian political analyst

Today they killed Khaled. If I don't act for his sake, tomorrow they will kill me.
— Wael Ghonim of Egypt, former Google executive

Angola is a rich country, but we don't get any of it. The people in power are eating all the money.
— Paulo Silva, Angolan citizen

As I've noted throughout this book, the sense of public betrayal cuts across nations and cultures. The world often seems perched on the brink of chaos, economically and politically, and the vacuum of leadership and authority makes everything worse. In what often seems a dark time, however, encouraging signs remain. One of the most compelling, to me, is that in numerous non-Western nations, many without much experience of democracy or high living standards, the popular movements have been almost entirely devoted to championing democracy and social openness. This makes for an ironic contrast with some of the movements in the West that we surveyed in the last chapter, like the

European extremist movements, which often seem to be arguing for *less* democracy.

In India, a political democracy but one with a rigid caste system and hundreds of millions living in deep poverty, a youthful grassroots movement has sprung up in protest against the corrupt political system. Protesters have rallied against the widespread practice of crony capitalism and the increasing gap between rich and poor generated by the nation's supercharged economy. Unlike most other movements, the Indian protests have a leader: social activist Anna Hazare, who launched a high-profile hunger strike in spring 2011.

Most Russians, meanwhile, now understand that their legal and economic system lacks basic elements of a free-market economy. The concept of private property is practically nonexistent, and loyalty to the regime too often determines whether one advances professionally. And, most worryingly, the Putin regime has become increasingly ruthless in suppressing free speech and persecuting political opponents. A brave and diverse protest movement has sprung up in response.

These movements, like the most democratic elements of the Arab Spring, have been inspired by a collective passion for freedom, liberty, and democracy. The citizen movements in Iran and the greater Middle East, for example, seek to promote fundamental social change, to facilitate openness in the most general sense, and to reform the political system into some form of legitimate, representative government. Democratic movements have also sprouted in African nations like Uganda, Ethiopia, and Angola, where immense natural wealth has been hoarded by corrupt regimes at the expense of ordinary people.

These are heartening signs, even as many of the protesters face intense and perhaps even insurmountable opposition. As I've noted earlier, those in the West who despair about the future of the democratic model haven't been paying close enough attention: the *only* model worth fighting for is the democratic one, whatever variations one puts on it. The brave individuals standing up against political oppression around the world seem to understand this better than some in the West today.

MOVEMENTS AGAINST REPRESSION AND CORRUPTION IN RUSSIA AND INDIA

On February 21, 2012, three young women wearing ski masks entered the Cathedral of Christ the Savior in Moscow and performed a punk rock "prayer" before the altar, a prayer whose words included "Mother of God, Virgin Mary, drive Putin away" and "The patriarch believes in Putin/Bastard, better believe in God." The authorities promptly arrested them and charged them with hooliganism. The Russian courts, which almost never fail to bring guilty verdicts, convicted the women and sentenced them to two years in prison.

Why did this seemingly marginal, naïve, and immature trio—a punk group named Pussy Riot—garner so much attention in Russia, and eventually worldwide? As a lengthy feature article that appeared in *Spiegel Online* put it,

> Revolution can be sexy, and doe-eyed female wannabe revolutionaries, especially when they quote Solzhenitsyn and Simone de Beauvoir from inside a glass cage, make for more appealing headlines than the tirades of a grey-bearded dissident, no matter how great the suffering he experienced. And it is undeniable that their story is also more accessible than the tragic fate of murdered female champions of human rights, like the journalist Anna Politkovskaya and activist Natalya Estemirova.[1]

Certainly the group's tactics offended some, especially older Russian citizens devoted to the Orthodox Church. As former deputy prime minister Boris Nemtsov put it, when many observers thought that the three women might get seven years in prison, "If they were my daughters, I would have slapped them across the backside. But seven years is an absurd sentence. Putin is simply afraid of his own people."[2]

From their scandalous-sounding name to their confrontational tactics, Pussy Riot may sound like a marginal political movement—but the group's future prospects are less important than what it represents in today's Russia. The three young women speak for millions of Russians fed up with a repressive government and judicial system, corrupt elites, and lack of political freedom. Those participating in protests against Putin include even "doctors, computer scientists, and lawyers," according to *Spiegel*—well-paid economic players who might be expected to approve of the regime's cronyism with business elites.

Vladimir Putin, who once enjoyed broad support from Russians, has seen his approval ratings plummet as the true nature of his political methods—including jailing political opponents and censoring the media—have become clear. The three young women, like the protesters in Moscow in March 2012, represent a population that has lost its trust in the nation's antidemocratic regime. United Russia, Putin's party, has become more reminiscent of the old Communist Party in Soviet Russia. After reassuming the Russian presidency that March, Putin quickly repealed the few democratic reforms his predecessor, Dmitry Medvedev, had instituted. United Russia's methods have become more and more crude, leading to what political analyst Vladimir Pastukhov calls "the return of political terror as an instrument of the government."[3] The methods include ruining political opponents—Alexander Lebedev, for example, a former intelligence official and harsh Putin critic, was humiliated with a sex video showing him with prostitutes.

Pussy Riot, which first made its presence known in January 2012, when it gave an "illegal" concert in Red Square during Moscow protests, is far from the only antisystemic movement in Russia. Kseniya Sobchak, for instance, the wealthy socialite daughter of the man who was once Putin's boss, former St. Petersburg mayor Anatoly Sobchak, has become, in the words of *Spiegel Online*, the "Joan of Arc for the protest movement." In June 2012 eight armed investigators ransacked her apartment for six hours and discovered that she had $1.8 million in cash at home. She suspects the government wants to bring her up on tax-evasion charges, although it has not yet done so. She says that she is innocent.

Sobchak is a star in Russia, where she has taken to TV, radio, the Web, and print to denounce Putin and celebrate the protest movements. "Please don't call me a revolutionary," she says—but in Russia today, that's exactly what she has become. Her defiance alone amounts to a revolutionary statement of independence.[4]

"Everyone understands that the law no longer protects people," says Pastukhov. "All business owners know that their companies can be taken away from them at any second, as can freedom and perhaps even their lives."[5]

Polls indicate that just one in three Russians see the country as a democracy.[6]

In this climate, the fate of three young "punk rock" women has taken on a symbolic significance far beyond what anyone—certainly including Vladimir Putin—could have imagined. The Russian antisystemic movements will no doubt continue, and confrontation (and perhaps brutal escalation) is a frightening but real possibility.

Whereas Russians predominantly object to what they see as the Putin regime's repression of political freedom and basic civil liberties, Indians have come together in huge numbers to protest their government's huge problem with political corruption. In January 2011, Indians in fifty-two cities marched against corruption, tearing up copies of government "anticorruption" bills—indicating their lack of faith in the government's efforts to address their grievances. The broken trust has a long history: most recently, a scandal in which the Telecommunications Ministry allowed mobile-phone companies to monopolize low-priced spectrum in return for bribes, costing the national treasury an estimated $7 billion—"hands down the largest episode of graft in Indian history," according to *Time*.[7]

Protests and demonstrations took place around the country even before the movement's most dramatic episode: the hunger strike, begun on April 5, 2011, of activist Anna Hazare, who became the nominal leader of the protest forces. The Indian movements are also remarkable for their lack of specific political affiliation. The activists, many affiliated with the nonideological movement India Against Corruption, refuse to join up with the nation's mainstream political parties. Like the protest efforts in Russia, India's movement attracted widespread support from prominent Indians, including pop-culture stars and numerous spiritual leaders.

Hazare's hunger strike was designed to pressure the government to adopt a reform known as the Jan Lokpal Bill, a set of anticorruption reforms that sought to create an ombudsman to deal with corruption issues. Remarkably, the government publicly agreed to do this, forming a commission to draft the legislation, and Hazare ended his strike just four days later. But the law the government produced did not satisfy the protest movement, and Hazare conducted another twelve-day fast in August 2011. In December 2011, the Indian parliament's lower house passed a version of the bill that Hazare and his supporters derided as watered down, with key provisions removed. The bill died in the upper house.

In 2012, the Indian protest movement began to splinter. Hazare's forces, now gathered into what was known as Team Anna, continued to pressure the government for adoption of Jan Lokpal. After several more false starts, Hazare announced that he was disbanding Team Anna to form a political party.

Many have described Hazare as "Gandhian," an identification made natural by his hunger-strike tactics. On closer look, however, he clearly does not share many of the great Indian independence leader's values. An army veteran, Hazare expressed readiness to go to war with Pakistan over Kashmir, and his own "model village" civil society enforced discipline through floggings and beatings. Moreover, as Pankaj Mishra wrote in an important analysis, Hazare's main target of government corruption seems not to be so much the government-business nexus but "wasteful" government spending on social services—that is, on social welfare for the poor, who number in the hundreds of millions in India. While India's poor have produced genuine social movements—including one from landless peasants protesting against impositions by mining companies—Hazare's movement gets the most political attention.

Hazare's followers, Mishra wrote, were "conspicuously middle class," and they tended to be the beneficiaries of India's globalization-fueled economic boom. During the global economic downturn, these Indians have seen some of their gains lost; for them, the anticorruption movement made sense principally as a reform that would help restart the Indian economic powerhouse. As Mishra puts it,

> In reality, the Indian government is paralyzed between its old promise of basic sustenance and justice to the poor majority, and its increasing—perhaps, unavoidable—embrace of a form of capitalism that, geared toward private wealth creation, makes such social democracy unsustainable. Hazare's insistence that the government, overruling parliament, adopt his plan for an anticorruption czar, was far less about protecting the rights of the masses than establishing the grounds for a Lee Kuan Yew-style technocracy: one that with arbitrary and unlimited power over all Indian citizens could bypass democratic institutions, enhancing the political power of an unelected, unaccountable, and fundamentally antipolitical elite.[8]

So the India protest movements offer an important insight about the antisystemic movements occurring worldwide: even when protesting antidemocratic forces, they may well be antidemocratic themselves; even when speaking out on behalf of the dispossessed, they may be content to dispossess other groups.

Still, Hazare and his movement, if nothing else, suggest that in the world's largest democracy, the status quo is about to change.

SPONTANEOUS MOVEMENTS IN THE MIDDLE EAST

The ongoing Arab Spring movements have ensured that the region remains roiling and in transition. While it would be beyond the scope of this book to chronicle all of the movements that have sprung up since the 2011 Tunisian revolution, we need to recognize that some movements—such as those in Iran and Egypt—may take decades to work themselves out. Few movements in the region are likely to resolve themselves as quickly and decisively as Tunisia's, which inspired all the others, starting with Egypt.

Spurred by the Tunisian example, the Egyptian revolution began on Tuesday, January 25, 2011, when protesters threw rocks at riot police and climbed atop armored trucks in protest of "poverty, rampant unemployment, government corruption, and autocratic governance of President Hosni Mubarak" and his thirty-year rule.[9]

The Egyptian democracy movement was perhaps best exemplified by Wael Ghonim, a thirty-one-year-old computer engineer and former Google marketing executive. In late 2010 he set up a Facebook page, "We Are All Khaled Said," named after a young man whom Egyptian police had beaten to death. Ghonim's first post read, "Today they killed Khaled. If I don't act for his sake, tomorrow they will kill me."[10] His Facebook page had three hundred readers *two minutes after he made his first posting*. In three months, he had two hundred fifty thousand readers.[11] "We Are All Khaled Said" would help spark the movement that eventually led to the ouster of Hosni Mubarak and the dissolution of his National Democratic Party, signature events of the Arab Spring. As the *New York Times* put it, Ghonim's story "resonates on two levels: it epitomizes the coming-of-age of a young Middle Eastern generation that has grown up in the digital era, as well as the transformation of an apolitical man from comfortable executive to prominent activist."[12] Ghonim was eventually released by Egypt's secret police after being held and interrogated for two weeks.

Another important instigator of the Egyptian democracy movement was Ahmed Maher, a sociology student and recent graduate of the American University in Cairo. Maher used Facebook to invite friends to demonstrate against the Mubarak regime, but for months he did not attract much participation. The Tunisian revolt changed that. When Maher began using images of Tunisia's Jasmine Revolution in his Facebook invites, he saw his participation rates skyrocket. "From one hundred," he said, "we jumped to one million."[13]

Of course, Egyptian democracy's prospects remain murky at best. In May 2012, Mohamed Morsi won the presidency, becoming the first Muslim Brotherhood member to head an Arab state. Before he was ousted in a coup in July 2013, Morsi substantially carried out his pledge to assert control over the Egyptian military, which had been running the country in the year since Mubarak's departure. He fired the Egyptian defense minister, army chief of staff, and several other military leaders. At the time, Morsi presented his moves as steps toward greater democratic control, but as he began to consolidate power more closely, millions of Egyptians turned against his regime. As of this writing, Egypt's future remains unsettled, with an interim government, installed by the military, governing the country. But in 2013, just as in 2011, millions of citizens had taken to the streets, suggesting that, whatever may happen next, the Egyptian democratic movement is likely to endure.

Some activists may flock to the new, left-leaning Constitution Party, formed in 2012 by Mohamed ElBaradei, who played an important role in the 2011 protests. ElBaradei's aim, he says, is to "unite Egyptians behind democracy and to take power in four years' time."[14] Meanwhile, Abdel Moneim Aboul Fotouh, who left the Muslim Brotherhood in 2011 because of political differences, started a new party, Strong Egypt. Fotouh says that his new party "seeks to perform its duty towards the [citizens] by providing them with security, and maintaining their dignity and humanity through justice without discrimination according to social class, geographical area, economic level, or religious or political affiliations."[15]

Meanwhile, the Islamist Construction and Development Party aims to express "the ideology and the goals of the Islamic group in Egypt and to bring together all the groups' members across the country in one place." More specifically, it promotes "the rejection of all Westernization and secularization attempts and finding ways to deal with what the Islamists describe as corruption, deviation, moral and values decay."[16]

Clearly, the future of democracy in Egypt, and what democracy truly means for Egyptians, remains unresolved. But the old order unquestionably is gone; subsequent regimes, of whatever ideology, will find it much harder to spurn public approval and trust. For this reason, if no other, Westerners can take some encouragement.

In Iran, the democratic opposition, the Green Movement, like other populist movements, enjoys support from a large portion of the country's middle class and educated citizens.[17] It originated in the 2009 presidential elections, when the *mowj-e-sabz*, or "green wave," arose in support of a reformist candidate, former prime minister Mir Hossein Mousavi, a rival of Iranian president Mahmoud Ahmadinejad.[18]

After Ahmadinejad won a disputed election against Mousavi in 2009, the movement tried to annul the results and then "to restore the civil liberties promised by the 1979 Islamic Revolution."[19] While the regime crushed the Greens' street protests, the movement has persisted as a political force. As the Ahmadinejad regime commits more crimes against its people and the economy crumbles under international sanctions, many of its supporters have begun to switch allegiances. Many so-called Blues—lower-class workers and farmers who once formed the base of the president's party—are now joining forces with the Greens, who have broadened their stance by "calling for free, fair, and competitive elections as well as the establishment of an accountable government that protects civil, minority, and women's rights."[20] The movement has remained steadfast in demanding human rights and political liberties, even as the regime continues its repressive (and frequently brutal) tactics.

But even a change in Iran's theocratic leadership might not lead to a change in Iranian foreign policy. "Seventy-eight percent of Mousavi supporters said Iran should not 'give up its nuclear activities regardless of the circumstances.'"[21] Furthermore, even if the regime dissolved, there is no guarantee that the Greens would win in elections (should free elections become possible), because polls show that Ahmadinejad supporters far outnumber Green supporters.[22]

It may be, as some analysts have argued, that the Greens are more of a civil rights movement than a political revolution like the Arab Spring movements. If so, then its progress is bound to be slower and more incremental.[23]

AFRICA: WEALTH NOT SHARED

The African continent's myriad problems—poverty, civil war, pandemics, Islamic radicalism—are beyond the scope of this chapter and this book. Yet the broader tide of antisystemic political energy is finding expression in Africa, too. While the continent's dozens of nations are far too diverse and complex to paint with a broad brush, many African citizens sense that their political leaders are not serving the needs of the people.

Consider Angola, a nation that, like many on the continent, has undergone enormous challenges since independence, with Cold War rivalries and civil war. But Angola, also like many of its neighbors, contains rich natural resources—in this case, petroleum. The country has become Africa's second-leading producer of crude oil. While history has shown that oil can be a bane as often as a boon, this is a development that, if managed properly, ought to be economically beneficial. So far, however, while oil has bolstered Angola's GDP, it has enriched only its economic and political elites. Few Angolans have experienced much of the new oil wealth, because the government decided to bring in cheap Chinese labor to fill most jobs arising from ambitious national construction projects.

"Angola is a rich country, but we don't get any of it," said Paulo Silva, a citizen of Luanda. "The people in power are eating all the money."[24]

Indeed, the nation's poverty statistics speak starkly to the fact that much of the nation's wealth is concentrated in very few hands: 60 percent of Angolan families live on less than $1.70 a day and lack proper shelter. Chinese-staffed construction projects have built housing that only upper-middle-class or wealthy Angolans can afford—this, in a nation that cannot provide most of the population with basic shelter.

So Angola, like other countries in Africa—Uganda and Ethiopia among them—has witnessed the rise of a national protest movement. In 2011, on the heels of the Arab Spring, young Angolans, in this case led by rap musicians, began utilizing now-familiar tactics—social media, text messaging, and other new communication tools—to speak out against government corruption and call for the end of the regime of José Eduardo dos Santos, who has ruled Angola for more than thirty years. The movement has since seen broader middle-class participation, including veterans of the Angolan military. The government, not surprisingly, has cracked down fiercely with arrests and violence.[25]

"The hope for Angola is a new generation that is rising up," says antigovernment activist Rafael Marques de Morais. "They are not afraid to cross political boundaries."[26]

That remains to be seen. But Angola's enormous wealth disparities and its government's refusal to address its people's grievances—except with further repression—mirror, in a starker way, the discontents that we see around the globe.

In Mozambique, a sudden coal boom has brought the Brazilian mining company Vale into the country, where it has invested in a major coal mine. But to do so, it had to displace hundreds of rural families, to whom it promised improved housing, services, and other amenities. When these promises turned out to be hollow, seven hundred families protested their resettlements, which they said had resulted in poorer access to water and power.[27] Though resource-rich, and with a booming economy, Mozambique remains a profoundly poor country, ranking near the bottom of the UN's Human Development Index.

Government repression has taken its most extreme form in South Africa, where in August 2012 police shocked the nation by firing into a crowd of striking platinum miners in Marikana, killing thirty-four. The massacre prompted bitter memories of the nation's apartheid era, when government forces routinely assaulted and killed democracy protesters and activists. But most of all, as the *New York Times* summarized it, the incident made larger the "fault line between the governing African National Congress and a nation that, eighteen years after the end of apartheid, is increasingly impatient with deep poverty, rampant unemployment, and yawning inequality."[28] That's a chorus that could be repeated, in different ways, around the African continent.

CONCLUSION

The combined conditions of political failure and economic instability have created the climate for a rebirth of antisystemic political activity—and sometimes extremist activity—around the world. Nationalist (and nativist) parties in Europe, radical progressive parties in Italy or Germany, and reenergized populist movements in the United States all share a common perspective that the established political order no longer works. While it's easy to point out the weaknesses of these movements, it's more difficult to refute their argument that governing institutions have failed.

Many regret the rise of these groups, seeing them, variously, as dangerous or frivolous. But for better or worse, they reflect how pervasively the trust breakdown has affected public attitudes. If the appeal of someone like Beppe Grillo or the Pirate Party or even the European nationalist parties baffles us from afar, we should remember this: One constant of human nature is that people will respond to something they regard as "authentic," someone or something they feel might, finally, be speaking to them in their language and sharing their concerns. Many of the answers they provide may be insufficient—or worse. But it doesn't change the fact that millions around the world are seeking an authentic, legitimate government that operates honestly and effectively.

However we might choose to describe the governing regimes in most countries, *authentic* or *legitimate* probably aren't the words that spring to mind.

NOTES

The epigraphs in this chapter are drawn from the following sources: Georg Diez, Walter Mayr, and Matthias Schepp, "The Path to Tyranny: Putin's Russia Is Becoming a Flawless Dictatorship," *Der Spiegel*, August 13, 2012, www.spiegel.de/international/europe/spiegel-cover-story-on-pussy-riot-trial-and-putin-a-849697.html; José Antonio Vargas, "Spring Awakening," *New York Times*, February 17, 2012, www.nytimes.com/2012/02/19/books/review/how-an-egyptian-revolution-began-on-facebook.html; and Lydia Polgreen, "Change Unlikely from Angolan Election, but Discontent Simmers," *New York Times*, August 31, 2012, www.nytimes.com/2012/09/01/world/africa/change-unlikely-from-angola-election-but-discontent-simmers.html.

1. Diez et al., "Path to Tyranny."
2. Ibid.

3. Ibid.

4. Andrew Meier, "Ksenia Sobchak, the Stiletto in Putin's Side," *New York Times*, July 3, 2012, http://www.nytimes.com/2012/07/08/magazine/ksenia-sobchak-the-stiletto-in-putins-side.html.

5. Diez et al., "Path to Tyranny."

6. Ibid.

7. Ishaan Tharoor, "Top Ten Abuses of Power: India's Telecoms Scandal," *Time*, May 17, 2011, http://www.time.com/time/specials/packages/article/0,28804,2071839_2071844_2071866,00.html.

8. Pankaj Mishra, "Indians Against Democracy," *New York Review of Books*, January 24, 2012, http://www.nybooks.com/blogs/nyrblog/2012/jan/24/indians-against-democracy/.

9. Cara Parks, "What's Going On in Egypt?" Huffington Post, January 28, 2011, http://www.huffingtonpost.com/2011/01/28/whats-going-on-in-egypt_n_815734.html

10. Antonio Vargas, "Spring Awakening."

11. Ibid.

12. Ibid.

13. Guy Sorman, "The New Rebellions," *City Journal* 22, no. 1 (Winter 2012), http://www.city-journal.org/2012/22_1_tech-empowered-protesters.html.

14. "Egypt's Mohamed ElBaradei Launches Egyptian Party," BBC News, April 28, 2012, http://www.bbc.co.uk/news/world-middle-east-17880367.

15. Virginie Nguyen, "Abouel Fotouh Takes Steps to Found Strong Egypt Party," July 5, 2012, *Egypt Independent*, http://www.egyptindependent.com/news/abouel-fotouh-takes-steps-found-strong-egypt-party.

16. "The Construction and Development Party," *Hiwar Online Magazine*, accessed July 8, 2013, http://hiwarportal.dedi.org.eg/key/the-construction-and-development-party-al-jamaah-al-islamiya/.

17. "Iran: U.S. Policy Options," Foreign Policy Initiative, April 6, 2012, http://www.foreignpolicyi.org/event/Iran/policyoptions.

18. Hooman Majd, "Think Again: Iran's Green Movement," *Foreign Policy*, January 6, 2010, http://www.foreignpolicy.com/articles/2010/01/06/think_again_irans_green_movement.

19. Ibid.

20. Dariush Zahedi and Hamed Aleaziz, "Foreign Policy: Iran's Green Movement Could Go Blue," NPR, April 8, 2011, http://www.npr.org/2011/04/08/135235930/foreign-policy-irans-green-movement-could-go-blue.

21. Robert Wright, "Why Regime Change Won't Work in Iran," *Atlantic*, January 18, 2012, http://www.theatlantic.com/international/archive/2012/01/why-regime-change-wont-work-in-iran/251603/.

22. Ibid.

23. Majd, "Think Again."

24. Polgreen, "Change Unlikely from Angolan Election."

25. Rafael Marques de Morais, "Growing Wealth, Shrinking Democracy," *New York Times*, August 29, 2012, http://www.nytimes.com/2012/08/30/ opinion/in-angola-growing-wealth-but-shrinking-democracy.html.

26. Polgreen, "Change Unlikely from Angolan Election."

27. David McKay, "Mozambique Coal Boom Caught UN Off Guard," Miningmx, November 22, 2012, http://www.miningmx.com/page/news/energy/ 1469634-Mozambique-coal-boom-caught-UN-off-guard#.ULFSeIfAeSo.

28. Lydia Polgreen, "Mine Strike Mayhem Stuns South Africa as Police Open Fire," *New York Times*, August 16, 2012, http://www.nytimes.com/2012/ 08/17/world/africa/south-african-police-fire-on-striking-miners.html.

10

TECHNOLOGY
Builder and Betrayer of Trust

We see more and more people around the globe using the Internet, mobile phones, and other technologies to make their voices heard as they protest injustice and seek to realize their aspirations.

—Hillary Clinton

Imagine a world in which every single person on the planet is given free access to the sum of all human knowledge. That's what we're doing.

—Jimmy Wales

For democracy to be true today, the application of technology is necessary. For a democracy to become vibrant and healthy, it is necessary that its citizens should be educated, informed, empowered, and enlightened.

—Indian People's Congress

It's probably no accident that the breakdown of authority worldwide is playing out in an era of unprecedented technological sophistication, in which Web-based communications tools allow citizens across the world to reach one another and put governments on notice that their actions can be viewed by millions. On the surface, such technology would seem to be the greatest boon to democracy and individual rights imaginable—and in many ways it is. But as we have also seen all too plainly in recent years, technology can be almost equally a force for repression. In such nations as Russia, China, and Iran, ruling regimes often see technology as an extension of their power, and they view its independent use by citizens as a direct threat to that power. Whether technology serves to empower or hinder us depends on whose hands operate the tools.

By now, nearly two decades after it became broadly available in the West, the Internet is one of the central realities of daily existence. Its transformative effect on daily life, culture, habits, economics, and politics is no longer disputed; the debate centers not on the fact of its influence but on the nature of that influence. From a global perspective, one of the Internet's most enduring effects is the way in which it has fostered an interconnectedness in which developments on one side of the world have genuine impact on the other. Websites, blogs, and social-networking sites have offered alternative universes of feedback and information to people everywhere. The Internet has made possible the forging of political communities and movements among people who previously would never have been able to communicate with one another. And Web-based technologies, like video-enabled cell phones, have made every citizen a potential reporter, lifting the veil on repressive governments around the world.

"Alaa is causing them trouble because he's been an activist for so long. He has many people around him he can influence. They don't want this voice now,"[1] said a supporter of Alaa Abd El-Fattah, an Egyptian blogger, software developer, and political activist. El-Fattah has become synonymous with the Egyptian revolution and has continued to plague the government long after Hosni Mubarak's fall. When the government shut down the Internet at the start of the Arab Spring protests in Egypt, El-Fattah, who was out of the country at the time, collected information from family and friends by landline phones and published information about events around Tahrir Square on his blog. Suddenly, we were all transported there, able to follow the protesters' struggle.

Indeed, all the Arab Spring uprisings relied heavily on new technologies—the Internet, social media, Twitter, TwitPic, Facebook, and YouTube—to accelerate social protest. Social media was so influential that U.S. senators questioned whether the CIA had failed to brief President Obama adequately on the Egyptian situation because of its failure to follow developments on Twitter. Democratic senator Dianne Feinstein referred to the intelligence community's performance as "lacking."[2] The United States's number two intelligence official could only respond that the CIA had "warned of instability" but that it "didn't know what the triggering mechanism would be." If CIA operatives had been following Twitter, they wouldn't have needed to worry about triggering mechanisms in the first place.

Events in the Middle East have also shown the darker side of technology and the way even ordinary citizens can use its power for pernicious ends. That's what happened in September 2012, with the explosion of YouTube-generated outrage over the *Innocence of Muslims* film trailer (actually produced by an Egyptian-born U.S. resident). As Steve Coll wrote in the *New Yorker*:

> The uproar over *Innocence of Muslims* matters not because of the deep pathologies it has supposedly laid bare but because of the way the film went viral. A sectarian auteur with modest means used the Web to provoke enemies directly. The filmmakers employed the same strategies that liberal bloggers and Facebook users seized upon during the Tunisian and Egyptian revolutions, and that Syrian revolutionaries use daily to rally resistance to the butchering government in Damascus. Free speech in a digital public square—not fringe violence—is what's new under the Mediterranean sun. And with free speech comes provocation.[3]

For the most part, though, ordinary citizens have used the new technology constructively. Among other capabilities, Web-based technologies have empowered citizen journalists to hold their governments to account. During the 2011 Japanese earthquake and the resulting disaster at Fukushima Daiichi nuclear plant, civilians and employees used technology to provide in-depth views of the crisis as it unfolded. User-generated content, including photos and flash videos, was not only disseminated through social networks but also picked up by professional news services as crucial elements of their coverage.[4]

In India, the now-famous website ipaidabribe.com has brought international attention to rampant corruption at all government levels. As of August 2012, more than twenty thousand reports had been made in nearly five hundred Indian cities.[5] A typical story goes like this:

Another respondent told of how he was forced to hand over cash when flying to Canada from Mumbai. At the immigration counter an official asked him if he had a police report. The man protested that he had a visa for Canada and did not require further documentation, but the official persisted. "He asked how much cash I am carrying—I say $200. The guy was like 'put it inside this envelope.' I had to leave and had no option, except putting that cash inside it."[6]

The site invokes one of the central messages coursing through the social media and technological revolution: data can help change the system, and sharing personal stories can help others. In fact, the site has already had some effect. At least one government minister, armed with a list of complaints from the website, issued warnings to twenty senior government officers.[7]

Technology's liberating impact is not confined to building awareness or political organizing. It can also play a direct institutional role in delivering goods and services to poor people. Alec Ross, senior advisor for innovation to former secretary of state Hillary Clinton, spearheaded the State Department's effort to take diplomacy digital. In conjunction with James Eberhard of Mobile Accord, the State Department set up the Text Haiti 90999 program within two hours of the 2010 earthquake, raising more than $40 million for the Red Cross through $10 donations. In Mexico, Ross is collaborating with the government, NGOs, and telecom companies to set up a system for tracking crimes that includes a cell phone–based tip system that will map the activities of criminals online and warn people about trouble spots.

Yet for all of its upsides, technology has also been adopted by autocratic regimes as a key tool to stifle popular expression and consolidate power.

In 2007, Russia hit the tiny Baltic nation of Estonia with a massive cyber attack. Websites for banks, newspapers, parliament, and government ministries were shut down through a distributed "denial-of-service" attack. One of the world's most wired countries, Estonia was completely destabilized. Russia's action was sparked by Estonia's decision to move a Soviet World War II memorial in Tallinn. Motivated by a mere grudge, Russia used the power of technology to effectively shut down a nation.[8]

After Iran's "Twitter Revolution" broke out in 2009, the Iranian government took steps to crush the popular protest. Clamping down on

Internet traffic by apportioning less bandwidth to the country and essentially shutting down the Web, President Mahmoud Ahmadinejad's regime showed how digital technology can become a tool of repression. In November 2012, after nearly two years of battling an insurrection, the Assad regime in Syria shut down all eighty-four of the country's ISP blocks for three days in an attempt to restrict rebel and opposition-group communications.[9] The shutdown went into force just as rebel forces were making substantial gains.

"The pattern seems to be that governments that fear mass movements on the street have realized that they might want to be able to shut off all Internet communications in the country and have started building the infrastructure that enables them to do that," said Andrew McLaughlin, a former technology adviser to the White House.[10]

Since its inception, the Internet has been regarded as an open platform, a communications and information tool without national boundaries. But more nations are beginning to assert their right, as they see it, to shut down Internet access for whatever reason—national security being the most popular. In an attempt to gain help in this effort, some authoritarian governments are appealing to a UN agency, the International Telecommunications Union (ITU), which is attempting to take a greater role in governing the Web. Russia, for instance, has sought the ITU's blessing for its efforts to control the Web for dubious goals like "decency" or "territorial integrity."[11]

Troublingly, efforts to clamp down on individual expression are not confined to such autocratic nations as Iran or Syria or North Korea, China, and Cuba. Well-established democracies, including the United States, the United Kingdom, and Germany, have all seen controversies over government abuses of Internet freedom. Recently, the South Korean government made news for removing a tweet in which a government critic used a curse word in reference to the president. The critic later found his Twitter account blocked.[12] This and other similar episodes of censorship led some observers to question the health of South Korea's celebrated democracy.

Clearly, then, technology is a double-edged sword: a force for good in many nations but also a tool for repression and censorship. The same qualities that make communications technology a source of goodwill and trust among citizens—especially the unrestricted freedom of discussion—are perceived by governments as endangering their power.

Governments see technology as problematic not only because of its well-established ability to mobilize opposition but also because it takes away their cherished ability to control the narrative, to exert authority over messaging and images (and perhaps over events themselves).

They don't seem to understand that this very control—and their own abuse of it—has played a crucial role in the loss of public trust.

HOW TECHNOLOGY MAGNIFIES THE TRUST CRISIS

In December 2011, nearly ten thousand Latvian depositors made a run on Latvia's largest commercial bank, Swedish-owned Swedbank. The panic resulted in withdrawals of more than ten million lats—the equivalent of roughly $20 million.[13] The day before, vague rumors had circulated on Twitter and other social-media networks that Swedbank's Estonian and Sweden arms "[were] facing legal and liquidity problems."[14] In this case, the rumors happened to be unfounded: Maris Mancinskis, the bank's Latvian head, called them "absurd," and no bank functionality was impeded. Perhaps fueling consumer fears, another Latvian bank, Latvijas Krajbanka, had undergone liquidation earlier in the year as a result of massive fraud, leaving its depositors stranded.

The run on Swedbank is just one example of how online technologies have redrawn the rules of trust and consumer confidence. While bank runs have a long history, the breakneck pace of the Swedbank panic shows how technological interconnectedness increases the risk of these kinds of events. It's easy to imagine how advanced technologies will make episodes like this unfold even faster in the future, making it much more difficult for banks or other institutions to guard against them.

The solution comes back to trust: in such a transparent communications environment, trust between constituents, shareholders, consumers, and depositors is more vital than ever before.

The new technologies offer some ground for optimism. For starters, the technology industry itself was the most trusted business sector in the 2012 Edelman Trust Barometer, garnering 79 percent trust globally.[15] Among individual countries, the United Kingdom, France, and Germany register the lowest trust in technology, at 67 percent[16]—a rate still higher than the second-most-trusted industry globally, the automotive sector, which stands at 66 percent. Banks, at 47 percent, and financial services, at 45 percent, ranked at the bottom of the industries list, with global trust in government a notch lower still, at 43 percent.[17]

The wide gap in trust between the technology and financial sectors helps explain the haste with which Latvians withdrew their savings from Swedbank: they trusted the source of the information (Twitter) while already harboring distrust of their bank. Edelman's 2012 report found that trust in social media jumped 75 percent from 2011 to 2012, rising from 8 percent to 14 percent globally. (Those figures may sound low, but millions, especially in older generations, still don't use social media and so lack the experience that enables trust; what's important is the huge spike upward in trust levels.) Moreover, a 63 percent majority reported needing to hear information repeated three to five times in order to overcome skepticism.[18]

While in the Swedbank case the rumor turned out to be untrue, too many cases abound in which a single institutional voice denies what hundreds or even thousands of ordinary people already know. The record of institutions in circulating false information is far longer and more damaging than that of social media, at least up to now. People will likely trust social-media sources over government sources for a long time to come, especially in less democratic nations.

Indeed, the ever-increasing number of Internet users makes it clear that technology will play a crucial role in resolving the crisis of authority. More than two billion people have used the Internet. Internet penetration varies greatly around the world, with 77 percent penetration in North America to just 11 percent in Africa; most other regions and countries fall somewhere in between. As of January 2012, 22 percent of the world's population used a social network. North America again tops the list at 50 percent penetration, while Africa has the lowest penetration rate at 4 percent, but that figure is growing.[19] As of March 2012, there were 835 million Facebook users.[20] People are spending more and more time managing their social networks, as well as using other social platforms, especially YouTube and other video sites.[21]

"Microblogging" services, such as Twitter or the Twitter equivalent Sina Weibo in China, are also growing quickly. The global penetration of microblogging among Internet users stands at 43 percent. China leads the way, with 72 percent of Internet users having microblogged in 2011, according to Universal McCann's 2012 social-media tracker.[22]

Other reports suggest that of China's more than five hundred million Internet users, half are microbloggers—a nearly 300 percent growth rate just since 2011.[23]

And social networks are growing quickly in the Middle East: more than three million people joined Facebook in Egypt and Syria alone in the first six months of 2012. Twitter membership in the Arab region nearly doubled between June 2011 and June 2012, growing to a total of two million users.[24]

The power of these technologies became abundantly clear during the Arab Spring.

TECHNOLOGY AND THE ARAB SPRING

Events of recent years have made clear that social media is uniquely effective at influencing trust both passively, through information consumption (as in the Swedbank example), and actively, through its use as a tool for activists. Nowhere has this dual power been more evident than in the Middle East, where the Arab Spring showed the world that technology and social media can spread democracy faster than soldiers or governments.

In Egypt and Tunisia, protesters' use of social media and other technologies, such as cell phones, was integral to the demise of autocratic regimes. Syria, Bahrain, and Kuwait also saw a sharp jump in politically motivated social-media activity: according to the Arab Social Media Report, the hashtag #bahrain, with more than half a million mentions in tweets in September 2011 alone, was the most popular hashtag of that month in the Arab region, followed by #egypt, #syria, #feb14 (the date on which demonstrations began in Bahrain), and #kuwait.[25] Globally, #egypt was 2011's most frequently used hashtag, with #jan25, the date of the Egypt uprising's start, rounding out the list of Twitter's global hot topics for 2011 at number 8. In world news, the most tweeted story of 2011 was Egyptian president Hosni Mubarak's resignation; Mu'ammar Gadhafi's death in Libya made number 5. Lastly, on the list of cities and countries most frequently tweeted, Cairo and Egypt took numbers 1 and 2, respectively, with Libya at number 4.[26]

These figures are remarkable when considering the relatively sparse Twitter membership in the Arab region—estimated at 652,333 active users, out of a global Twitter membership of one hundred million.[27] In other regions, social-network use is enormously varied; in the Arab world, its most potent usage has been for political activity. The hashtag #egypt, for example, became globally prominent in part because users in the West picked it up—but it wouldn't have reached Western attention had it not been in heavy rotation among Egyptian Twitter members.

This niche political activity has spread into the developed nations from which Twitter emerged.[28] For example, the three days of unrest in August 2011 in London, during which poor citizens rose up against what David Cameron referred to as "Broken Britain"—an enshrined system of inequality and injustice—were largely organized online. In fact, two men were jailed for attempting to incite disorder via Facebook.

Social media can even outsmart censorship in certain cases. According to the Facebook User Penetration and Internet Freedom Rankings, the three Arab nations with the highest Facebook user penetration—United Arab Emirates, Bahrain, and Qatar—have some of the lowest Internet freedom rankings in the Arab region.[29] "Social media tools do not fall under Internet restrictions in these countries," the report found. They "provide an outlet for discussion, communication, and protest, especially among youth," and with a frequency that "rise[s] during times of conflict and unrest."[30] This was the case in Tunisia, where, despite Web-censorship laws, informal online networks were abuzz with activity after Mohamed Bouazizi's self-immolation in January 2011.

To be sure, Arab Spring protesters were no physical match for the militaries and police forces they faced. Although the conflicts grew bloody in some instances, the Arab Spring movements seem to represent an historic turning point in the region. Their political outcomes remain at issue, but the movements clearly indicate the size and strength of a vast, technology-savvy younger population. Some critics, like Malcolm Gladwell and Fareed Zakaria, downplayed the influence of social media in the Arab protests, but Wael Abbas, an Egyptian blogger, provided a more balanced assessment: "Social media is a tool. But revolution is the decision of many people. Once we decided to have a revolution, once people decided to stay in the square, social media was a helpful tool to call for support, ask lawyers for help. I will not give social media all the credit, nor will I take away all the credit from social media."[31]

As Nabil Al Sharif, Egypt's former minister of state for communications, said, "The most important outcome of the Arab Spring has been the destruction of the old media regime"—not merely the destruction of the old political regime.[32] Distrust of the national media led citizens "to rely on self-generated news," which could be easily spread domestically and globally.[33] Even coverage of the Egyptian revolt by independent television stations lacked the "transparent record" of the authentic, guerilla-style mobile-phone images and videos that protesters produced on the scene. It was ultimately these images that shaped accounts of the historic events in Cairo.[34]

The impact of social media on Middle East politics also makes clear the importance of a new U.S. State Department project: "Internet in a suitcase," a global Obama-administration initiative designed to support free speech and democracy by creating new pathways for communication. Specifically, it would distribute "shadow" Internet and mobile-phone systems that dissidents can use across the Arab world and beyond to undermine repressive regimes. Financed with a $2 million grant, the "suitcase" enables activists to communicate outside the reach of governments in Iran, Syria, and Libya. The initiative's leader, Sascha Meinrath of the Open Technology Initiative at the New America Foundation, commented, "We're going to build a separate infrastructure where the technology is nearly impossible to shut down, to control, to surveil. . . . The implication is that this disempowers central authorities from infringing on people's fundamental human right to communicate."[35]

What some call a "liberation-technology movement" has the potential to influence political change more broadly (and perhaps more democratically) than ever before. Technology is unquestionably changing the way that dissidents operate and how governments respond to them.

Although the dramatic events of the Arab Spring have moved off the front pages, the activists have battled on. El-Fattah was released from prison in Egypt in December 2011 after two months behind bars. The charge against him was inciting Christian protesters to attack soldiers in Cairo. His case brought attention to the Egyptian practice of trying civilians in military courts—which has sparked a growing opposition, driven significantly, again, by social media. The hashtag #nomiltrial is now widely known, and videos from the No Military Trials group are linked on the *New York Times* and BBC websites, among others. Social media's capacity to advance political causes and spread awareness cannot be underestimated.

SOCIAL MEDIA, SOCIAL MOVEMENT

"Without Weibo there would be no Wukan," says Ting Luo, a specialist on village elections in China at the London School of Economics.[36]

Sina Weibo, the Chinese version of Twitter, played a central role in the 2011 Wukan Village protests, in which several thousand residents of the coastal fishing village protested against the government's sale of their land to developers without compensation. The protesters, especially the younger generation, knew how to attract media attention through social networking. Their use of Weibo helped transform the Wukan protest into an international cause. Eventually the protests were resolved when the Chinese Communist Party allowed the village to hold elections for new leadership.

The Internet was also central to the efforts of twenty well-educated young Chinese activists who masterminded the 2011 Chinese Jasmine Revolution. Calling themselves the Initiators and Organizers of the Chinese Jasmine Revolution after a phrase used in the Arab Spring, the activists, spread across half a dozen countries, called for demonstrations every Sunday against the Chinese Communist Party's autocratic rule and rising inequality within the country. The first calls for a Chinese Jasmine Revolution came from an anonymous Twitter post and an anonymous appeal on a U.S.-based Chinese news site, Boxun.com. The protests, which took place in over a dozen Chinese cities in February and March 2011, would never have been possible without the Internet.

One of the organizers, known as Forest Intelligence, works on his laptop from a café in Seoul. He told the AP, "People born in the late eighties and the nineties have basically decided that in their generation one-party rule cannot possibly outlive them, cannot possibly even continue in their lifetimes. This is for certain."[37] Such confidence, whether justified or not, is infectious: Forest Intelligence recruits volunteers and maintains the website for the movement. Members in China include an expert in online search engines and a former government employee.

They also have the support and assistance of Wang Juntao, the dissident sentenced to thirteen years in prison for helping students during the 1989 prodemocracy protests in Tiananmen Square.

The CCP responded quickly to the Jasmine protests, increasing Internet monitoring and beefing up police presence. The government crackdown led ultimately to the disappearance or arrest of two hundred people. Chinese artist Ai Weiwei was one: he was arrested in April 2011 on suspicion of "economic crimes" after expressing support for the Jasmine Revolution through his blog and Twitter accounts.[38]

The Occupy Wall Street movement in the United States was also an Internet project from the start. Jeff Jarvis, a professor of journalism at the City University of New York, calls OWS "a hashtag revolt." As Jarvis argues, "a hashtag has no owner, no hierarchy, no canon or credo. It is a blank slate onto which anyone can impose his or her frustrations, complaints, demands, wishes, or principles."[39] Indeed, this ability to customize helped make OWS a different movement in different cities. The protest had its own character in New York City and London, Barcelona and Sydney, Mexico City and Tel Aviv. The Internet provided the platform while allowing local and national movements to express themselves in different ways. Organizers and participants didn't try to control the message, and technology let it take on a powerful life of its own.

Similarly, the Indignant Movement (*indignados*) in Spain was born over the Internet. Beginning with the Real Democracy Now! Internet experiment, people across Spain who wanted to have a say in how their government makes decisions came together to voice their anger over massive income inequality and the country's ineffective and often corrupt political leadership. Thanks to Facebook and Twitter, the Spanish *indignados* movement spread across Europe. Some version of it now operates in about seventy cities around the world. Without the Internet, the "worldwide protest against the greed of politicians and banks, which has brought the planet into financial crisis,"[40] as the *indignados* somewhat clumsily call their movement, would only be a series of unconnected demonstrations.

After the 2011 Russian parliamentary elections, citizens flooded YouTube with videos alleging vote rigging by Vladimir Putin's United Russia party. According to a report by Yandex, a Russian search-engine giant, Russia has more than one million Twitter users—a five-fold jump since 2010. Internet users formed the backbone of the protests, and organizers were acutely aware of the impact the Web was having on the size and scope of the movement. Writer Sergei Shargunov said, "I want to say a big hello to Twitter and Facebook. Hoorah Internet! Today they [points at Kremlin] can't control us thanks to social-networking sites and us."[41]

Also at the Moscow protests was Danila Lindele, a twenty-three-year-old Russian activist, who stood by tweeting on his iPad. "When it comes to the rally today, [the] Internet has played an extremely vital role in making it happen because nothing was broadcast on television. Everything is disseminated through Twitter, Facebook, and through our VK site,"[42] he said, referring to Vkontakte, a European social network especially popular in Russia.

Putin's regime understands well the challenge social media poses to its power. The Russian authorities' ongoing attacks against Alexei Navalny, one of Putin's fiercest critics and social-media activists, are a case in point. In March 2012, ahead of Putin's third presidential victory, Navalny spearheaded a series of rallies that drew more than one hundred thousand supporters. In July 2012, shortly after he used his blog to make fraud and corruption accusations against Investigative Committee chief Alexander Bastrykin, the government accused Navalny of embezzlement and barred him from leaving Russia. He remains defiant in the face of a potential ten-year prison sentence. "I will continue doing what I did before," he says. "Nothing has changed for me."[43]

Navalny still plans to create his own political party that will harness the power of new technologies. In an interview with *Time*—which included him as the only Russian on its 2012 Most Influential Persons in the World list—he said, "We need to use new technologies, first of all the Internet, for the practical functions of the party, like a reconstituted Facebook. Many people call it Democracy 2.0. I'm a lobbyist and fanatic of this system. It should allow people to register online and verify their identities through a bank card or by some other means and then let them take part in [the party's] decision making, voting, and so on."[44]

In the United States, Barack Obama's 2008 campaign revolutionized American politics with its use of technology. After Howard Dean's 2004 campaign broke new ground by raising money through hundreds of thousands of small donors via the Internet, Obama took things to a new level. Obama's team, for instance, took advantage of a tool not available in 2004—free YouTube advertising, a potentially more effective outlet than TV ads. YouTube viewers, unlike regular TV viewers, choose to watch political ads, rather than being forced to watch them when their programs are interrupted. As Joe Trippi, a political consultant who ran Howard Dean's digital campaign, told the *New York Times*, "The campaign's official stuff they created for YouTube was watched for 14.5 million hours. To buy 14.5 million hours on broadcast TV is $47 million."[45]

Obama is the first true "Internet president": his leveraging of the technology has been sustained, innovative, and enormously effective, getting his message out constantly through multiple platforms to people who can watch or listen at their convenience. More than seven million people have watched Obama's 2008 speech on race, for example. As Arianna Huffington argues, "Were it not for the Internet, Barack Obama would not be president. Were it not for the Internet, Barack Obama would not have been the [Democratic] nominee."[46]

All American politicians are increasingly making communications technologies work for them: many blog or tweet in the hopes of painting a more flattering picture of themselves and their embattled institutions. Clearly, the Internet and all its facets—social media, online journalism, citizen videography—has transformed the political landscape. It has given voice to movements that would have been drowned out by the mainstream and ignored by disinterested elites. For ordinary people who so often feel powerless, the Internet is the great gift of the technological age, one that promises to break down barriers—social, cultural, and political.

But as with any powerful, transformative new technology, it has also prompted a determined pushback.

TECHNOLOGY FOR OPPRESSION

"According to relevant laws, regulations, and policies, search results for *the truth* cannot be displayed." This is the message that appeared on the screen of the more than three hundred million registered users of Sina Weibo in July 2012 when they searched for the term *the truth* on the Chinese social-media site. First disappearing in late June, *the truth* joined the long list of blocked phrases under what has been called

China's Great Firewall—a list that includes *Tiananmen Square*, *Tibet*, and the name of the disgraced politician *Bo Xilai*, among others.

While China's constitution affords its citizens freedom of speech and press, Chinese law enables authorities to suppress whatever it views as dangers to the state. In April 2010, the CCP revised its Law on Guarding State Secrets to tighten control over information flows.[47] Further, the CCP's first white paper on the Internet in May 2010 required all Internet users in China to abide by Chinese rules and regulations. As Rebecca MacKinnon, an expert in global Internet policy, argues, "the [Chinese] regime actually uses the Internet not only to extend its control but to enhance its legitimacy."[48]

Ranked 171st out of 178 countries in an index of press freedom compiled by the watchdog group Reporters Without Borders,[49] China is closely policed by more than a dozen government bodies. From the Internet to movies, Beijing is watching it all. Google's longstanding dispute with China over linking to its uncensored search page, and China's decision to launch its own state-owned search engine in 2011, showed the regime's determination and persistence. The government's censorship choices often seem illogical or impulsive. Qi Zhenyu, head of social media for *iSun Affairs*, a Hong Kong–based current-affairs magazine, told the *Telegraph*, "Whenever this is a word that upsets them, they just go ahead and block, [but] most of the time you can't really explain why they censor a certain word."[50]

Ordinary Chinese citizens would like to see an expansion of press freedom and relaxation of censorship over social media. Then premier Wen Jiabao even made public statements in favor of free speech. "The people's wishes for, and needs for, democracy and freedom are irresistible," he said in an interview with CNN—but his words were censored in China! According to Columbia professor Andrew Nathan, "It's impossible to know exactly what Wen means . . . he probably envisions a great deal less reform and a great deal less human rights than we would think such words imply."[51]

To be sure, information slips through government censors in China. Movements like the Chinese Jasmine Revolution show how concerted efforts can circumvent the imposed political orthodoxy at times. Nevertheless, the CCP's reach remains formidable, and the party is determined to maintain strict control—as the party reminded the world again in November 2012, when it arrested a blogger, Zhai Xiaobing, and confiscated his computer after he made a joke on Twitter about the Communist Party Congress. A party official explained that Zhai was being investigated for "spreading terrorist information."[52]

No matter what public outcry results, Beijing is unlikely to halt its use of technology to spy on citizens and undermine political organizing.

While China is often cited as the chief practitioner of state censorship and manipulation of technology, it's far from alone. Interestingly, a June 2012 report by Google shows that the majority of requests it receives from governments to remove specific content and speeches, including those on YouTube, *come from democracies.* The company's "Transparency Report," which covers takedown requests between July and December 2011, shows almost 7,000 requests from the U.S. government, 1,722 from government agencies in Germany, and 255 from India—while less than ten came from Jordan, Bolivia, and Ukraine. The United States also led the way in requests for user data, with 6,231 separate requests. Dorothy Chou, a senior policy analyst at Google, found the results alarming,

> not only because free expression is at risk, but because some of these requests come from countries you might not suspect—Western democracies not typically associated with censorship. . . . We realize that the numbers we share can only provide a small window into what's happening on the Web at large, but we do hope that by being transparent about these government requests we can continue to contribute to the public debate about how government behaviors are shaping our Web.[53]

These figures are not the only indication of the U.S. government's apparently growing desire to monitor citizen behavior on the Internet. The controversy over the 2012 Stop Online Piracy Act (SOPA), a U.S. bill that would allow law enforcement to fight online trafficking by shutting down websites without trial or a court hearing, exemplifies Chou's point. Wikipedia, Google, Mozilla, and Reddit, among others, went "dark" to protest the bill, posting anti–SOPA imagery on their home pages to symbolize what the bill would allow the government to do to sites it accuses of copyright infringement. "The solutions are draconian. There's a bill that would require [Internet service providers] to remove URLs from the Web, which is also known as censorship last time I checked," Google CEO Eric Schmidt said in a speech last November.[54] I agree.

The Russian government has recently been engaging in Internet censorship similar to China's. Putin announced plans in June 2012 to create an Internet blacklist for websites running "banned content," a proposal backed by all four factions of the State Duma. Wikipedia's Russian-language site went black in protest. And since the protests against United Russia and Putin began in 2011, the government has been shutting down blogs and spamming protest hashtags on Twitter with progovernment propaganda.[55] Faced with a technology-savvy opposition, the Russian government has fought back with those same technologies to repress political activity.

Many countries have professed their devotion to free and open digital platforms, but their deeds don't always match their words. In May, Pakistani authorities blocked Twitter for an entire day in response to so-called "blasphemous" tweets concerning the Prophet Muhammad. This move came *just twelve hours* after Interior Minister Rehman Malik said that no restrictions would ever be imposed on Twitter. Some were able to get around the ban by using proxy servers, but the move highlights an increasingly aggressive government agenda. The Pakistani government invited bids for an Internet-filtering system that could block up to fifty million URLs and attempted to ban fifteen hundred "immoral" terms from use in cell phone text messages. In 2010, Pakistan banned Facebook and other social-networking sites for two weeks; it also made YouTube crash worldwide after trying to block the site for streaming the now infamous Danish cartoons of Muhammad.[56] With the Twitter ban, Pakistan's IT Ministry may have been testing the limits of censorship as general elections loomed.[57]

As Joel Simon, executive director of the Committee to Protect Journalists, puts it: "In the name of stability or development, these regimes suppress independent reporting, amplify propaganda, and use technology to control rather than empower their citizens . . . because the Internet and trade have made information global, domestic censorship affects people everywhere."[58] The organization's 2012 report put North Korea and Syria atop the list of most censored societies, along with Myanmar, Iran, and Cuba, among others.

Myanmar has seen some progress in this area. The ruling regime abolished censorship of private publications in August 2012, and its other reforms—including releasing the heroic dissident Aung San Suu Kyi, now a member of parliament—led to a visit by President Obama shortly after his reelection. But it's too early to say whether these moves constitute genuine reform. Control over the Internet and digital publications remain at the forefront of the government's censorship policy: Myanmar's Electronic Transactions Law carries a prison sentence of up to fifteen years for distributing information deemed "detrimental to the interest of or that lowers the dignity of any organization or any person."[59] As in the case of China, the parameters for what constitutes a violation are, at best, vague.

Troubling as they are, government abuses are not the only dark side of the new technologies. While I've been a longtime, vocal opponent of censorship and the infringement of the right to free expression, I also believe it's important to consider some of the complications that technology brings.

For one thing, open-source technologies can be a mixed blessing for revolutionaries. In August 2012, a YouTube video went viral showing Syrian rebels—who have been waging a civil war against the tyrannical regime of Bashar al-Assad—throwing the bodies of postal workers off a roof. Another showed a man's throat being cut.[60] The videos made plain that the Syrian rebels were quite murderous themselves and demonstrated how recording a revolution can bring unintended consequences.

Social media also presents authenticity challenges. Farai Chideya, the founder of PopandPolitics.com, points to the issue of "verification" on Twitter. How can you really know that your source is authentic when Twitter is so effective at overcoming censorship by allowing users to change or hide their locations? In fact, many Middle East Twitter users don't list a country at all in order to protect themselves. Tweeters can even ask Western followers to mask their activity by changing their location en masse. During the 2009 Iranian rebellion, this tweet appeared: "RT Iran: pls everyone change your location on tweeter to IRAN inc timezone GMT+3.30 hrs - #Iranelection."[61]

While these tactics make it nearly impossible for the Iranian government to identify "subversive" tweets, they also lock out followers looking to get involved: they're unable to differentiate between imposters, Westerners covering for protesters, and government agents from the genuine activists. The technology can also facilitate misinformation, as shown by the initial reports that U.S. Representative Gabrielle Giffords had been killed in the 2011 Tucson shooting.

Is it possible to have too much openness? In principle, I'm in agreement with Wikipedia's Jimmy Wales, who has said that every person on the planet should be given access to "the sum of all knowledge." But there comes a point when such access goes too far. Julian Assange and WikiLeaks (no affiliation with Wikipedia) is a case in point.

WikiLeaks's mission to publish classified documents is an abuse of free expression. Hillary Clinton has said that "in almost every profession, people rely on confidential communications to do their jobs." She argues that WikiLeaks puts lives in danger and compromises national security, and not just for the United States.[62] Assange's reckless disregard for the importance of confidentiality—and yes, in some cases, secrecy—has jeopardized the security of nations across the globe. He told *Time* that WikiLeaks "tries to make the world more civil and act against abusive organizations that are pushing in the opposite direction."[63] Unfortunately, his half-baked vision has garnered some prominent support. Filmmakers Oliver Stone and Michael Moore have argued that Assange has given us valuable insight into the uglier actions of the U.S. government that the media cover up.[64]

The media certainly leave much to be desired in their coverage (or lack thereof) of important stories. But I see no reason to laud the so-called "accomplishments of WikiLeaks," to say nothing of Ecuador's appalling decision to grant Assange diplomatic asylum. It's telling that Assange calls WikiLeaks a tool for freedom of expression, yet he could only find refuge in a government known for censorship and repression. Assange is no hero. That he used the Internet as the tool of his warped vision is a sobering reminder of the limits of transparency.

Finally, there is the destabilizing influence of "hacktivist" groups like Anonymous, which have wrought havoc around the world by targeting and bringing down the websites of governments and private organizations whose ideas or policies they oppose. The political goals of Anonymous are even more amorphous than those of Occupy Wall Street, a movement with which it shares certain assumptions about entrenched power—against it, in other words—and a decentralized, anyone-can-join-us vibe. If there is a unifying idea to the actions of Anonymous, it is opposition to censorship—thus its hacking of U.S. government websites, including the Department of Justice, around the time SOPA was being debated. But its reach and range of targets are vast: it has committed cyber attacks on the Pentagon and News Corp., MasterCard, and Amazon; threatened to "destroy" Facebook; and disabled the website of an agricultural-research collective conducting a trial on genetically modified foods—among many other cases.[65]

Anonymous also launched attacks on Israeli-government websites in November 2012 in opposition to the Israelis' latest battle with Hamas, and it aided the efforts of a fifteen-year-old Gazan, Nour Haridy, who used Twitter to explore how to keep the Internet running in Gaza in the event the Israeli government disabled it. "They helped us a lot," Haridy said. "Without Anonymous we would not have reached the surface."[66]

Regardless of one's views on the Israeli-Palestinian conflict, the actions of groups like Anonymous ought to be deeply troubling. Like Assange and WikiLeaks, the group apparently feels that its political views are self-evidently righteous, thus justifying any actions it should choose to commit—no matter how destructive to the livelihoods or safety of innocent people, to say nothing of the damage to national security.

HOW TECHNOLOGY CHANGED THE GAME

The technological revolution in communications and the phenomenon of globalization—the "death of distance"—have wrought both exciting and frightening outcomes. Technology has been a great democratizer, opening up opportunities for countless people who would not otherwise have been heard from, lifting the veil on repressive societies, and enabling democratic movements to gel and link up with one another. At the same time, autocratic governments have grown adept at manipulating the technology for their own ends. And open-source technology, so liberating in so many respects, can itself sometimes be destructive of social and governmental stability.

Even in censored societies, the international media and some brave citizens have taken advantage of the new technology to get their stories out. This development has made the organization of national and international movements easier. It has linked protesters to one another and disseminated messages broadly. Governments and armies can't stop it from happening. Even the most authoritarian governments seem to understand that the technology will continue to evolve despite their efforts to control it. Yet many still resort to repression, censorship, and sometimes deadly violence.

Modern technologies form an obvious pathway to more transparency and accountability—whether through open-data strategies that harness the power of these technologies or, more ambitiously, a global fight against censorship and a coordinated system of support for democratic movements.

But, in the end, it is governments, not just citizens, that must adapt to the new political universe that technology has ushered in. Individuals around the world already get it when it comes to technology—their familiarity and comfort with these tools is evident in the novel and often ingenious ways in which they have put them to use. For people everywhere, technology offers a doorway to a future of vast possibility, expanded personal freedom, and greater justice.

Will their governments let them walk through?

NOTES

The epigraphs in this chapter are drawn from the following sources: James Glanz and John Markoff, "U.S. Underwrites Internet Detour around Censors," *New York Times*, June 12, 2012, www.nytimes.com/2011/06/12/world/12internet.html; Roblimo, "Wikipedia Founder Jimmy Wales Responds," Slashdot, July 28, 2004, http://slashdot.org/story/04/07/28/1351230/wikipedia-founder-jimmy-wales-responds; and "Vision Document: Humans' Evolutionary Ascent: On Collective Human Living: Technology's Impact on Democracy and Economy," Indian People's Congress, 2011, http://indianpeoplescongress.org/technologys_impact_on_democracy_and_economy.php.

1. Sarah El Deeb, "Egpyt: Activist Alaa Abdel Fattah Detained by Military, Thousands March in Protest," Huffington Post, October 21, 2011, http://www.huffingtonpost.com/2011/10/31/egypt-alaa-abdel-fattah_n_1067804.html.

2. Greg Miller, "Senators Question Intelligence Agencies' Anticipation of Egypt Uprising," *Washington Post*, February 3, 2011, http://www.washingtonpost.com/wp-dyn/content/article/2011/02/03/AR2011020305388.html.

3. Steve Coll, "Days of Rage," *New Yorker*, October 1, 2012, http://www.newyorker.com/talk/comment/2012/10/01/121001taco_talk_coll.

4. Simon Owens, "How CNN's iReport Enhanced the Coverage of the Japan Earthquake and Its Aftermath," Nieman Journalism Lab, March 22,

2011, http://www.niemanlab.org/2011/03/how-cnns-ireport-enhanced-the-networks-coverage-of-the-japan-earthquake-and-its-aftermath/.

5. http://ipaidabribe.com/.

6. Andrew Buncombe, "ipaidabribe.com—India's Front Line in the War on Corruption," *Independent*, October 30, 2010, http://www.independent.co.uk/news/world/asia/ipaidabribecom-ndash-indias-front-line-in-the-war-on-corruption-2120527.html.

7. Ibid.

8. "The Cyber Raiders Hitting Estonia," BBC News, May 17, 2007, http://news.bbc.co.uk/2/hi/europe/6665195.stm.

9. Martin Chulov, "Syria Shuts Off Internet across the Country," *Guardian*, November 29, 2012, http://www.guardian.co.uk/world/2012/nov/29/syria-blocks-internet; "Internet Back Up in Damascus," *Herald Sun*, December 2, 2012, http://www.heraldsun.com.au/news/breaking-news/internet-back-up-in-damascus/story-e6frf7k6-1226528215098.

10. Tom Gjelten, "Shutdowns Counter the Idea of a World-Wide Web," NPR, December 1, 2012, http://www.npr.org/2012/12/01/166286596/shutdowns-raise-issue-of-who-controls-the-internet.

11. Ibid.

12. "How to Get Censored in South Korea," Storify, November 2012, http://storify.com/nytimesworld/censorship-in-south-korea.

13. "Latvia's Biggest Bank Fights Off Deposit Run," CNBC, December 12, 2011, http://www.cnbc.com/id/45637136/.

14. Lori Spechler, "In Twitter We Trust?" CNBC, December 12, 2011, http://www.cnbc.com/id/45643376/In_Twitter_We_Trust.

15. "Trust Barometer Global Results," Edelman Trust Barometer 2012 Annual Global Study, January 19, 2012, http://trust.edelman.com/trust-download/global-results/.

16. Ibid.

17. Ibid.

18. Ibid.

19. Ibid.

20. "Facebook Users in the World," Internet Stats, accessed July 9, 2013, http://www.Internetworldstats.com/facebook.htm.

21. Glen Parker and Lindsey Thomas, *The Business of Being Social: Social Media Tracker 2012* (London: Universal McCann, 2012), http://www.universalmccann.de/wave6/downloads/wave6_insights_international.pdf.

22. Ibid.

23. Stan Schroeder, "China Has 500 Million Internet Users, Half of Them Are Microbloggers," Mashable, January 17, 2012, http://mashable.com/2012/01/17/china-500-million-web-users/.

24. Luke Richards, "Stats: Social Media Growth and Impact across the Middle East," Econsultancy, August 8, 2012, http://econsultancy.com/us/blog/10491-stats-social-media-growth-and-impact-across-the-middle-east.

25. "Mapping Twitter," *Arab Social Media Report* 3 (2011), http://www.dsg.fohmics.net/en/asmr3/ASMR_MappingTwitter3.aspx.

26. "Hot Topics," Twitter, 2011, http://yearinreview.twitter.com/en/hottopics.html.

27. "Mapping Twitter."

28. Jamila Boughelaf, *Mobile Phones, Social Media, and the Arab Spring* (United Kingdom: Credemus Associates, n.d.), http://www.credemus.org/images/stories/reports/mobile-phones-and-the-arab-spring.pdf.

29. Ibid.

30. Ibid.

31. "Twitter, Facebook and Youtube's Role in Arab Spring," Social Capital Blog, updated July 7, 2013, http://socialcapital.wordpress.com/2011/01/26/twitter-facebook-and-youtubes-role-in-tunisia-uprising/.

32. Carol Huang, "Facebook and Twitter Key to Arab Spring Uprisings: Report," *National*, June 6, 2011, http://www.thenational.ae/news/uae-news/facebook-and-twitter-key-to-arab-spring-uprisings-report.

33. Ibid.

34. Ibid.

35. Glanz and Markoff, "U.S. Underwrites Internet Detour."

36. Ting Luo, interview by Jessica Tarlov, London, February 2012.

37. Gillian Wong, "Voices behind China's Protest Calls," Huffington Post, April 6, 2011, http://www.huffingtonpost.com/2011/04/06/voices-behind-chinas-protest-calls_n_845923.html.

38. "A Digital Rallying Cry," April 12, 2011, *Economist*, http://www.economist.com/blogs/prospero/2011/04/ai_weiwcis_blog.

39. Ben Berkowitz, "To Occupy Wall Street, Occupy the Internet First," Reuters, October 4, 2011, http://www.reuters.com/article/2011/10/04/us-wallstreet-protests-media-idUSTRE79377W20111004.

40. "Indignados," Elections Meter, accessed July 9, 2013, http://electionsmeter.com/polls/indignados.

41. Japhet Weeks, "Moscow Protests Get Legs with Social Media," Voice of America, December 12, 2011, http://www.voanews.com/content/moscow-protests-gets-legs-with-social-media-135549658/149497.html.

42. Ibid.

43. Will Stewart, "Charismatic Putin Opponent Could Face Ten Years in Jail after Being Charged with Embezzlement," *Daily Mail*, July 31, 2012, http://www.dailymail.co.uk/news/article-2181545/Alexey-Navalny-charged-embezzlement.html.

44. Simon Shuster, "The Anti-Putin Movement: An Interview with the Blogger in Chief," *Time*, January 18, 2012, http://www.time.com/time/world/article/0,8599,2104445-2,00.html.

45. Claire Cain Miller, "How Obama's Internet Campaign Changed Politics," *New York Times*, November 7, 2008, http://bits.blogs.nytimes.com/2008/11/07/how-obamas-Internet-campaign-changed-politics/.

46. Ibid.

47. Li Jing, "China Tightens State Secrets Law," *Epoch Times*, October 9, 2010, http://www.theepochtimes.com/n2/china-news/china-tightens-state-secrets-law-43968.html.

48. Rebecca MacKinnon, "China's Internet White Paper: Networked Authoritarianism in Action," RConversation, June 15, 2010, http://rconversation.blogs.com/rconversation/2010/06/chinas-Internet-white-paper-networked-authoritarianism.html.

49. "Europe Falls from Its Pedestal, No Respite in the Dictatorships," Reporters Without Borders, 2010, http://en.rsf.org/press-freedom-index-2010,1034.html.

50. Tom Philips, "The 'Truth' Deleted from Internet in China," *Telegraph*, July 12, 2012, http://www.telegraph.co.uk/news/worldnews/asia/china/9394684/The-truth-deleted-from-Internet-in-China.html.

51. Tania Branigan, "Wen Jiabao Talks of Democracy and Freedom in CNN Interview," *Guardian*, October 4, 2010, http://www.guardian.co.uk/world/2010/oct/04/wen-jiabao-china-reform-cnn-interview.

52. "China Arrests Blogger for Twitter Joke," *Guardian*, November 21, 2012, http://www.guardian.co.uk/world/2012/nov/21/china-arrest-blogger-twitter-joke.

53. Carl Franzen, "Google: Most Censorship Requests Come from Democracies," Talking Points Memo, June 18, 2012, http://idealab.talkingpointsmemo.com/2012/06/google-transparency-democracies-censorship.php.

54. Zach Carter and Ryan Grim, "SOPA Blackout Aims to Block Internet Censorship Bill," Huffington Post, January 18, 2012, http://www.huffingtonpost.com/2012/01/18/sopa-blackout-Internet-censorship_n_1211905.html.

55. "Russian Twitter Political Protests 'Swamped by Spam,'" BBC News, December 9, 2011, http://www.bbc.com/news/technology-16108876.

56. Huma Yusuf, "Twitchy about Twitter," *New York Times*, May 22, 2012, http://latitude.blogs.nytimes.com/2012/05/22/pakistans-ban-on-twitter-is-a-test-of-censorship-ahead-of-elections/.

57. Ibid.

58. Erin Conway-Smith, "Press Freedom: Eretria, North Korea, Syria 'Most Censored Countries,'" *Global Post*, May 2, 2012, http://www.globalpost.com/dispatch/news/regions/africa/120502/press-freedom-eritrea-north-korea-syria-most-censored-countries-.

59. Thomas Fuller, "Myanmar to Curb Censorship of Media," *New York Times*, August 20, 2012, http://www.nytimes.com/2012/08/21/world/asia/myanmar-abolishes-censorship-of-private-publications.html.

60. "Uproar as Footage Shows Syrian Rebel Attrocities," ABC News, August 14, 2012, http://www.abc.net.au/news/2012-08-14/outrage-as-grisly-syria-video-shows-bodies-thrown-from-roof/4196550.

61. Farai Chideya, "Iran + Twitter = Trust, but Don't Verify," Huffington Post, June 17, 2009, http://www.huffingtonpost.com/farai-chideya/iran-twitter-trust-but-do_b_216970.html.

62. Massimo Calabresi, "WikiLeaks' War on Secrecy: Truth's Consequences," *Time*, December 20, 2012, http://www.time.com/time/magazine/article/0,9171,2034488,00.html.

63. Ibid.

64. Michael Moore and Oliver Stone, "WikiLeaks and Free Speech," *New York Times*, August 20, 2012, http://www.nytimes.com/2012/08/21/opinion/wikileaks-and-the-global-future-of-free-speech.html.

65. Adam Vaughan, "GM Crop-Trial Website Taken Down by Cyber-Attack," *Guardian*, May 28, 2012, http://www.guardian.co.uk/environment/2012/may/28/gm-crop-trial-website-cyber-attack.

66. Eli Lake, "15-Year-Old Egyptian Cyber-Activist Takes On Israel," Daily Beast, November 21, 2012, http://www.thedailybeast.com/articles/2012/11/21/gaza-s-internet-boy-wonder-takes-on-israel.html.

11

THE NEED FOR BOLD SOLUTIONS

Yes, democracy matters. But . . . democracy is so much more than just winning an election. It is nurturing a culture of inclusion and of peaceful dialogue, where respect for leaders is earned by surprising opponents with compromises rather than dictates. . . . Elections without that culture are like a computer without software. It just doesn't work.

—Thomas Friedman

The world's greatest global-governance challenge is to establish shared responsibility for the most intractable problems of our postunipolar world.

—Michael Fullilove, executive director,
Lowey Institute for International Policy

If this book has made anything clear in enumerating the ways that governments and institutions around the world have failed, it is that we need bold new solutions to twenty-first-century global problems. At this point, anything short of such remedies won't do—as we have seen, when governments attempt half measures on economic issues or address corruption merely by reshuffling personnel, nothing changes. The problems we face today are too deep seated and broad ranging for that kind of approach. Whether the issue is broadening educational opportunities to all populations, solving the climate-change crisis, ensuring clean water and low-cost drugs, or managing the ongoing security challenges of a multipolar world, we must think big and act accordingly.

The challenges are especially daunting in a time of global transition: we have clearly moved, over the last twenty years, into an era in which the nation-state, once the all-but-omnipotent unit of power, has seen its autonomy and even its relevance challenged by the globalization of economies and institutions. Problems that could once be confined to discrete nations or regions now increasingly take a global cast because of the transnational integration of economies and governing institutions, mass communication, and travel. The crises I've described in this book are a perfect example: failures of governance and loss of public trust are global problems, not national ones.

Yet the nation-state and local governance remain vital, as they are the institutions closest to the people they serve and often the best situated to take effective action. If we need much better leadership internationally—and we do—we also need to find solutions tailored to work within nations, and even more targeted efforts that can apply locally. Thus, we need a three-pronged strategy:

- *Reform and improve international institutional leadership— whether the UN, the European Union, or the World Bank.* We simply must make international institutions more effective, whether in mediating violent disputes or enforcing fair trade and currency practices. When this effort requires new institutions, this, too, should be pursued.
- *Strengthen nation-state governance.* We may live in a global economy and, increasingly, a global mass culture, but the nation-state, changed as its role may be, is not going away; people of vastly different cultures demand governments that speak to their needs and aspirations, and the nation-state remains the best vehicle for this task.
- *Direct specific reform and relief efforts, wherever feasible, as locally as possible, in order to ensure that the benefits of these policies reach the people for whom they're intended.* In an age of technological wizardry, microtargeting of resources, if done well, can deliver results efficiently and effectively.

As I have argued, if we don't act soon, we will be facing a deeper crisis than we have ever seen—locally, nationally, and globally. The longer we wait, the more complex our problems will become and the more limited our options.

So there is much to be done. I'll offer some specific recommendations in this chapter for solutions we should pursue. But, more than any policy recommendation, I want to stress that the West must defend democracy; open societies; freedom of speech, press, and religion; and free-market, free-trade economics under the rule of law. Fundamental to these goals of economic growth and opportunity and political freedom is expanded access to quality education. Nothing that has happened over the last decade—not ill-fated wars, not financial catastrophes, not natural disasters—has undermined the core truth of these timeless principles. We clearly gain wherever democratic principles are put into practice, and the explosion of popular movements globally should remind us of the appeal of these values. As I said in my introduction, without democracy and freedom, process-oriented microreforms will amount to not much more than Band-Aid solutions.

I don't pretend that, in calling for a reaffirmation of these values, I am breaking new ground. Rather, I seek to remind readers of how essential the Western birthright is both to our own resurgence and to the hopes and dreams of hundreds of millions of people around the world. Democratic, promarket, secular values apply at each of the three governance levels I have identified: global, national, and local. If we commit to these principles and embed them in the solutions we pursue, then we can significantly restore authority, legitimacy, and trust to our governing institutions.

REVITALIZING—AND DEMOCRATIZING— THE NATION-STATE

Unless we revitalize the nation-state as an effective entity, attempts to redress injustice or bring greater stability internationally are doomed to failure. The community of nations is, after all, made up of *nations*, and in recent years the nation-state model has faced severe challenges. So much so, in fact, that it's become fashionable to declare the nation-state obsolete in a networked age of global markets, multinational corporations, and international free-trade agreements.

As Simon Kuper argued in an important *Financial Times* column, "The nation-state is shrinking to just a flag, some sports teams, and a pile of debts." Pointing to what he called "the waning of the nation-state," caused by new technologies and a globalized world, Kuper wrote that "people are gradually replacing nationalism with an array of transnational loyalties. Someone might identify with the global community of English-speakers, or as a Londoner, black person, Muslim, Justin Bieber fan, member of the global elite, or possibly all these things. Most people also still identify with a nation, but that's becoming just one identity among many."[1]

Kuper has a point. Clearly, the nation-state is struggling as a viable institution, and even its best assets are not entirely equal to global challenges. That said, however, I think we are deluding ourselves if we believe that international or corporate structures are going to supplant nations as we have always known them. In fact, in a way Kuper's argument contradicts itself: he cites a number of secessionist movements in Europe—the Catalans in Spain, Scots in England, and Flemish nationalists in Belgium—saying that they "aim to ditch old redundant nation-states in order to create new redundant nation-states. The history of nationalism in Europe looks to be creaking to an end."

On the contrary, while nation-states may be changing in their function and even their composition, the secessionist movements indicate nothing so much as a reaffirmation of the desire of people sharing common bonds to live among one another. This is especially true when we remember the resistance in so many countries, especially in Europe, to growing numbers of nonnative groups and the cultural challenges they bring (see chapters 8 and 9). Nations, as coherent organizations of cultural or ethnic affinity groups bound by history and political structure, will need to adapt to the new global arrangements—but in doing so they will become more, not less, relevant.

One should be able to recognize, then, that the nation-state is a troubled institution without declaring its imminent demise.

The problem dominating the landscape in dozens of nations today is the same one that bedevils the international community—the fiscal crisis and the challenge of restarting and stabilizing the global economy. I will offer some ideas for economic reform in the global section. Nationally, reforms will vary depending on the circumstances, of course, but one overarching idea should govern all efforts: a recommitment to democracy, rule of law, vital civil societies, a free press, and economic opportunity.

No other reform matters as much as this essential commitment—a commitment that I feel has been sorely lacking on the part of the West for many years.

As I have argued throughout this book, millions around the world are clamoring for democracy. Across the Middle East and North Africa, we have seen uprisings in pursuit of democratic goals; likewise, on the streets of affluent cities in the developed world, victims of the economic crisis have demonstrated in favor of a more equitable system. As Moncef Marzouki, the president of Tunisia, wrote in the *New York Times* regarding the Arab Spring, "These are difficult tasks for any country, and the challenge is even greater for new democracies in the postrevolutionary Arab world. We are in a race against poverty. At this crucial moment, the West must not abandon us. It must continue to aid Tunisia in strengthening democracy and the rule of law, securing our borders to stop arms from reaching extremists, and creating economic opportunities that give our citizens hope."[2]

It should be a global priority to push for democracy in all nations that seek it and ensure that the international community supports democratization. Western leaders do, of course, voice support for these goals: President Obama made a forceful plea for open societies in response to the September 2012 attack on the American consulate in Libya, and Jens Stoltenberg, prime minister of Norway, responded to the 2011 Norway massacres by calling for more democracy, not less. I don't question the sincerity of these expressions. The problem, however, is not only that such statements are intermittent but also that they are rarely tied to substantive, sustained action.

Consider the issue of democratization in Iran: President Obama's much-touted "leading from behind" approach has not served the aspirations of the Iranian people. This was especially shown in 2009, when the Ahmadinejad regime effectively crushed the Green Revolution without so much as a cross word from the White House. The administration claimed its silence helped the Iranian democracy movement behind the scenes, but the results speak for themselves: activists beaten or killed or jailed, free expression snuffed out, and a complete failure on the regime's part to deal with the grievances of its people.

But while it's fashionable, especially on the political right, to criticize Obama's Iranian policy, conservatives haven't performed much better. They may talk louder, but what have they done? Under President Bush, we dug into our pockets for a paltry $65 million to support the Iranian democracy movement.

Such a weak commitment sends a message not just to our allies but also to our adversaries. And the West's weakness of commitment and staying power extends well beyond Iran: we have done precious little to support the strengthening of civil society in Egypt and other Arab societies, many of which, as we saw during the Arab Spring, eagerly look to the West for some endorsement. We have also stayed mostly silent about Russian and Chinese human-rights abuses as well as a host of corrupt practices, from election fraud to unfair trade policies.

At best, we have become incrementally instrumental in shaping developments. Our vacillation weakens the democratic institutions that do exist in these countries. We have no permanent focus, it seems, no permanent "skin in the game" that would foster a long-term effort to push the values that we know, better than anyone in the world, can lead nations to democratic reform, freedom, and prosperity.

This Western tentativeness is especially apparent when contrasted with the vigor with which Russia and China, among others, pursue their interests and goals. They vigorously and unapologetically defend their values. The West, and especially the United States, must be every bit as committed to our own—especially because these values represent the best hope for a decent life for millions around the world. Even George Soros—with whom I rarely agree—seems to understand this better than the U.S. government. His Open Society Institute has done more to promulgate democratic values and practices around the world than the last two presidential administrations. That fact ought to appall all those who wish to see democracy advance.

Without committed, democratic leadership that leads from the front—in words, in deeds, and, above all, in consistency and focus—the withering away of the nation-state that Kuper envisions might just become a reality. Alternatively, nation-states, in the absence of sustained democratic movements, will simply emulate the Russian and Chinese model and become more autocratic. Nature abhors a vacuum, and the West is leaving one right now with its failure to pursue energetically the democratic reforms that—ironically—most people want. They have made that aspiration clear, again and again, around the world.

Ultimately, of course, even a staunch commitment to democratic values cannot solve, on its own, the problems that plague the international community. To address the challenges that affect us all, we must make changes to the way our international institutions do things—and, in some cases, change those institutions themselves.

STRENGTHENING GLOBAL AND INTERNATIONAL GOVERNANCE

Many around the world have questioned the legitimacy of major international organizations, whether the United Nations, the World Bank, or the International Monetary Fund, especially on the grounds that their leaders are not democratically elected. A top-down governing structure and a lack of democratic accountability have often hampered these organizations. Global and international organizations also have often reacted slowly to changing circumstances that have required altering their charters or structures. But, more crucially, these institutions have frequently failed to deliver effectively on their responsibilities. The UN has all too often proved ineffective in peacekeeping, in mediating conflicts, or in providing effective humanitarian relief, and its reputation has been tainted by multiple scandals. The World Bank's touted investments in underdeveloped nations often produce little or no improvement in living standards or reduction of poverty. And the IMF can be too intrusive in attempting to influence exchange rates rather than letting markets determine the value of national currencies; the organization also has an unfortunate record of lending to nations with atrocious human-rights records.

These are just some of the many criticisms of these major international organizations over the years. International faith in such institutions cannot afford to get much weaker; we must bolster both their effectiveness and their reputations. And here the nation-state issue is relevant as well: as much as we need robust national entities, the reality is that we also face challenges that nation-states will be hard pressed to solve.

As nation-states struggle to govern effectively, they contend with heightened demands from their citizens, who have been gaining increased access to communications and political representation. The combination of rising individual power and weakened national governments is, after all, one of the underlying dynamics behind the end of authority—demands unfulfilled, needs not met, failures of governance. As Philip Stephens pointed out in the *Financial Times*, it's not all the nation-states' fault. Many of the problems they face are of global scope: "Uncontrolled migration, economic offshoring, financial instability, climate change, unconventional weapons proliferation, cross-border crime and terrorism—none of these are problems within the capacity of individual states to resolve. To reclaim power governments will have to act in concert."[3]

All of this points, in my view, to the central role that international institutions are likely to play in the future—but only if they can demonstrate the ability to perform. Fortunately, there may be a model to follow in, of all places, Europe. In fall 2012, Mario Draghi, president of the European Central Bank, finally did what the political class has failed to do for years—he led. He not only may have helped end the European financial crisis but also provided a model for others to emulate.

Put simply, what Draghi did, after a crisis that has gone on for years, was make it clear that he would do whatever it took to support the euro. That pledge would include essentially unlimited funds to embattled European governments—but not without conditions. Those governments would have to agree to austerity measures; they would have Draghi's pledge never to desert them, but in turn they had to promise to reform their fiscal and economic policies.

For years preceding Draghi's announcement, the euro's instability had hovered over financial markets. Fear of a euro collapse, along with potential national insolvencies in Ireland, Spain, or Italy, made investors tentative, stifled business activity, and cast a pall over any sustained global economic recovery. The European Union never appeared more like the image its detractors often painted of it: as a vast collection of states of wildly divergent economic strength and incompatible priorities. The economic powerhouses, like Germany and the United Kingdom, pressed for austerity; the weaker nations, like Greece, Spain, and Italy, all urged more spending and rallied against austerity. The only consistent result was stalemate.

Amid the uncertainty, the need for leadership couldn't have been clearer. And not a moment too soon, in September 2012, Draghi stepped forward with his famous announcement that "the euro is irreversible," creating an "unlimited" new bond-buying program, called Monetary Outright Transactions. Eurozone countries choosing to enter the bond-buying program would be subject to the austerity requirements under the new bailout fund, the European Stability Mechanism.[4]

Draghi's leadership was notable for going against the wishes of the Germans, who criticized the bond-buying plan for overstepping the ECB's responsibilities by intervening in state budgets. But Draghi was undeterred, insisting that the ECB's mandate was to protect the euro: "Let me repeat what I said last month. We are strictly within our mandate to maintain price stability over the medium term."

Economist Zachary Karabell applauded Draghi's move: "In a system that depends on the willingness of markets to extend credit, and the faith that governments will not default, the role of central banks in providing security and stability cannot be underestimated." He lauded Draghi for his willingness to "ensure that the deficiencies of politicians, the limitations of governments, and the unreasonableness of people do not completely torpedo social stability."[5] Under Draghi's leadership, the European Central Bank helped alleviate the euro crisis, even without substantial bond purchases.

Throughout this book, I've highlighted failures of governance and failures of leadership. Draghi's leadership has certainly not solved all of the problems of the European Union, but it does provide a clear indicator of how successful international institutions can work, and how they must work if we are to solve the crisis of authority.

RESTARTING THE ECONOMY

Since 2008, the economic, fiscal, and currency crisis has hovered over all other problems. As bad as the conditions are in First World nations, the economic downturn has presented even harsher challenges to the developing world. Until the global economy stabilizes, we can't resolve other major challenges.

Again, core democratic principles should guide us here. Free and open markets have led to the greatest creation of wealth and improvement in living standards the world has seen. We can do more to foster markets by reaching more broad-based trade agreements and dismantling protectionism. The United States and Europe, for instance, while enjoying a longstanding and lucrative trade relationship, could boost economies on both sides of the Atlantic by agreeing on a formal free-trade agreement that eliminates or streamlines many costly regulations that stifle innovation and hurt companies.

Also on the regulatory side, it's past time for the United States, in concert with the IMF and WTO, to take a strong stand against Chinese currency manipulation. By manipulating their currency, the Chinese have ensured that their exports have a major competitive advantage over goods manufactured in the United States and elsewhere. Such manipulation, as U.S. senator Sherrod Brown and a host of economists argue, constitutes a subsidy of Chinese exports, perhaps as much as 40 percent.[6] I agree with Robert Lighthizer, a trade representative under President Reagan, who argues that the United States should challenge Chinese currency manipulation at the IMF and "bring a WTO case on the grounds that currency manipulation is a prohibited export subsidy."[7] The IMF and WTO must act as honest brokers to curtail the damage China has done to the economies of other nations.

We won't achieve true economic recovery until entrepreneurship has regained the momentum it had in the 1990s, and not just in the United States. The entrepreneurial spirit has not only lifted the American economy but also propelled innovation and progress globally. The financial crisis hit entrepreneurs and start-up industries hard, drying up investment and venture capital. Unfriendly immigration laws in the United States and elsewhere make it hard for foreign-born entrepreneurs to start businesses and gain citizenship. The tech sector in former start-up hotbeds like Israel is shrinking, creating a much more difficult path for entrepreneurs looking for financing.

In their new book, *Better Capitalism*, Robert Litan and Carl Schramm argue that the United States should give green cards to all foreigners coming to America to study science, technology, engineering, or math. Universities should give professors more freedom to exploit their innovations.[8] Governments should provide subsidies to small businesses and start-ups and encourage competition among banks and local financiers to back innovative projects. Policies also should offer incentives to female entrepreneurs and programs that connect them with investors and capital. The percentage of women involved in start-ups has been rising, while the percentage of males has been dropping off.[9]

Encouraging entrepreneurship is also vital for promoting stability in such trouble spots as the Middle East.[10] According to the Center for International Private Enterprise, negative economic shocks of just 5 percent can raise the risk of a civil war by as much as 50 percent in fragile environments.[11] And because international aid and donor assistance cannot last forever, building local business capacity and supporting local entrepreneurs can help combat the risk of continued civil unrest. Small-business owners drive economic growth in developed nations; they could do the same in areas facing political unrest and transition. Providing fledgling businesses with access to capital and the tools to run their own businesses should be a major focus in volatile nations.

The United States should work with foreign entities to create a pro-entrepreneurship environment. This work could involve promoting the rule of law and free-market norms, as well as capital infusions into local businesses and communities through such vehicles as microloans. Rather than trusting a national government, which may be unreliable, to distribute aid, the United States and its partners should work directly with local communities. This approach would foster economic stability while also undercutting a primary criticism of the United States— that it supports abusive governments.

Another way to promote economic growth is by fostering education, especially in the developing world. One way to do this, as Tom Friedman argues, is to use incentive-based grants. Friedman argues compellingly that countries that lag behind in development and educational attainment—particularly those in the Middle East, but not only there— need a kind of "Race to the Top" for educational reform. These nations desperately need to acknowledge that they are being held back not by political adversaries (like, say, Israel) but by their own failure to educate their people and provide an environment conducive to human development. These nations must recognize, Friedman argues, that when it comes to economic progress, Islamic devotion is not the answer: "Math is the answer. Education is the answer. Getting the Middle East to focus on that would do more to further our interests and their prosperity than anything else. As we are seeing in Egypt, suddenly creating a

mass democracy without improving mass education is highly unstable."[12]

Such grants would both help foster development in these nations
and be more practical uses of our own dwindling resources. "We will
have to tell needy countries that whoever comes up with the best ideas
for educating their young women and girls or incentivizing start-ups or
strengthening their rule of law will get our scarce foreign-aid dollars,"
Friedman suggests. "That race is the future of foreign aid." And education isn't the only area in which we should rethink foreign aid.

RETHINKING FOREIGN AID

While the violent conflicts taking place today have many causes, most
take place in countries with stagnant or broken economies. The United
States has long played a leading role in offering assistance in these
conflicts, but the U.S. record on foreign aid, while often impressive in
preventing short term catastrophe, has been dismal in terms of fostering long-term growth. This is because we usually see foreign aid
through an exclusively humanitarian lens. A more strategic use of
foreign aid would help reduce the likelihood that troubled nations will
slip into conflict in the first place.

Expeditionary economics is a new and developing field in foreign-
aid theory. It argues that the United States and other powers should
switch from a top-down to a bottom-up approach when it comes to
rebuilding postconflict nations—specifically, by having militaries over-
haul their approach to nation building. Expeditionary economics rests
on several key assumptions:

- *Preference for the free market.* The free market is always the best
  distributor of goods and services. People are natural entrepreneurs who will generate value as soon as the government ceases to
  be in the way.
- *A new understanding of aid.* During the Cold War, foreign aid
  was designed to prop up economies to prevent them from falling
  to Communism. Today, the primary concerns of foreign aid are
  stopping terrorism, preventing state failure, and enforcing humanitarian norms. Yet despite this radical reorientation of goals,

foreign-aid policy has changed very little. Policymakers must re-think the place of economics in national security, focusing more effort on successful or even preemptive economic intervention.

- *Seeing every economy as unique.* A successful foreign-aid model must appreciate the particular history, culture, and conditions in the nations in which it is applied. One-size-fits-all models are ineffective and enormously wasteful.
- *Creating a different role for the military.* Militaries must be trans-formed into potent economic as well as martial forces. Troops should be organized to bring aid to the communities they patrol.

The West should also make better use of foreign direct investment, a woefully underused tool. Our failure to recognize its benefits is hurting not only needy people but also ourselves. The developed world is miss-ing out on an opportunity to do some good in developing economies and make money at the same time. FDI robustly increases local pro-ductivity and offers an untapped labor force.

Consider what China is doing in Africa.

Over the past few years, China has seized on the opportunity that FDI offers and is reaping the benefits. As Zambian-born economist Dambisa Moyo argues, China's growing investment across Africa has made the Beijing regime much more popular than Washington there and provided China with a dedicated, hardworking labor force. For example, in Uganda, twin high-rises, both funded by the Chinese, will house the offices of the president, vice president, and prime minister. China's influence can be seen everywhere: the Chinese are providing the Ugandans with tangible items like roads, bridges, buildings, house-hold items, and cell phones while the United States is offering only abstract "aid."[13]

Moyo cautions that Africans cannot wait for Bill Gates to rescue them from poverty. The United States must write checks for *invest-ment*, not just for aid.[14] Although aid is indeed important, it does not jumpstart communities in the same way that FDI does. While I'm not a fan of China's political system, the approach that Beijing has taken in Africa has delivered results. The United States and its allies should emulate the best aspects of the policy, consistent with our values.

Public/Private Partnerships

The private as well as the public sectors have felt the effect of the economic crisis, but they can fare better by pooling their efforts. Public/ private partnerships (PPPs) do just that, offering societies the prospect of using private capital for the public good: to build roads, fund health care, deliver clean water, and support the work of valuable NGOs, among other ventures. PPPs are a critical means of delivery for long-term infrastructure projects as well as an important means of generating economic activity. PPPs make it a primary function of governments to support entrepreneurship and private investment, mutually benefiting both the public and the private sectors.

To be fair, some PPPs have failed to produce the desired results, especially in terms of health-care delivery and the privatization of water. Failures often arise out of the unequal partnership agreements between governments and private corporations: while governments have the upper hand on policy issues, business providers tend to prevail on contractual issues related to delivery.

Business leaders and government officials should create an international PPP negotiation committee. The committee could negotiate initial terms of PPP contracts and also monitor the quality of service delivery through the duration of the contract. The sharing of resources and delivery of goods and services are now global concerns, because failures to deliver in one country affect others. An international PPP committee could help ensure that PPPs create the most benefits for governments, businesses, and citizens.

GLOBAL HEALTH

As Bill Clinton describes it, the "troika" of government, the private sector, and foundations is making the greatest strides in improving health care. It's important to recognize what we've accomplished and build on it. Polio is the latest in a long line of diseases that are on their way to elimination. We have successfully tackled chicken pox, smallpox, measles and SARS. "We have reduced polio by 99 percent worldwide," UN secretary-general Ban Ki-moon said in September 2012. "Just as the entire world will benefit from polio eradication, the world must stand shoulder-to-shoulder with Nigeria, Pakistan, and Afghanistan to finish the job."[15]

University of Cape Town researchers believe that they have finally found a single-dose cure for malaria, a major killer in Africa. The new "super pill" could cure millions each year and save health-care systems in the developing world billions of dollars.[16]

We're also winning the global HIV/AIDS fight because of shifts in the pharmaceutical industry from a low-volume, high-margin business to a low-margin, high-volume one. Today, it only costs $200 per patient, per year, to treat HIV/AIDS (with the exception of South Africa), including all the drugs, tests, personnel, and outpatient costs. Thanks to the work of such NGOs as the Bill and Melinda Gates Foundation, national governments, and such companies as Coca-Cola, we are on the precipice of an AIDS-free generation. And drug companies see a profit from these efforts.[17]

All of these successes make clear the importance of collaboration. Advances will come about faster through sharing and global-research efforts. Innovations in health-care-service delivery and research advances in one country will help elsewhere. What works in Rwanda may work in Haiti and in Mexico. The time has come for health-care efforts to link up, through such organizations as the Clinton Global Initiative and on their own, to tackle the world's health-care crises.

Catalytic Philanthropy

"I am a true believer in the power of capitalism to improve lives. Where the free market is allowed to operate, it is agile and creative. It can meet demand the world over and plays a central role in increasing living standards," Bill Gates told 161 billionaires and near-billionaires at the Forbes 400 Summit last summer.[18] As Bill Clinton has argued for years, private wealth is key to promoting the public good because it can supplement the work of governments, NGOs, and businesses to share expertise and implement long-lasting solutions.[19]

Catalytic philanthropy, as Bill Gates calls it, unleashes the free market for purposes beyond just making money. Enabling market forces to work on behalf of the poor is the future of charitable giving. Catalytic philanthropy will rely on governments, though, to create these market incentives. For instance, if drug companies factor the developed world into their business models, they can find new markets for their products while also helping to improve global health. Targeted philanthropic money will trigger action from both governments and businesses. The charitable community should shift toward employing the catalytic philanthropy model wherever possible.

Global Poverty and the Challenge of Food Security

As the startling statistics in previous chapters make clear, the economic crisis has most victimized the world's poor. Today, more than one billion people live on less than $1 a day, while "eight hundred million others experience hunger following the global economic and financial crisis," according to IPP Media.[20] As the World Bank's poverty and hunger strategy outlines, the poor require technical assistance, interest-free development grants, and a boost in spending on agriculture.[21]

Inexorably linked to the problem of global poverty is the issue of food security. Food-delivery initiatives such as the World Food Program, the Global Food Crisis Response Program, and Feed the Future—a $3.5 billion commitment by the Obama administration to supporting agricultural development worldwide—deserve more support. New programs such as the UN Zero Hunger Challenge deserve generous backing. We must ensure that food systems are resilient. As Ban Ki-moon contends, we need climate-smart and climate-resistant agriculture as well as water-smart, energy-efficient policies.[22]

Population growth expected by 2050 will require a 70 percent increase in global food production—intensifying the need for more investment in agriculture in poor countries. Private and public investment in innovation will help develop more efficient approaches. The UN and the World Bank are encouraging more partnerships among farmers, businesses, governments, civic groups, and international organizations in the quest to alleviate hunger.

Addressing Climate Change

By now, most politicians, leaders of international institutions, NGOs, and businesses recognize that climate change exists and must be addressed. We've seen high-level summits and heard ambitious talk, but we need more action.

As the UN's Ban Ki-moon argued in 2012, we need a global, robust, and legally binding climate regime. Unfortunately, 2012's Rio+20 summit failed to secure a global commitment to a responsible environmental policy, producing a watered-down document without enforcement mechanisms. We need to do more than shine a light on these issues and talk about them—we must create an innovative, far-reaching treaty that governments and corporations will implement.

As Richard Haas, president of the Council on Foreign Relations argues, "It is becoming increasingly clear that efforts at mitigation are not just falling short but that the gap between what is needed and what is likely to happen is widening. Prospects for a grand bargain here look as remote as they do in the trade and cyber realms. This argues for developing a multipronged approach to deal with the problem (i.e., slowing deforestation, increasing reliance on nuclear power, sharing technology to promote cleaner coal, introducing a carbon tax, etc.), as well as increased international efforts to help vulnerable countries deal with the effects of climate change."[23]

CYBER SECURITY: THE NEW BATTLEGROUND

Since 2000, staggering quantities of sensitive information have been digitized. Ranging from customer financial data to classified U.S. military documents, this information is highly valuable and heavily guarded. Despite these defenses, cyber-security breaches have multiplied, as private individuals and hackers employed by foreign governments redouble their efforts to gain access to private data.

Although the United States is the world's largest target, the problem is not confined to the United States. Many Asian financial firms suffered embarrassing breaches of customer data in the early 2000s. As I write, the Canadian government is investigating two cyber attacks that it believes originated in China, home to the world's most-advanced hackers. As the scope and dangers of cyber warfare grow, powerful entities are investing time and money in developing offensive and defensive cyber capabilities. The U.S. government, for instance, almost certainly was the primary player in the 2010 Stuxnet attacks that damaged Iranian nuclear centrifuges.

International cyber security simply must be enhanced. Failing to do so risks catastrophic consequences, from economic damage to disabled governments. Some steps we could take include the following:

Establishing an international cyberspace doctrine. In order to better defend against cyber attacks, the United States and other nations must establish a cyberspace doctrine. This would be the first step toward a consensus that might one day produce a Geneva Convention–like set of norms. Because cyber security is such a new and changing field, a set of standards by which to judge and respond to cyber attacks is a necessity. The Obama administration has moved to establish such a doctrine, but it is neither fully formed nor internationally accepted.

Establishing a more robust mechanism. The field of cyber security remains in its infancy, and many of the world's cyber-defense efforts are ad hoc and uncoordinated. President Obama has appointed a cyber security czar to oversee all operations, but further international coordination is necessary. Governments should establish separate cabinet ministries or agencies to deal with cyber threats.

Planning for the future. The foundation of cyber security is technical know-how. The United States will lag behind China and South Korea in the cyber war if it does not beef up its math-, science-, and technology-education programs. Less than 5 percent of Americans graduate with degrees in STEM (science, technology, engineering, mathematics) fields, compared with almost 50 percent of Chinese. Unless this imbalance changes, the United States will have difficulty finding the talent to support cyber-security missions.

Engaging with allies. Cyber security is a global problem, with information flowing freely across borders. Many nations now work together on cyber security, but international coordination must become much more comprehensive.

At the same time, it is vital that cyber-security efforts be pursued in such a way that they don't threaten the open networks and free exchange of information that have made the Internet such a powerful economic and democratic force. As Richard Haass of the Council on Foreign Relations (CFR) argues, the emphasis should be on maintaining the flow of information while ensuring that national governments don't use the security issue to "curb the flow of information for political purposes."[24]

LOCAL REFORMS

Reforming Education Locally

In a high-tech economy, education becomes a necessity—and not just for economic advancement. Greater educational attainment also brings social benefits, including a reduction in crime, improved public health, and more civic participation. For example, in America, for every added year of schooling a citizen enjoys, voter registration rises by 30 to 40 percent.[25] In Uganda, a child completing basic education is three times less likely to become HIV positive later in life.[26]

Education also closely tracks one of the greatest challenges we face today: population growth. Female education retards fertility like nothing else. As Bill Clinton discussed at the Aspen Ideas Festival, population growth complicates everything that we want to do on climate change, food security, and health care. Simply putting more girls in school would slow world population growth—giving them access to the labor market and jobs, thereby delaying the age of marriage and the age at which they give birth to their first child. This social-science phenomenon has no exception in any culture.

Technology offers a number of innovative approaches to increasing the quality of education and, especially, the availability of early education globally.

Ventures such as Khan Academy, a nonprofit organization with the mission of "providing a high-quality education to anyone, anywhere," is one example. The Khan Academy website supplies a free collection of more than 3,400 microlectures via video tutorials stored on YouTube. The subjects range widely. Khan Academy also offers peer-to-peer tutoring. Salman Khan, the school's founder, might turn his model into a charter school. In the meantime, he's expanding his teaching faculty and adding more subject content. Ventures like Khan Academy and the University of the People—the first tuition-free, peer-to-peer institution based on Open Educational Resources—offer global access to better educational opportunities.

Microloans for the Poor: The Grameen Bank Model

Many of the world's poor are victims of circumstance, living in economically stagnant societies lacking adequate education and plagued by corruption, disease, and decrepit infrastructure. Lack of planning for the future is central to the vicious cycle of poverty: without clear, achievable goals, impoverished societies often remain stuck in the status quo. Making things worse is the myth that poor people lack motivation and a work ethic.

Nobel Peace Prize–winning Grameen Bank, founded nearly thirty years ago in Bangladesh, delivers life-changing microloans to millions of poor people. The bank extends credit only to start or expand businesses. It fosters mutual accountability, with members joining in groups of five so that they are supported and responsible to one another. (The bank's loan-repayment rate is 97 percent.) Perhaps the key to Grameen's success is that the bank's borrowers are also its majority owners. Those who rely on the bank's credit play a role in its management, fostering a deeper sense of loyalty than in traditional microbanking models. The fact that the borrowers are also the managers creates a sense of empowerment for those involved, especially among the women who form the largest group of borrowers.

Grameen Bank serves as the primary source of capital for women entrepreneurs and has also supported education, affordable health care, and nutrition initiatives.[27] The Grameen Bank model deserves broad emulation: it is a testament to how the world's poor can lift themselves out of poverty if given the tools to do so.

CONCLUSION

Around the world, people are looking for some sign that better days are ahead and that the worst of the post-2008 economic crash is behind us.

Japanese citizens, for instance, having lost confidence in their government because of a nuclear disaster, want to know that there is hope. Disenfranchised Arabs want to believe that Western, democratic ideals offer hope for a better future and prospects for change after decades of autocratic and repressive governments. The citizens of Europe eagerly search for a sign that their children's future won't be overshadowed by the threat of insolvency and political dissolution. Millions more who have come to believe that nihilistic violence, or worse, is the only way to express outrage with unrepresentative and oppressive governments would welcome a sign that policies are finally being directed toward constructive ends. Even citizens in affluent America fear that the future holds scant promise for betterment, especially with a government that seems categorically unable to address serious problems.

Despite enormous setbacks and difficulties, democracy and representative government remain the overwhelming aspiration of the world's people, and no coherent alternative exists. But democracy has not been working well and desperately needs reform. Governments must work to regain public trust by increasing transparency, fostering political participation and economic opportunity, and promoting democracy, both in the United States and overseas. The stakes are clear: we're either going to strengthen our democratic institutions—nationally and internationally—or the most significant global crisis since the 1930s could lead in any number of damaging directions.

While many focus on political structures and processes, my sense is that most citizens are less concerned with process than they are with finding solutions to large-scale problems. Most would embrace a political body, whether a national government or a multilateral institution, energetically taking steps that would reempower ordinary people politically and economically. What citizens see instead, however, is a dysfunctional and often seemingly rigged system that works against them. Until that changes, authority and trust will remain endangered, if not obsolete—and the enormous problems facing us will go unsolved.

NOTES

The epigraphs in this chapter are drawn from the following sources: Thomas Friedman, "Egypt: the Next India or the Next Pakistan?" *New York Times*, December 16, 2012, www.nytimes.com/2012/12/16/opinion/sunday/friedman-egypt-the-next-india-or-the-next-pakista-.html; and Michael Fullilove, Richard Haass, Jiemian Yang, and Igor Yurgens, "Challenges for Global Governance in 2013," Council on Foreign Relations, January 7, 2013, www.cfr.org/

global-governance/challenges-global-governance-2013/p29742?cid=nlc-public-the_world_
this_week-link21-20130104.

1. Simon Kuper, "A Question of Identity," *Financial Times*, November 23,
2012, http://www.ft.com/intl/cms/s/2/34783668-3370-11e2-aa83-
00144feabdc0.html#axzz2DWzTGGm3.

2. Moncef Marzouki, "The Arab Spring Still Blooms," *New York Times*,
September 27, 2012, http://www.nytimes.com/2012/09/28/opinion/the-arab-
spring-still-blooms.html.

3. Philip Stephens, "State versus Citizens in Tomorrow's World," *Financial
Times*, December 13, 2012, http://www.ft.com/intl/cms/s/0/75dfa02c-448d-
11e2-932a-00144feabdc0.html.

4. "ECB to Buy Sovereign Bonds in New Program to Save Euro," CNBC,
found online at SGT Report, http://sgtreport.com/2012/09/ecb-to-buy-
sovereign-bonds-in-new-program-to-save-euro/.

5. Zachary Karabell, "Mario Draghi May Become the Man Who Saved
Europe and the World," Daily Beast, September 7, 2012, http://www.
thedailybeast.com/articles/2012/09/07/mario-draghi-may-become-the-man-
who-saved-europe-and-the-world.html.

6. Sherrod Brown, "Currency Manipulation Gives Chinese an Unfair Advantage," July 11, 2012, The Hill, http://thehill.com/blogs/congress-blog/
economy-a-budget/237423-currency-manipulation-gives-chinese-an-unfair-
advantage.

7. Robert Lighthizer, "Testimony before the U.S.-China Economic and
Security Review Commission," U.S.-China Economic and Security Review
Commission, accessed July 9, 2013, http://www.uscc.gov/hearings/
2010hearings/written_testimonies/10_06_09_wrt/10_06_09_lighthizer_
statement.php.

8. "Fixing the Capitalist Machine," *Economist*, September 17, 2012, http://
www.economist.com/node/21563704.

9. Joe Van Brussel, "Women Entrepreneurs Increasingly Part of Job Crisis
Solutions," Huffington Post, September 28, 2012, http://www.huffingtonpost.
com/2012/09/28/women-entrepreneurs-jobs-crisis-zuckerberg_n_1920527.
html.

10. Gayle Tzemach Lemmon, *Entrepreneurship in Postconflict Zones: A
Working Paper* (New York: Council on Foreign Relations, 2012), http://www.
cfr.org/entrepreneurship/entrepreneurship-postconflict-zones/p28257.

11. Aleksander Shkolnikov and Anna Nadgrodkiewicz, *Building Democracies and Markets in the Post-Conflict Context* (Washington, DC: Center for
International Private Enterprise, 2008), http://www.cipe.org/sites/default/files/
publication-docs/IP0806.pdf.

12. Thomas Friedman, "My Secretary of State," *New York Times*, November 27, 2012, http://www.nytimes.com/2012/11/28/opinion/friedman-my-secretary-of-state.html.

13. Shirley Jahad, "How China and the US Pave Different Roads to Development in East Africa," Southern California Public Radio, August 16, 2012, http://www.scpr.org/news/2012/08/16/33873/china-builds-influence-uganda/.

14. Jake Whitney, "Dambisa Moyo and Why Western Aid Is Killing Africa," Huffington Post, April 1, 2009, http://www.huffingtonpost.com/jake-whitney/dambisa-moyo-and-why-west_b_180964.html.

15. Edith Lederer, "Gates Hopes Polio Will Be Eradicated by 2018," Salon, September 27, 2012, http://www.salon.com/2012/09/27/gates_hopes_polio_will_be_eradicated_by_2018/.

16. Steve Boyes, "University of Cape Town Researchers Believe They Have Found a Single Dose Cure for Malaria," *National Geographic*, August 29, 2012, http://newswatch.nationalgeographic.com/2012/08/29/university-of-cape-town-researchers-believe-they-have-found-a-single-dose-cure-for-malaria/.

17. Bill Clinton, "The Case for Optimism," *Time*, October 1, 2012, http://www.time.com/time/magazine/article/0,9171,2125031,00.html.

18. Randall Lane, "Bill Gates: My New Model for Giving," *Forbes*, September 18, 2012, http://www.forbes.com/sites/randalllane/2012/09/18/bill-gates-my-new-model-for-giving/.

19. Bill Clinton, "Charity Needs Capitalism to Solve the World's Problems," *Financial Times*, January 20, 2012, http://www.ft.com/cms/s/0/544c317a-42a2-11e1-93ea-00144feab49a.html#axzz27lrlrJMt.

20. "Global Recession Puts 1 Bn People Under Poverty Line," IPP Media, September 28, 2012, http://www.ippmedia.com/frontend/index.php?l=46334.

21. "Goal 1: Eradicate Extreme Poverty and Hunger by 2015," World Bank, 2011, http://www.worldbank.org/mdgs/poverty_hunger.html.

22. "Africa: Action on Climate Change Crucial to Water and Food Security, Ban Stresses at UN Event," All Africa, September 27, 2012, http://allafrica.com/stories/201209281358.html.

23. Michael Fullilove, Richard Haass, Jiemian Yang, and Igor Yurgens, "Challenges for Global Governance in 2013," Council on Foreign Relations, January 7, 2012, http://www.cfr.org/global-governance/challenges-global-governance-2013/p29742?cid=nlc-public-the_world_this_week-link21-20130104.

24. Michael Fullilove, Richard Haass, Jiemian Yang, and Igor Yurgens, "Challenges for Global Governance in 2013," Council on Foreign Relations, http://www.cfr.org/global-governance/challenges-global-governance-2013/p29742.

25. Kevin Milligan, Enrico Moretti, and Philip Oreopoulos, "Does Education Improve Citizenship? Evidence from the United States and the United Kingdom," *Journal of Public Economics* 88 (2004): 1667–95.

26. "Facts on Education in Africa," Achieve in Africa, April 15, 2009, http://achieveinafrica.wordpress.com/2009/04/15/facts-on-education-in-africa/.

27. George Schultz and Madeleine Albright, "A Nobel Prize Winner Under Siege," *Wall Street Journal*, September 5, 2012, http://online.wsj.com/article/SB10000872396390443759504577629620737997542.html.

CONCLUSION
No Time to Lose

As I have attempted to show in the preceding chapters, both the democratic and the nondemocratic worlds are clearly facing a crisis of governance, a crisis of legitimacy, and, indeed, a crisis of authority. The challenges are broader and more pervasive than most commentators have recognized. To be sure, the underlying issues have been exacerbated by a worldwide economic downturn. But it would be a profound mistake to conclude that a weak economy is solely responsible for the crisis of authority in government. That's simply wrong.

What has happened is that around the world, citizens in democratic and nondemocratic societies, rich and poor, of all different racial and ethnic groups, have lost confidence in those charged with the responsibility of governing them.

This book has tried to outline the reasons for this across-the-board decline in confidence, which include the inadequate and unfair distribution of resources, the inability of governments to moderate and meet citizen needs, and, equally important, a level of corruption on a national and international basis that seems to have rendered many governing regimes all but dysfunctional.

That being said, this book is not intended to be merely a catalog of woes and problems or a laundry list of issues. It is meant to offer clear, unambiguous solutions. I've emphasized a set of multilateral approaches that are essential. It has been shown time and again that we are not going to solve the problems of climate change, financial regulation, inequality, health care, clean water, education, and nutrition on a nation-by-nation basis. These are transnational problems; they demand transnational responses.

Book after book, article after article, has chronicled the weakness of the United Nations. This book is meant to go beyond that valid but limited critique. What I've sought to do is to underscore where international institutions have, on either an ad hoc or a systematic basis, addressed the critically important problems of governance, legitimacy, and resource allocation. Efforts to strengthen international governance must continue—and, more crucially, they must begin to bear fruit.

At the same time, however, the nation-state remains vitally relevant. I've argued here that individual steps need to be taken not only to maintain the legitimacy and responsiveness of individual states but also to promote institutions that allow those states to work together on common problems. So far, we've seen some success, though not nearly enough, in developing new institutions for these purposes. But this effort remains very much a work in progress.

My emphasis on institutions is, I believe, well placed, as the scale of our problems cannot be addressed without effective institutional action. However, we shouldn't lose sight of the role of the individual. Chrystia Freeland and others have chronicled the evolution of a "super elite": a small, transnational coterie of the ultrarich that has played a disproportionate role—sometimes constructive, sometimes not—in philanthropy and in facilitating the kinds of institutions I have argued for here. There is very clearly a role for these individuals, both in their home countries and globally, to develop solutions to some of today's major challenges.

George Soros, for example, whom I've mentioned earlier, does not share my political views, but he recognizes better than most the importance of fostering democratic institutions and open societies. I was also struck recently by something Bill Clinton said. He described what he called "creative cooperators," by which he meant individual citizens who can harness resources—using national institutions, international institutions, or, more likely, the power of the Internet—to solve problems.

Technology has a crucial role to play here. I've been particularly taken with the work of the State Department's Alec Ross, whose work I discussed in chapter 10. Ross's innovative technology programs have helped allocate resources systematically, whether to Africans devastated by natural disasters or, more broadly, to improve quality of life in societies where mere survival is a struggle. Technology is also the lynchpin behind the success of Salman Khan's Khan Academy, which offers the promise of a free, world-class education for every child through the power of the Internet.

In spotlighting promising efforts, however, I don't mean to suggest that there is a right answer or a singular answer. There are *many answers*. And if this book has a concluding message, it is that individuals—wealthy or poor, in government or out of government—using creative, out-of-the-box solutions can make a difference.

This book has stressed repeatedly that we are facing a crisis. But I've tried to underscore that, from the individual to the state to multilateral institutions, roles are changing and new roles are evolving. Within all of the uncertainty and seeming chaos of change, there is opportunity as well. We need to seize it if we're going to alleviate a crisis that threatens to undermine our global order. I remain hopeful that we will address our most pressing challenges in a way that, ten years from now, will give people greater confidence than they have today.

But make no mistake: there is a crisis, and it requires immediate attention.

INDEX

9/11, 40, 42, 43, 67

Ababene, Ali, 1
Abbas, Wael, 203
Abdullah II (king), 5
Abramoff, Jack, 143
Acemoglu, Daron, 50
Activist News Association, 70
Afghanistan, 43, 135
Africa, 2, 12; AIDS crisis in, 34;
    antisystemic politics in, 190–191;
    China and, 233; democracy in, 225;
    democratic movements in, 182;
    electoral fraud in, 136; famine, 12, 28;
    immigration and, 36; protest
    movements, 6, 190–191; sub-Saharan,
    30; technology and, 201. *See also
    specific countries*
African National Congress, 6, 131
Ahmadinejad, Mahmoud, 135, 189, 199
AIDS, 31, 34, 35, 86, 235
Ai Weiwei, 206
*American Casino: The Rigged Game that's
    Killing Democracy* (Schoen), 143
Amin, Ahmed Raafat, 70
Angola, 45, 159, 182, 190–191
Anonymous, 213–214
anticorruption, 138, 185
anti-Semitism, 162, 173
antisystemic politics, 157–160, 181–192;
    in Africa, 190–191; in Europe, 159,

160–175; French nationalism,
    161–163; in Germany, 163–165; Greek
    nationalism, 174–175; Hungarian
    nationalism, 172–174; in India,
    185–187; in Italy, 165–167; in Middle
    East, 187–190; in Netherlands,
    168–169; in Russia, 183–185;
    Scandinavian nationalism, 169–172; in
    United States, 160, 176–177
Arab News (newspaper), 70
Arab Social Media Report, 202
Arab Spring, 5, 69, 70, 85, 146, 182, 187,
    226; Marzouki on, 225; Sorman on,
    8–9; technology and, 196, 202–205
Asia, 41; cyber security and, 237; South,
    30. *See also specific countries*
al-Assad, Bashar, 6, 148, 212
Assange, Julian, 213
Aung San Suu Kyi, 212
autocracies, 67, 77, 92–93; China and,
    72–74, 85–89; crony capitalism and,
    132; Egypt and, 89–92; Middle East
    and, 68–71; reform in, 151; Russia and,
    71–72, 83–85; trust in, 68–74
Avlon, John, 41

Bahrain, 202, 203
Bajaj, Rahul, 100
bank bailouts, 149–151
Ban Ki-moon, 234, 236, 237
Bank of England, 12